Survival

GLOBAL POLITICS AND STRATEGY

Volume 62 Number 6 | December 2020–January 2021

'Conquering the Baltic states would just make Europeans angry, not end the war. To end the war through military victory, Russia would need to reconquer much of Eastern Europe, even perhaps eastern Germany, and do it quickly, before Europe's superior resources could be mobilised.'

Barry R. Posen, Europe Can Defend Itself, p. 17.

'America and the world have survived the Trump administration, the United States' latest Jacksonian revival. Voting patterns from 2020 suggest that Republicans have an opportunity to revive the expansive coalition that brought electoral and policy success in the 1980s … But they may miss the chance if Trump continues to dominate the Republican landscape.'

Kori Schake, Republican Politics and Policy After Trump, p. 48.

'The Soviet Union sought not only to constrain external alignments but to transform internal structures too. This was an *ideological* empire in which Soviet power spread Marxism–Leninism to other states while imposing communist systems on them to help ensure their subordination to Soviet control.'

Nigel Gould-Davies, Belarus and Russian Policy: Patterns of the Past, Dilemmas of the Present, p. 182.

Survival

GLOBAL POLITICS AND STRATEGY

Volume 62 Number 6 | December 2020–January 2021

Contents

Cover: Jim Bourg-Pool/Getty Images

Survival

A world after Trump

On the cover
Donald Trump and Joe Biden participate in their final debate of the presidential campaign on 22 October 2020, before Biden was elected president in November.

On the web
Visit www.iiss.org/publications/survival for brief notices on new books on the United States, Europe, and Counter-terrorism and Intelligence.

***Survival* editors' blog**
For ideas and commentary from *Survival* editors and contributors, visit www.iiss.org/blogs/survival-blog.

Survival
GLOBAL POLITICS AND STRATEGY

The International Institute for Strategic Studies

2121 K Street, NW | Suite 801 | Washington DC 20037 | USA
Tel +1 202 659 1490   Fax +1 202 659 1499   E-mail survival@iiss.org   Web www.iiss.org

Arundel House | 6 Temple Place | London | WC2R 2PG | UK
Tel +44 (0)20 7379 7676   Fax +44 (0)20 7836 3108   E-mail iiss@iiss.org

14th Floor, GBCorp Tower | Bahrain Financial Harbour | Manama | Kingdom of Bahrain
Tel +973 1718 1155   Fax +973 1710 0155   E-mail iiss-middleeast@iiss.org

9 Raffles Place | #51-01 Republic Plaza | Singapore 048619
Tel +65 6499 0055   Fax +65 6499 0059   E-mail iiss-asia@iiss.org

Survival Online www.tandfonline.com/survival and www.iiss.org/publications/survival

Aims and Scope *Survival* is one of the world's leading forums for analysis and debate of international and strategic affairs. Shaped by its editors to be both timely and forward thinking, the journal encourages writers to challenge conventional wisdom and bring fresh, often controversial, perspectives to bear on the strategic issues of the moment. With a diverse range of authors, *Survival* aims to be scholarly in depth while vivid, well written and policy-relevant in approach. Through commentary, analytical articles, case studies, forums, review essays, reviews and letters to the editor, the journal promotes lively, critical debate on issues of international politics and strategy.

Editor **Dana Allin**
Managing Editor **Jonathan Stevenson**
Associate Editor **Carolyn West**
Assistant Editor **Jessica Watson**
Production and Cartography **John Buck, Kelly Verity**

Contributing Editors

Ian Bremmer	Toby Dodge	John L. Harper	Jeffrey Mazo	Angela Stent
Rosa Brooks	Bill Emmott	Matthew Harries	'Funmi Olonisakin	Ray Takeyh
David P. Calleo	Mark Fitzpatrick	Erik Jones	Teresita C. Schaffer	David C. Unger
Russell Crandall	John A. Gans, Jr	Hanns W. Maull	Steven Simon	Lanxin Xiang

Published for the IISS by
Routledge Journals, an imprint of Taylor & Francis, an Informa business.

About the IISS The IISS, a registered charity with offices in Washington, London, Manama and Singapore, is the world's leading authority on political–military conflict. It is the primary independent source of accurate, objective information on international strategic issues. Publications include *The Military Balance*, an annual reference work on each nation's defence capabilities; *Strategic Survey*, an annual review of world affairs; *Survival*, a bimonthly journal on international affairs; *Strategic Comments*, an online analysis of topical issues in international affairs; and the *Adelphi* series of books on issues of international security.

SUBMISSIONS

To submit an article, authors are advised to follow these guidelines:

- *Survival* articles are around 4,000–10,000 words long including endnotes. A word count should be included with a draft.
- All text, including endnotes, should be double-spaced with wide margins.
- Any tables or artwork should be supplied in separate files, ideally not embedded in the document or linked to text around it.
- All *Survival* articles are expected to include endnote references. These should be complete and include first and last names of authors, titles of articles (even from newspapers), place of publication, publisher, exact publication dates, volume and issue number (if from a journal) and page numbers. Web sources should include complete URLs and DOIs if available.
- A summary of up to 150 words should be included with the article. The summary should state the main argument clearly and concisely, not simply say what the article is about.

- A short author's biography of one or two lines should also be included. This information will appear at the foot of the first page of the article.

Please note that *Survival* has a strict policy of listing multiple authors in alphabetical order.

Submissions should be made by email, in Microsoft Word format, to survival@iiss.org. Alternatively, hard copies may be sent to *Survival*, IISS–US, 2121 K Street NW, Suite 801, Washington, DC 20037, USA.

The editorial review process can take up to three months. *Survival*'s acceptance rate for unsolicited manuscripts is less than 20%. *Survival* does not normally provide referees' comments in the event of rejection. Authors are permitted to submit simultaneously elsewhere so long as this is consistent with the policy of the other publication and the Editors of *Survival* are informed of the dual submission.

Readers are encouraged to comment on articles from the previous issue. Letters should be concise, no longer than 750 words and relate directly to the argument or points made in the original article.

ADVERTISING AND PERMISSIONS

For advertising rates and schedules

USA/Canada: The Advertising Manager, Taylor & Francis Inc., 530 Walnut Street, Suite 850, Philadelphia, PA 19106, USA Tel +1 (800) 354 1420 Fax +1 (215) 207 0050.

UK/Europe/Rest of World: The Advertising Manager, Routledge Journals, Taylor & Francis, 4 Park Square, Milton Park, Abingdon, Oxfordshire OX14 4RN, UK Tel +44 (0) 207 017 6000 Fax +44 (0) 207 017 6336.

SUBSCRIPTIONS

Survival is published bimonthly in February, April, June, August, October and December by Routledge Journals, an imprint of Taylor & Francis, an Informa Business.

Annual Subscription 2020

	UK, RoI	US, Canada Mexico	Europe	Rest of world
Individual	£162	$273	€ 220	$273
Institution (print and online)	£585	$1,023	€ 858	$1,076
Institution (online only)	£497	$869	€ 729	$915

Taylor & Francis has a flexible approach to subscriptions, enabling us to match individual libraries' requirements. This journal is available via a traditional institutional subscription (either print with online access, or online only at a discount) or as part of our libraries, subject collections or archives. For more information on our sales packages please visit http://www.tandfonline.com/page/librarians.

All current institutional subscriptions include online access for any number of concurrent users across a local area network to the currently available backfile and articles posted online ahead of publication.

Subscriptions purchased at the personal rate are strictly for personal, non-commercial use only. The reselling of personal subscriptions is prohibited. Personal subscriptions must be purchased with a personal cheque or credit card. Proof of personal status may be requested.

Dollar rates apply to all subscribers outside Europe. Euro rates apply to all subscribers in Europe, except the UK and the Republic of Ireland where the pound sterling rate applies. If you are unsure which rate applies to you please contact Customer Services in the UK. All subscriptions are payable in advance and all rates include postage. Journals are sent by air to the USA, Canada, Mexico, India, Japan and Australasia. Subscriptions are entered on an annual basis, i.e. January to December. Payment may be made by sterling cheque, dollar cheque, euro cheque, international money order, National Giro or credit cards (Amex, Visa and Mastercard).

Survival (USPS 013095) is published bimonthly (in Feb, Apr, Jun, Aug, Oct and Dec) by Routledge Journals, Taylor & Francis, 4 Park Square, Milton Park, Abingdon, OX14 4RN, United Kingdom.

The US annual subscription price is $1,023. Airfreight and mailing in the USA by agent named WN Shipping USA, 156-15, 146th Avenue, 2nd Floor, Jamaica, NY 11434, USA. Periodicals postage paid in Jamaica NY 11431.

US Postmaster: Send address changes to Survival, C/O Air Business Ltd / 156-15 146th Avenue, Jamaica, New York, NY11434.

Subscription records are maintained at Taylor & Francis Group, 4 Park Square, Milton Park, Abingdon, OX14 4RN, United Kingdom.

ORDERING INFORMATION

Please contact your local Customer Service Department to take out a subscription to the Journal: **USA, Canada:** Taylor & Francis, Inc., 530 Walnut Street, Suite 850, Philadelphia, PA 19106, USA. Tel: +1 800 354 1420; Fax: +1 215 207 0050. **UK/ Europe/Rest of World:** T&F Customer Services, Informa UK Ltd, Sheepen Place, Colchester, Essex, CO3 3LP, United Kingdom. Tel: +44 (0) 20 7017 5544; Fax: +44 (0) 20 7017 5198; Email: subscriptions@tandf.co.uk.

Back issues: Taylor & Francis retains a two-year back issue stock of journals. Older volumes are held by our official stockists: Periodicals Service Company, 351 Fairview Ave., Suite 300, Hudson, New York 12534, USA to whom all orders and enquiries should be addressed. *Tel* +1 518 537 4700 *Fax* +1 518 537 5899 *e-mail* psc@periodicals.com *web* http://www.periodicals.com/tandf.html.

The International Institute for Strategic Studies (IISS) and our publisher Taylor & Francis make every effort to ensure the accuracy of all the information (the "Content") contained in our publications. However, the IISS and our publisher Taylor & Francis, our agents, and our licensors make no representations or warranties whatsoever as to the accuracy, completeness, or suitability for any purpose of the Content. Any opinions and views expressed in this publication are the opinions and views of the authors, and are not the views of or endorsed by the IISS and our publisher Taylor & Francis. The accuracy of the Content should not be relied upon and should be independently verified with primary sources of information. The IISS and our publisher Taylor & Francis shall not be liable for any losses, actions, claims, proceedings, demands, costs, expenses, damages, and other liabilities whatsoever or howsoever caused arising directly or indirectly in connection with, in relation to or arising out of the use of the Content. Terms & Conditions of access and use can be found at http://www.tandfonline.com/page/terms-and-conditions.

The issue date is December 2020–January 2021.

The print edition of this journal is printed on ANSI-conforming acid-free paper.

Europe Can Defend Itself

Barry R. Posen

US President Donald Trump has regularly expressed dissatisfaction with NATO and the European Union over the last four years. The palpable distress this has caused among European officials has created room to ask the question of whether Europe could look after itself on security matters. Could it dispense with the services of the US military? More specifically, could Europe cope on its own with Russia's querulous foreign policy and revived military?

There are many facets to this question – political and military, nuclear and conventional.[1] The conventional military question attracts a lot of attention, because it is the question most closely connected to the enduring debate on whether the Europeans spend enough on defence. Conventional forces are very expensive, consuming the lion's share of the defence budgets of even the strongest nuclear powers, and Europe has long been accused of woefully under-investing in defence.[2]

Below I review and critique one widely cited and pessimistic assessment of Europe's ability to defend itself without US assistance: the International Institute for Strategic Studies' (IISS) 'Defending Europe: Scenario-based Capability Requirements for NATO's European Members'.[3] I briefly summarise the IISS's methodology and conclusions. I argue that the study's choice of scenario, as well as many of its critical assumptions, largely

Barry R. Posen is the Ford International Professor of Political Science in the Security Studies Program at the Massachusetts Institute of Technology. He is the author of numerous articles and three books, including *Restraint: A New Foundation for US Grand Strategy* (Cornell University Press, 2014).

Survival | vol. 62 no. 6 | December 2020–January 2021 | pp. 7–34   https://doi.org/10.1080/00396338.2020.1851080

determine the conclusions. I then develop an alternative scenario, and using the same methodology as the IISS demonstrate that Europe may already have a very good autonomous capability to defend itself.

In general, observers agree that the Europeans could not go it alone.[4] This would seem to follow logically from NATO's official pre-pandemic goal that all members should spend 2% of GDP on defence – a demanding objective given that the European average is 1.5%. If a 25% shortfall currently exists, with the prospect of US assistance, how could the Europeans be competitive with Russia on their own? I argue that the Europeans could indeed be competitive with Russia. There is sufficient force structure in terms of brigades and squadrons, armed with relatively modern equipment. But there are also well-known problems with Europe's military forces, including poor readiness and poor sustainability due to inadequate stocks of ammunition and spare parts. Details are closely held, so the evidence is largely anecdotal. It does suggest, however, that the Europeans have not spent enough to bring their forces up to their full potential.[5] Due to the scarcity of granular readiness information, open-source analysts have focused on larger questions for which data is more plentiful. In particular, are extant European brigades and squadrons roughly adequate to address a Russian challenge? The headline answer is no. Yet on closer inspection, depending on the scenario, I find that the answer is probably yes. On its face, this conclusion seems plausible, given that even 1.5% of Europe's collective GDP is a great deal of money. It is important because if the extant force structure is broadly sufficient, Europeans could expeditiously address their readiness problems if they chose to do so.

To an extent, of course, strategic point of view affects the answer to the 'go it alone' question. Those strongly committed to the transatlantic Alliance, on both sides of the Atlantic, like analyses that show all of Europe's shortcomings. Though these shortcomings highlight Europe's failure to reach the 2% headline goal, and thus elicit a degree of ire even from committed Atlanticists, this is a small price to pay for sustaining the impression of European helplessness, which makes the US military commitment seem essential. Partisans of EU strategic autonomy, though far from satisfied with Europe's efforts, prefer to highlight all that Europe has already done.

Critics of the transatlantic Alliance, including myself, stress Europe's failure to meet the 2% goal. We see this as cheap-riding on the US, enabled by the excessive military insurance that the US provides to Europe.[6] At the same time, we argue that whatever shortfall in immediate European military resources there may be, it is not an inevitable, natural fact but a choice. In my view, Europe is much better situated to look after itself than it is often portrayed to be.

The balance of inputs

The main security problem for Europe is Russia. We should be curious as to how Europe's situation could be so bad, given that Europe's main military inputs – people and money – exceed Russia's. Including Turkey and Canada, and excluding the US, NATO has nearly 1.9 million military personnel. Excluding Turkey and Canada, NATO has nearly 1.4m military personnel.[7] Russia has about 900,000 troops in the active forces, and another 500,000 in paramilitary units, the main purpose of which is internal security, for a total of 1.4m.[8] The Stockholm International Peace Research Institute assesses that Russia spent perhaps $65 billion on defence in 2019, measured at market exchange rates.[9] The non-US NATO members spent roughly $300bn on defence that year, about $280bn without Turkey and Canada. Indeed, combined German and French defence spending alone is $100bn, which exceeds that of Russia. In crude terms, then, the Europeans out-resource Russia in military inputs. Furthermore, Europe draws its inputs from a much larger and more diverse base. The pre-Brexit GDP of the EU (which excludes NATO members Canada, Norway and Turkey, and includes neutrals such as Finland and Sweden) was about $16 trillion, compared with Russia's $1.7trn. The pre-Brexit population of the EU was 513m, while Russia's is about 145m. Overall, then, any inability on the part of European members of NATO to muster the military wherewithal to oppose Russian aggression involves more than a mere incapacity to allocate sufficient national resources to the challenge. It would be a defence-management failure of truly heroic proportions.

Two reasons are generally offered to explain why Europe would logically get less for its total defence spending than would a single country.

Firstly, whether counting NATO members or EU members, every European state has its own defence ministry and its own array of military headquarters, schools, depots and bases. Given that some of these countries are quite small, considerable duplication of effort is plausible. The superficial evidence does not support the argument that superfluous European civilian employees are the problem, however. The ratio of civilians employed by EU ministries of defence to the number of troops under arms is considerably lower than that of the United States. The US has 758,000 direct-hire civilians, 1,363,000 active troops and 804,000 reservists. Even if all reservists are included, the ratio of civilians to military personnel is 0.35. Europe employs 372,000 civilians to manage 1,400,000 troops, for a ratio of 0.25. Thus, by the numbers, Europe appears to be more efficient at management and support than the US.[10] This may seem off base intuitively, but the similarity in the ratio of civilians to uniformed personnel is suggestive.

Secondly, European spending might yield suboptimal results due to a lack of standardisation in the acquisition of weaponry and the consequent loss of scale economies of production. This too seems plausible. A frequently cited, though methodologically opaque, study by the European Parliament suggested that in the early part of the last decade, eliminating such inefficiencies would save $26bn a year.[11] Nevertheless, there is reason to question the extent of Europe's inefficiency. European sources are fond of claiming that the Europeans collectively field 17 different types of main battle tank to the United States' one.[12] This is a false comparison, as it arrays many different types of European armoured vehicle against only one US type, the M1 *Abrams* main battle ank. More tightly comparing like to like, European militaries field five types of modern tank, almost half of them the excellent German-designed and -manufactured *Leopard* II tanks.[13] Many former members of the Warsaw Pact, now in NATO, still field some of the Soviet-designed T72s, which are still widely in service in Russia.[14] The same kind of argument is often advanced with respect to combat aircraft. Europe is credited with 20 types and the US with six, which again exaggerates the disparity: most EU combat aircraft are US-designed F16s and European *Tornado*s, *Typhoon*s and *Rafale*s. And only the latter two were acquired since the end of the Cold War. *Tornado*s and *Typhoon*s were produced by

European consortia in reasonably long production runs. European military procurement may be less efficient than the United States' because higher US spending enables longer production runs. But how much less efficient is unclear. All modern fighter aircraft are wildly expensive, no matter where they are produced. European militaries would doubtless profit from greater standardisation from the standpoint of both efficient acquisition and ease of maintenance and supply on the battlefield. However, these shortfalls seem insufficient to explain the general pessimism about Europe's autonomous military capabilities.

Judging relative military power: campaign analysis

Although inputs and inventories can give us a sense of the military balance, soldiers, intelligence analysts and force planners much prefer to assess the adequacy of military preparations based on specific contingencies. Some use the term 'campaign analysis' for this process. Campaign analysis first identifies the key potential battles implied by a state's foreign policy. It then tries to simulate the possible outcomes of such battles with the forces on hand. Simulation can rely on multiplayer war games, simple or complicated computer programmes, or analytic models that integrate a few key variables suggested by historical experience. Planners prefer to use more than one approach, and defence ministries and military staffs have the money, personnel, time, computer power and high-resolution information to do quite a lot of campaign analysis if they wish. More analysis is probably better, because war is a complicated business, and one would rather not fail should the occasion for war arise. The conduct of multiple analyses allows planners to triangulate judgements about the adequacy of forces and assess where to make constructive new investments. Those seeking to formulate independent assessments must rely on the simple end of the analytic spectrum and open-source material.[15] The IISS's 'Defending Europe' is such an analysis.[16]

Any campaign analysis considers five factors. First, there is the mission. For example, is it offensive or defensive? Second comes the place, including geography, topography and lines of communication. The third factor is time. Is the element of surprise salient, or will there likely be time for preparations? Is a short war or a long war expected? The fourth consideration involves the

Table 1: **Summary: IISS counter-offensive vs alternative defence of Poland**

	IISS concept	Alternative concept
MISSION	Offensive	Defensive and coercive
PLACE	Baltic states and Belarus	Northwest Poland, Kaliningrad, Lithuania and Belarus border
DURATION	90 days + immediate offensive	90 days + open-ended defence
RUSSIAN FORCES	Most forces in western Russia, reinforced from all over Russia	Most forces in western Russia, reinforced from all over Russia (discounted slightly for lacunae in combat-service support and command elements)
NATO-EUROPE FORCES	Extant NATO command structure (discounted for readiness and modernisation shortfalls)	Extant NATO command structure (discounted for readiness and modernisation shortfalls, augmented with infantry units)
ANALYTIC HEURISTIC	Theatre-wide force ratios	Theatre-wide force ratios
ASSESSMENT	NATO PROSPECTS POOR	NATO PROSPECTS GOOD

quantity and quality of forces that each side can bring to the fight. Finally, how are opposing forces likely to clash? The ways these factors interact are assessed through war games, computer simulations or analytic models based on relevant military experience. A thorough campaign analysis is a tall order. The more refined the desired answer, the more comprehensively the underlying questions need to be addressed. Neither the IISS analysis nor my own seeks a refined answer. Rather, we are simply asking, what does it take for NATO Europe to have a fighting chance? I will review the IISS analysis, and then show how changes in a limited number of important assumptions alter the assessment of the adequacy of NATO Europe's forces. Table 1 summarises the two approaches.

The IISS approach

'Defending Europe' assesses NATO's military power absent the US. To test NATO Europe's capability versus Russia, it selects a demanding scenario. Lithuania and Poland get themselves into a war with Russia that starts with little warning, and ends with Russia's conquest of Lithuania and parts of northwest Poland. NATO Europe is compelled to reconquer this lost territory. The IISS analysts infer this requirement to liberate from NATO's Article V commitment to its members and the assumption that if NATO could not liberate these territories, other member states would lose confidence in the Alliance, whereupon it would dissolve. Presumably, the possession of such a counter-offensive capability is taken to be essential to deter Russian attack.

The scenario is demanding for two reasons. Firstly, the Baltics are inherently hard to defend. They became members of NATO and the EU prior to the resurgence of geostrategic competition. Little thought was given to the grave difficulty of successful defence against an even moderately well-resourced Russian effort to retake them. These states constitute a long, narrow finger of land, with the northernmost states bordering Russia and access to Lithuania constricted to a narrow land corridor – the Suwalki Gap – between Kaliningrad, a heavily armed Russian exclave, and Belarus, which is often regarded as a Russian satellite. Secondly, the Baltic states have small populations relative to Russia, and could put up only limited resistance on their own.

Although the Estonian border provides some natural defences in the form of lakes, ponds and swamps, the Baltic states simply cannot hope to defend themselves successfully. And unlike Finland, which has the strategic depth to support a strategy of delay and extended attrition, Baltic military forces have no space to which they could withdraw so as to regroup and continue the fight. Because of the geography, NATO would have to station very large forces in the Baltics along a 700–800-kilometre border to have a hope of defending them.[17] But given the area's geography and topography, even large NATO forces would be highly vulnerable to catastrophic failure because a single Russian success could cut them off from assistance. The maritime approaches to the Baltic states do not solve the problem because Russian bases are so close to them. Forces in Russia proper and in Kaliningrad could exploit the full panoply of the country's coastal-defence weapons, including modern naval mines, anti-ship missiles and land-based air-defence missiles, to make naval operations along the coast quite costly.[18]

The authors of the IISS study seem to accept that the Baltics are indefensible, but then assess NATO Europe's capabilities against a mission almost as hard as defending them: retaking the lost territory.[19] Furthermore, Russia is credited with completing its conquest and occupation of Lithuania, settling militarily into conquered terrain in Poland and building out a powerful military occupation of Belarus. NATO is then tested against the requirement to counter-attack these positions 90 days later. In this case, it is reasonable to attribute, as the authors do, a significant advantage to the defender, in this case Russia.

Russia is also assumed to have a significant advantage in military forces available for this contingency. Half of all the ground forces of the Russian army are committed to the theatre, which comes to 75 'battalion tactical groups' (BTGs).[20] Russia withholds a third of these units for a variety of security missions, and, at the time the scenario unfolds, 51 BTGs are in Belarus, Kaliningrad and Lithuania. These forces, equivalent to 18 NATO brigades, are assumed to be well armed, well trained and in a high state of readiness (see Table 2).[21] The scenario invokes a series of special measures that Russia undertakes, including drawing personnel from across Russia to fully man combat units and airlifting an entire airborne division into Kaliningrad.[22] These activities are either unnoticed or ignored by NATO, which does not increase the readiness of its own forces. Russia does have the initiative in this scenario, and has worked for several years to improve the readiness of its forces. And the Russian army has done well recently in small, carefully controlled fights against markedly inferior forces in Donbas and Syria, as well as in the slow-motion, largely unopposed seizure of Crimea. But it has not geared up for even a minor operation against serious resistance since its unimpressive performance in Georgia in 2008. In this light, the IISS's assumptions seem very favourable to Russian forces.

The assumptions seem favourable to Russian forces

Overall, NATO's available forces are assumed to be limited. The study does make one assumption that some would consider advantageous to NATO Europe, however. Although the US has exited the Alliance in this scenario, the NATO command structure – staffs, communications hardware and plans – has passed intact to the Alliance (less the US complement) and is available to coordinate the operation. The authors rightly observe that without this assumption, the Europeans would have a difficult time managing a large operation, as the 'shadow' structures maintained by the EU probably are not sufficiently developed to run a large operation. With regard to available European forces, however, the IISS study is very pessimistic. While it attributes to NATO's European members nearly 100 armoured and mechanised brigades, it asserts that about 75% of them could not contribute to the operation because they are equipped with 'obsolescent tank, infantry-fighting-vehicle, or armoured-personnel-carrier designs'.[23] Of the 22 remaining adequately equipped mechanised brigades, the IISS observes that under normal conditions, European units are not particularly 'ready', and therefore assumes that only 50%, or 11 brigades, could deploy to Poland and be ready to fight within 90 days.[24]

Thus, the study casts Russia as working hard, creatively and effectively to ready its forces for combat in short order, and Europe as far less determined.[25] One-third of all Russian ground combat units, indeed the best third, are assumed to be on the front line, whereas perhaps 10% of European units are judged available for the campaign. No wonder things look bleak.

Simulating combat is not a simple matter. The IISS adopted some rules of thumb to assess the adequacy of NATO Europe's forces to the task of liberating Lithuanian and Polish territories conquered by Russia. 'Defending Europe' posits that offensive success becomes plausible when the attacker enjoys a material superiority in the theatre of 1.5:1, and more certain at 2:1.[26] The authors apply this ratio to major ground-force elements and to tactical air forces. No source is provided for the origin of these rules of thumb, but one can find such ratios cited frequently in Cold War-era assessments for ground forces.[27] The 1.5:1 theatre-wide force ratio emerged from many different analyses of the same problem: what it would take to break through on a front that was thickly defended, a problem that first emerged during the First World War on the Western Front. A possible criticism of the use of that ratio in this hypothetical theatre is that neither Russia nor NATO has sufficient brigades to thickly defend the entire front. Thus, it is quite possible that the scope for manoeuvre is greater than assumed, in which case the requirements for offence and defence might be better assessed through a series of war games.[28]

The IISS analysts calculate the forces required for NATO Europe by multiplying the Russian force by 1.5 and 2. They then subtract their estimate of available European forces to come up with NATO Europe's force deficit. To meet the 1.5:1 criterion, Europe would need 27 mechanised brigades, and for the 2:1 criterion 36 brigades.[29] Given that Europe only has 11 ready mechanised brigades, the shortfall is between 17 and 26 brigades.

(Strikingly, the entire active US Army could now provide only another 10–14 armoured or mechanised brigades.[30] So the IISS analysis implicitly holds that NATO's ground forces would be inadequate even with active US participation.) Based on their pessimistic view of the general level of readiness (50%) achievable in European military units, the authors have to double the brigade shortfalls to generate their hypothetical overall shortfall and the budget necessary to remedy it. Europe needs to either stand up, or thoroughly re-equip, between 34 and 52 brigades, at an initial capital cost of $150–200bn.[31] Finally, the analysis rightly calls attention to often overlooked combat-support assets that European countries effectively liquidated from their armies after the Cold War. The most notable of these are short-, medium- and long-range surface-to-air missile batteries to defend against combat aircraft, drones, cruise missiles and tactical ballistic missiles.[32] European ground forces have none of these assets, and would certainly require some to mount a counter-offensive.

'Defending Europe' chooses a demanding scenario against which to measure Europe's autonomous capabilities. In the authors' view, to meet NATO's Article V commitment to its members, NATO must have the capability, available in short order, to liberate the territory of any member state that has fallen to an adversary offensive. In this scenario, the authors want very high confidence of success, so significant material superiority is required. Because European forces have faced challenges in maintaining peacetime readiness since the end of the Cold War, only half are assumed available at any one time. Meanwhile, Russia's forces are deemed well armed and highly ready. The standards for NATO are so exacting that even if the US were included in NATO's forces, they could not be met.

Table 2: **NATO Europe's counter-offensive: IISS ground-force assumptions and requirements**

Available Russian heavy brigades	18
Available NATO heavy brigades	11
NATO–Russia force-ratio requirement	1.5–2:1
NATO heavy-brigade requirement	27–36
NATO deficit	-16 to -25 (if 50% readiness, -32 to -50)
Actual NATO:Russia force ratio	0.6:1
ASSESSMENT	NATO EUROPE CANNOT COUNTER-ATTACK WITH EXTANT FORCES

Using similar heuristics, however, I contend that the European members of NATO possess sufficient combat capability to marshal a spirited defence of the Alliance in the east.

Alternative assessment: European defence and dissuasion

The European members of NATO, and the members of the EU, collectively have much larger populations and a much larger GDP than Russia. They also enjoy a favourable geographic position relative to Russia, whose paths to the sea are blocked by European power in the Mediterranean, the Baltic and the north Norwegian seas, as well as the Atlantic Ocean.[33] Two European members of NATO, the United Kingdom and France, possess nuclear weapons. A decision to take on a European coalition in war would be a weighty one for Russia. Nuclear weapons on both sides make efforts to settle a war with decisive offensives mutually suicidal. Furthermore, a long war of attrition would do egregious damage to Russia's economy and, ironically, turn it into a vassal state of China – hardly a nationalist success for Russian President Vladimir Putin or his successor. Europe can plausibly dissuade Russia from aggression with the threat to wage such a war. That threat is credible if Russia cannot win a short war.

Conquering the Baltic states would just make Europeans angry, not end the war. To end the war through military victory, Russia would need to reconquer much of Eastern Europe, even perhaps eastern Germany, and do it quickly, before Europe's superior resources could be mobilised. Even this might not produce a strategic success, because the bulk of Europe's land, wealth and population is situated even farther to the west, affording it strategic depth. Rather than quixotic attempts to defend the Baltics, or self-destructive early offensives to take them back, European conventional forces should be rated by their ability to deny major offensive successes for Russia against its eastern members. The concomitant threat of a long, grinding war of attrition against an economically, demographically and even geographically advantaged Europe is the deterrent against Russian aggression, even in the vulnerable Baltic states.

The analytic framework of 'Defending Europe' can be applied to the task of assessing whether Europe possesses the force structure to defend itself in the east. The question is not whether Europe can quickly muster a 1.5–2:1 superiority over Russia. It is whether Russia can muster a 1.5–2:1 superiority over Europe. Simply reversing the problem from offence to defence changes Europe's prospects. But switching roles also may reduce the size of the Russian force available for the fight, and increases the size of the available European force.

Adapting the 'Defending Europe' scenario

'Defending Europe' assumes that Russia conquers Lithuania and part of Poland. NATO troops positioned forward fight as best they can, but succumb to superior Russian numbers. I accept this as the opening phase of conflict and agree that NATO Europe's counter-move is to reinforce in Eastern Europe. I submit, however, that the smart play is to prepare to defend Poland from subsequent Russian military moves, build up European military power and harass Russia around its periphery, at sea, in the air and on land. Russia has to consider whether to mount an offensive in Poland in an attempt to cow Europe into negotiating an end to the war that recognises Russian gains. Can Europe make this prospect daunting? In this scenario, it is Russia that needs the 1.5–2:1 advantage in ground and air forces. Put another way, if the IISS is correct, and 11 mechanised brigades are all Europe could deploy to Poland, Russia would need between 16 and 22 heavy brigades for a credible offensive capability. How close is Moscow to that capability?

The IISS study credits Russia with the equivalent of 18 heavy brigades in Belarus, Kaliningrad and Lithuania at the end of the first phase of its offensive. Thus, Russia would have forward-deployed forces that sufficiently outnumbered Europe's 11 ready mechanised brigades to mount an offensive, a force ratio of 1.6:1. This NATO numerical disadvantage, if real, is much less expensive to rectify than the NATO force deficit for offensive operations. As noted earlier, there the deficit is between 17 and 26 brigades in theatre, and double that if NATO is assumed unable to achieve more than 50% readiness. Should NATO choose defence as a mission, its shortfall to reduce the Russian advantage to under 1.5:1 is a mere one or two brigades, or two to four assuming 50% readiness. Readiness is not, however, a fact of nature but a choice. Rather than buying new brigades, NATO Europe could simply invest in marginally increasing the readiness of its extant force of 22 properly equipped mechanised brigades from 50% to perhaps 60%.

Altering the Russian army's task from defence to offence should also affect the estimate of available Russian and European combat power. Russian units would have to do a bit more than they seem designed to accomplish, and NATO could profitably employ lighter forces for defensive rather than offensive tasks. Modest but analytically defensible changes in estimates of each side's available forces thus paint a different picture of relative combat power.

During the Cold War, Western analysts came to understand that Russian units were not identical to Western units, even if they carried the same name. Russian divisions were much smaller than Western divisions. Their principal combat sub-unit, the regiment, was smaller than its NATO counterpart, the brigade. To be fair, these units often had equal or even superior numbers of major weapons systems. But they were missing command and logistics elements. Thus, their flexibility and staying power were in doubt. Indeed, until very recently, the Russian army itself seemed to have absorbed this lesson, and began reorganising its forces into brigades that looked more like their Western counterparts. This change is not complete, however, and the army even appears to have reversed it in some cases. Many Russian units today, especially heavy divisions and their attached regiments, look much like their Cold War predecessors; indeed, they seem even leaner in terms of personnel.

'Defending Europe' credits Russia with four heavy divisions plus two independent brigades deployed in Kaliningrad, occupied Poland and Belarus up to the border with Ukraine. The divisions are assumed to have four regiments or brigades each, and each one of these is assumed to be the equal of a NATO brigade. Though the report's authors are a bit cryptic, they seem to believe that four Russian divisions in the West are reinforced with units and individuals from all over Russia, and capable of growing into hugely powerful and capable formations of a kind never seen in either the Soviet or the Russian army.[34] In normal times, however, US intelligence reports that Russian divisions range from 5,500–8,500 strong, whereas NATO divisions typically have twice that level of personnel.[35] The additional personnel now, as in the Cold War, are what it takes to engage in intense combat. It is hard to 'derate' the combat power of these Russian divisions and regiments; there is no handy way to do it.[36] But for offensive operations, it is more plausible that a typical Russian division could generate, command, control and supply two or three 'NATO brigade equivalents' than four of them.[37] Assuming the Russians can manage three brigades, this would bring the theatre-wide force ratio down from 20:11 to 14:11, or 1.3:1, or less (see Table 3).

If the IISS front-wide 1.5–2:1 force-ratio heuristic is valid, NATO European forces seem competitive. NATO's publicly announced rapid-reinforcement objective for ground forces is 30 mechanised battalions in 30 days.[38] In Western militaries, this would typically imply ten brigades. If ten brigades is NATO's official solution to the Russia problem, and if the IISS heuristic roughly captures the thinking of NATO planners, then NATO is unlikely to have assessed the plausible Russian force in theatre as larger than 15 brigades.

Changing the mission from offence to defence, however, also permits NATO Europe to take advantage of the large number of 'light' infantry units in Western armies (see Table 3). These units typically have no tanks, and though they can have light armoured vehicles, these are not well suited to offensive operations. Some are airborne units, which in most Western armies are considered elite troops. While these units are often among the readiest in any army, 'Defending Europe' rightly does not count them as useful for the counter-attack scenario. Most NATO European armies maintain one or more additional infantry brigades. Some of these specialise in mountainous terrain and are considered elite. There are also many infantry brigades that travel by truck or light armoured vehicle, and fight on foot. For defensive operations, especially where urban or forested areas are available for cover and concealment, these units can be effective, even against mechanised forces. Indeed, they are sometime preferable.[39] Such brigades are not the equal of armoured brigades in open country, but assigning them half the combat power of their heavier brethren when fighting defensively on ground of their choosing seems fair. France, Germany, Italy, the Netherlands, Spain and the UK collectively have at least another dozen of these types of brigades.[40] If half are assumed ready, then six more brigades are available to fight, and even if their combat power is discounted

Table 3: **NATO Europe's defence of Poland: ground-forces assumptions and requirements**

	IISS order-of-battle assumptions	Modified order-of-battle assumptions (1)	Modified order-of-battle assumptions (2)
Available Russian heavy brigades	18	14	14
Available NATO heavy brigades	11	11	14 (if six infantry brigades available and assumed 50% of heavy-brigade combat power on appropriate terrain)
Russia–NATO force-ratio requirement	1.5–2:1	1.5–2:1	1.5–2:1
Russian brigades needed	16.5–22	16.5–22	21–28
Russian surplus (or shortfall)	1.5 (-4)	(-2.5 to -8.0)	(-7 to -14)
Actual Russia:NATO force ratio	1.6:1	1.3:1	1:1
NATO heavy-brigade requirement	9–12	7–9	7–9
NATO surplus (or shortfall)	+2 (-1)	+2 to +4	+5 to +7
ASSESSMENT	NATO EUROPE COULD DEFEND WITH MINOR REFORMS	NATO EUROPE PROBABLY CAN DEFEND	NATO EUROPE IN A GOOD POSITION TO DEFEND

by another 50%, three brigade equivalents can be added to the NATO total, bringing the Russia–NATO force ratio down to 14:14, or one to one.

Airpower and air defence

Whether NATO's objective is to recapture territory taken by Russia, or to defend Poland, airpower will be a critical element of the campaign. This has been true of modern ground-force operations since the advent of combat aircraft early in the First World War. Airpower is particularly important in mechanised warfare, in which the responsiveness of airpower can be a useful counter to the sudden changes on the battlefield that armoured and mechanised clashes often produce. This dynamic could prove particularly salient in any campaign in Eastern Europe under present conditions, because, in contrast to the Second World War and the Cold War, the ratio of ground units to space is low, producing a greater possibility of fast-moving battles of manoeuvre.

'Defending Europe' uses the same front-wide force-ratio heuristic to assess European airpower as it does to assess land power. 'All other things being near equal', say the authors, 'platform numbers around parity favour the defender strongly. A force structure 50% larger than that assessed to be currently deployable would offer an uncertain outcome, while a deployed force double the size of the current estimate would provide a generally favourable outcome.'[41] They cite no source for this statement and I could find none myself. After counting available Russian and European aircraft, they conclude that NATO needs an additional 264 top-quality tactical fighters in combat units to achieve a 2:1 superiority and thus be able to take the offensive with hope of success.[42] The study offers a narrative about the kind of air operations that would attend a NATO counter-offensive. Quite rightly, it notes that they would be complex and demanding, as modern Russian surface-to-air missile systems are quite good, and Russian forces would be fighting on their own ground, with hardened and redundant communications systems and an integrated air-defence system. These assets would need to be suppressed in order to operate aircraft against ground targets while avoiding potential losses that could be high enough to scuttle the operation.

If we apply the IISS heuristic that the attacking air force should outnumber that of the defender by 2:1, NATO would experience no shortage of aircraft for a major defensive operation in Poland. 'Defending Europe' credits Russia with roughly 296 combat aircraft, and NATO with 400, a ratio of 1.35:1 in NATO's favour, which would be defending.[43] By the very criteria of the IISS analysis, Russian air forces are plainly inadequate to support a ground offensive deep into Poland. This is not to say that Russia could not attempt such a ground offensive. Russia has many assets to put in play, including cruise missiles and tactical ballistic missiles.[44] And Russian ground forces typically drag along with them mobile air-defence assets that would give NATO's supporting aircraft a tough time. Nevertheless, establishing a NATO defensive umbrella over Poland, and employing tactical aircraft to directly support NATO's ground forces in that country, are much easier tasks than trying to crack open prepared Russian air and ground defences in Belarus, Kaliningrad and Lithuania.[45] Indeed, NATO's air forces should, in some measure, be able to compensate for the mobile surface-to-air missile systems largely missing from NATO's ground forces.[46]

*　　　*　　　*

A single, relatively simple, analysis cannot settle fundamental questions about any balance of military power. European security, including the Russian military, fell out of favour as a subject of analysis after the Cold War. Even weighty decisions, such as bringing the Baltics into NATO, were not subjected to serious military scrutiny. Russia's actions have brought renewed attention to the problem, and the analytic community has begun to assess the balance, but publicly available material remains thin. NATO's ability to defend the Baltics is a favourite scenario, and the IISS has moved the debate beyond that particular military project, which may be futile. Indeed, it has chosen to test two good questions at a time. What would it take to liberate lost territory? And could NATO Europe do it alone? The institute's answer to the first question is, unsurprisingly, a lot. And its answer to the second is no. But from the point of view of Europe's ability to defend itself, the IISS's deck is stacked. What we really want to know is, if Europe alone were responsible for providing the military forces to stop a Russian campaign to reconquer its Soviet-era empire in Eastern Europe – and threaten the ultimate prize, which is Germany – could it do so? Employing the IISS's own methodology, the answer is a qualified yes.

We should not make too much of this answer, however. The challenge here is unavoidably big and lumpy, asking only whether the present force structure seems sufficient to the task. It does, but that does not mean that European militaries are in great shape, or that there are no critical vulnerabilities that need attention. Anecdotally, we know there are readiness issues in Europe's military forces, and that sustainability is in question. Furthermore, the IISS and I have made critical assumptions about the availability of any appropriate European forces from across the Alliance for combat along the Polish border. In the actual event, some European member states might be loath to send their best forces, especially their best ground forces, for this dangerous and demanding contingency. The IISS study presents many good ideas about things that need major improvement, including readiness, sustainability and, more particularly, ground-based air-defence assets. But the IISS team also draws from its analysis several grandiose and hugely expensive ideas for ramping up European counter-offensive capabilities that seem unnecessary.

Although many expect European defence budgets to drop due to COVID-19-related expenses, this is in fact a very good time to address NATO Europe's military-readiness shortfalls. High-end European military hardware suffers from an absence of tender loving care – to wit, parts and maintenance. The European civilian-aircraft industry and the airlines it supports are now contracting. All over Europe, highly skilled workers are losing their jobs. Factories are underutilised. These assets can be diverted to the task of bringing military aircraft, helicopters and missiles up to high standards of readiness. Additional orders could be placed for critical supporting assets that would serve as force multipliers in any contingency. Examples include Airbus Multirole Tanker Transports based on the A330 airframe, and A400 military-transport aircraft with refuelling capability. The project to replace NATO Europe's ageing fleet of Airborne Warning and Control System surveillance aircraft could be accelerated. Such initiatives are unlikely to arise unless Europe feels the heat. But there are many possible heat sources, including Russian bellicosity, consistent American demands for greater European contributions and evidence that US interest in Europe is simply waning.

I have painted a picture of a Europe that is surprisingly close to being able to defend itself militarily, especially given the weight of public commentary to the contrary. I have used the same heuristics that the IISS, in 'Defending Europe', employed to support the widespread pessimism. European civilian and military practitioners seem to have been surprisingly deft at insuring against the United States' departure, and hiding the effort behind public protestations of helplessness. True, my analysis may be somewhat generous to European forces, but not so generous as to vitiate the main conclusion: as far as conventional defence is concerned, European defence autonomy is not an unachievable and unaffordable goal. Indeed, it is within reach.

Notes

[1] For a concise summary of the conventional, nuclear and political issues, see Margriet Drent, 'European Strategic Autonomy: Going It Alone?', Policy Brief, Clingendael–Netherlands Institute of International Relations, August 2018, https://www.clingendael.org/sites/default/files/2018-08/PB_

European_Strategic_Autonomy.pdf.

2   See Barry R. Posen, 'Trump Aside, What's the US Role in NATO?', *New York Times*, 10 March 2019, https://www.nytimes.com/2019/03/10/opinion/trump-aside-whats-the-us-role-in-nato.html.

3   Douglas Barrie et al., 'Defending Europe: Scenario-based Capability Requirements for NATO's European Members', IISS Research Paper, April 2019, https://www.iiss.org/blogs/research-paper/2019/05/defending-europe.

4   See, for example, Pauli Järvenpää, Claudia Major and Sven Sakkov, 'European Strategic Autonomy: Operationalising a Buzzword', International Centre for Defence and Security, October 2019, p. 38, https://icds.ee/wp-content/uploads/2019/10/ICDS_Report_European_Strategic_Autonomy_J%c3%a4rvenp%c3%a4%c3%a4_Major_Sakkov_October_2019.pdf. The authors write: 'A 2019 study from the International Institute for Strategic Studies (IISS) demonstrates that Europe would face substantial capability shortfalls in taking on high-end military tasks such as the protection of global sea lines of communication or the conduct of collective defence.' See also Nick Witney, 'Strategic Sovereignty: Building Europeans' Capacity to Defend Themselves', European Council on Foreign Relations, June 2019, https://ecfr.eu/wp-content/uploads/5_Building_Europeans_capacity_to_defend_themselves.pdf. Referring to the same study, Witney states: 'The problem is the scale of Europeans' defence deficiencies:

making up for what the US currently provides and achieving genuine defence autonomy would be the work of decades rather than years.'

5   Accounts of unready European units and equipment are legion, especially in Germany. Germany is particularly well placed by virtue of geography, internal transportation infrastructure and wealth to contribute to any operation in Eastern Europe, so it is vexing that the Bundeswehr has chronic readiness problems. See, for example, German Bundestag, 'Information from the Parliamentary Commissioner for the Armed Forces', Annual Report 2019 (61st Report), 19th electoral term, Printed Paper 19/16500, 28 January 2020, pp. 7–10, 42–7, https://www.bundestag.de/resource/blob/692052/3ebc4bc657d328c1db223f430e63b839/annual_report_2019_61st_report-data.pdf.

6   See Barry R. Posen, *Restraint: A New Foundation for U.S. Grand Strategy* (Ithaca, NY: Cornell University Press, 2014), pp. 33–40.

7   Personnel and spending data is drawn from NATO Public Diplomacy Division, 'Defence Expenditure of NATO Countries (2013–2019)', Press Release PR/CP (2019)123, 29 November 2019, https://www.nato.int/nato_static_fl2014/assets/pdf/pdf_2019_11/20191129_pr-2019-123-en.pdf.

8   IISS, *The Military Balance 2020* (Abingdon: Routledge for the IISS, 2020), p. 194.

9   Nan Tian et al., 'Trends in World Military Expenditure, 2019', SIPRI Fact Sheet, April 2020, https://www.sipri.org/sites/default/files/2020-04/

fs_2020_04_milex_0.pdf. Some cavil at the use of market exchange rates to compare the magnitude of inputs, because exchange rates fluctuate. Instead, they prefer purchasing-power parity (PPP), a measure that is used to compare the productive output of economies of different levels of development. PPP thus makes the Russian and Chinese economies look larger, because it assigns Western prices to locally inexpensive civilian goods and services. Once the share of GDP taken by the national defence budgets in local currencies is assessed, devotees of PPP then multiply that figure by total GDP at PPP in dollars, and come up with a much larger 'defence input' figure in dollars, as much as $160bn in the case of Russia. NATO Europe would still outspend Russia by this metric, but the arithmetical gap obviously shrinks. See Fredrik Westerlund and Susanne Oxenstierna (eds), *Russian Military Capability in a Ten-year Perspective – 2019* (Stockholm: Swedish Defence Research Agency, 2019), pp. 103–4. For a lucid explanation of why SIPRI uses market exchange rates, see SIPRI, 'Frequently Asked Questions', no. 12, https://www.sipri.org/databases/milex/frequently-asked-questions#PPP. Seeing some merit in both positions, I view the median between defence spending at PPP and defence spending at market exchange rates as a reasonable indicator of relative effort. This would credit Russia with about a $110bn defence budget.

10 See US Department of Defense, 'Number of Military and DoD Appropriated Fund (APF) Civilian Personnel Permanently Assigned by Duty Location and Service/Component', Defense Manpower Data Center, 31 March 2020, https://www.dmdc.osd.mil/appj/dwp/dwp_reports.jsp; and European Union, 'Defence Data 2016–2017: Key Findings and Analysis', European Defence Agency, p. 13, https://www.eda.europa.eu/docs/default-source/brochures/eda_defencedata_a4.

11 Blanca Ballester, 'The Cost of Non-Europe in Common Security and Defence Policy', CoNE 4/2013, European Parliamentary Research Service, European Added Value Unit, December 2013, p. 78, https://www.europarl.europa.eu/RegData/etudes/etudes/join/2013/494466/IPOL-JOIN_ET%282013%29494466_EN.pdf.

12 Federica Mogherini and Jyrki Katainen, 'Reflection Paper on the Future of European Defence', European Commission, June 2017, p. 9, https://ec.europa.eu/commission/sites/beta-political/files/reflection-paper-defence_en.pdf.

13 Austria, Denmark, Finland, Germany, Greece, Norway, Poland, Portugal, Spain and Sweden collectively field roughly 1,650 *Leopard* II tanks. All these countries except for Austria, Finland and Sweden are NATO members. Tank aficionados will be quick to point out that there are different variants of this tank; they are not perfectly standardised.

14 The UK, France and Italy do each field different models in small numbers (200 French *Leclercs*, 227 British *Challenger* IIs and 160 Italian *Arietes* respectively). Had they too bought *Leopard* IIs, a good deal of money would no doubt have been saved in

procurement and maintenance costs. All these designs were procured near the end of the Cold War; every major power has reduced the number of tanks it has in service. Many of the remaining tanks have been refurbished and modernised over the last two decades. There are even older tanks still in the inventories of some NATO members.

15 For recent examples of open-source campaign analysis, see Joshua R. Itzkowitz Shifrinson and Miranda Priebe, 'A Crude Threat: The Limits of an Iranian Missile Campaign Against Saudi Arabian Oil', *International Security*, vol. 36, no. 1, Summer 2011, pp. 167–201; and Caitlin Talmadge, 'Closing Time: Assessing the Iranian Threat to the Strait of Hormuz', *International Security*, vol. 33, no. 1, Summer 2008, pp. 82–117. For a comprehensive treatment of the methodology of campaign analysis, see Rachel Tecott and Andrew Halterman, 'The Case for Campaign Analysis: A Method for Studying Military Operations', Research Paper No. 2020-4, Massachusetts Institute of Technology Political Science Department, 19 October 2020, https://andrewhalterman.com/files/Tecott_Halterman_Campaign_Analysis-merged.pdf (forthcoming in *International Security*).

16 Barrie et al., 'Defending Europe', chapter 3.

17 During the Cold War, planners would have assigned two dozen armoured/mechanised divisions to a front of this length. The Baltics could not afford a force of this size; indeed, the entire US active army has but ten divisions today.

18 See Robert Dalsjö, Christofer Berglund and Michael Jonsson, 'Bursting the Bubble: Russian A2/AD in the Baltic Sea Region: Capabilities, Countermeasures, and Implications', Swedish Defence Research Centre, March 2019. This paper offers an excellent primer on anti-access/area-denial (A2/AD) weaponry and its utility to the Russians in this contingency. The authors conclude that Russian capabilities are overstated, both by the West and by Russia. While their analysis supports this conclusion, it is not entirely reassuring since admittedly 'the prospects for defending or resupplying the Baltic States in a crisis or war are not as bleak as is often claimed'. *Ibid.*, p. 11.

19 The study assesses the adequacy of NATO European ground, air and naval capabilities for this task, but the bulk of its analysis is on the first two, so I do not treat the naval analysis in this critique.

20 Barrie et al, 'Defending Europe', pp. 19–20. These 75 units are assessed as having 1,000 tanks and 1,000 infantry fighting vehicles. Students of the Russian army now like to aggregate its combat power in terms of 'battalion tactical groups' or BTGs. See Lester W. Grau and Charles K. Bartles, *The Russian Way of War: Force Structure, Tactics, and Modernization of the Russian Ground Forces* (Fort Leavenworth, KS: Foreign Military Studies Office, US Army, 2016), pp. 30–8, https://www.armyupress.army.mil/Portals/7/Hot%20Spots/Documents/Russia/2017-07-The-Russian-Way-of-War-Grau-Bartles.pdf. These are small combined-arms task forces

assembled within standing Russian army combat organisations, such as brigades, regiments and divisions. This is the way Western militaries have fought since at least the Second World War, but it is somewhat new to the Russians. The size and combat power of these groups are a bit elusive, though they usually consist of one mechanised infantry battalion, one or more companies of tanks, and some or all of a mechanised artillery battalion, perhaps with 50 armoured fighting vehicles in total. Because the IISS analysis jumps back and forth from discussing actual Russian units and BTGs, it is sometimes difficult to figure out how the analysts are actually counting and comparing combat power. After laboriously counting BTGs, the authors then shift to 'brigades' as the unit of comparison. Apparently they believe that a Russian division in this scenario will command and control forces equivalent to four NATO brigades, each of which deploys three BTGs.

21 Mechanised brigades, relatively independent units of 3,000–6,000 personnel and perhaps 150 major combat vehicles, have become the most commonly employed major ground-force formation in Western armies. In recent years, Russia has largely but not entirely emulated this practice, so 'Defending Europe' uses brigades as its unit of comparison.

22 Barrie et al., 'Defending Europe', pp. 18–19.

23 Ibid., p. 4. Although the authors do not say it, this assumption may also simply be a proxy for the unlikelihood that forces from Turkey or Greece,

both large NATO armies, would actually be made available for combat in Poland under any circumstances. From the point of view of political practicality and geographical proximity, one would expect British, Dutch, French and German forces to be available, and perhaps some contingents from Italy and Spain. Judging from the country entries in The Military Balance 2020, these countries have about 23 armoured and mechanised brigades; each also has at least one airborne or air-assault brigade, and often a number of infantry brigades. Though Polish units are inevitably in the war, many of their dozen armoured and mechanised brigades seem undermanned and equipped with a significant number of older Soviet-pattern armoured vehicles, so the IISS probably discounts their utility in some way.

24 Barrie et al., 'Defending Europe', pp. 4, 27. In the IISS scenario, the Russians destroy two or three Polish and other NATO ready mechanised brigades in the first phase of the campaign.

25 Some confusion has been caused by the EU's effort to track publicly the ability of European countries to generate combat power. The European Defence Agency published a collection of data that included some readiness statistics. See European Union, 'Defence Data 2016–2017'. On the basis of its interpretation of national reporting, the agency asserted that 405,000 members of EU ground forces were 'deployable', but that 94,000, or roughly 25%, were 'sustainable'. The definitions of these categories are somewhat vague, but

the first seems to refer to uniformed army troops in units that could be sent abroad for national missions, and the latter figure to the estimated steady-state force that Europe could support in the field for relatively long deployments or keep highly ready in case of sudden deployment requirements. See European Defence Agency, 'Definitions', https://www.eda.europa.eu/info-hub/defence-data-portal/Definitions. There is no obvious inference to be drawn from either figure about the immediate employability of troops in a true Europe-wide security crisis.

26 Barrie et al., 'Defending Europe', pp. 27–9.

27 The intuition informing this rule of thumb is that front-wide superiority allows the attacker to fix most of the defender's forces in place across the front, and then concentrate its own surplus in narrow sectors to overwhelm the defender. This was the problem as NATO planners saw it during the Cold War. See Congressional Budget Office, 'Strengthening NATO: Pomcus and Other Approaches, Background Paper', February 1979, pp. 9–13, https://www.cbo.gov/sites/default/files/96th-congress-1979-1980/reports/79doc644.pdf. This study cited a then-common use of this heuristic at the Pentagon. An annual report, for instance, states that 'certain ratios … should not be allowed to favor an attacker by too great a margin. For example, if an attacker could achieve a favorable overall ratio of perhaps 1.5:1 in several of these respects, he could embark on such large local con-

centrations that the defender would find it difficult to prevent one or more breakthroughs.' US Department of Defense, 'Annual Defense Department Report, FY 1976 and FY 1977', chapter 3, p. 15, https://history.defense.gov/Portals/70/Documents/annual_reports/1976-77_DoD_AR.pdf?ver=2014-06-24-150722-417. Note, however, that the IISS analysts seem to believe that even a 1.5:1 ratio in favour of NATO would provide insufficient assurance of success.

28 See, for example, David A. Shlapak and Michael Johnson, *Reinforcing Deterrence on NATO's Eastern Flank: Wargaming the Defence of the Baltics* (Santa Monica, CA: RAND Corporation, 2016), p. 12, https://www.rand.org/pubs/research_reports/RR1253.html. The authors note: 'RAND developed this map-based tabletop exercise because existing models were ill-suited to represent the many unknowns and uncertainties surrounding a conventional military campaign in the Baltics, where low force-to-space ratios and relatively open terrain meant that maneuver between dispersed forces – rather than pushing and shoving between opposing units arrayed along a linear front – would likely be the dominant mode of combat.' One might say the same of either an offensive or a defensive campaign along the border between Poland and Kaliningrad–Lithuania–Belarus.

29 Barrie et al., 'Defending Europe', table 3.1, p. 28.

30 IISS, *The Military Balance 2020*, p. 47. There are seven additional brigades in the US Army National Guard, but

these are reserve units, and by the readiness standards of 'Defending Europe' ought not to be counted as ready for such a contingency.

31   Barrie et al., 'Defending Europe', table 4.10, p. 41. This would be more armoured forces than existed in the entire US active army at the height of the Reagan-era build-up.

32   *Ibid.*, pp. 27–8. The study simply assumes that each major combat unit, from brigade through corps, requires a surface-to-air missile unit of some kind. Major installations also require their own air-defence units.

33   *Ibid.*, on pp. 33–4, also offers an assessment of the maritime forces NATO Europe would require to support its counter-offensive ground and air operations. It sees NATO as having significant shortfalls in this regard – on the order of $100bn of capital stock. Interestingly, though naval forces are quite expensive, this shortfall is much less than the shortfall in ground forces, implying that Europeans may already be somewhat over-invested in naval power. Revisiting the maritime analysis is beyond the scope of this paper, but the defensive scenario would also reduce the requirement for maritime forces. Finally, though US forces are excluded from both the IISS scenario and my alternative, in a real war the Russians could not operate on the assumption that US naval forces were irrelevant. This reality would likely impose considerable constraints on the Russians.

34   *Ibid.*, p. 19. It also appears that the readiest BTGs are stripped from units all over Russia to bring these brigades and regiments up to 100% readiness, each capable of deploying three full BTGs. Though this is a murky area, Western analysts seem inclined to accept Russian claims about the readiness and quality of its military organisation at face value. I doubt that Russia is capable of generating the number of ready BTGs assumed in the IISS analysis, but developing an alternative estimate is beyond the scope of this paper.

35   For example, the French 7th armoured brigade has 7,500 personnel, nearly as many as a Russian division. The French 1st and 3rd divisions are credited with personnel strengths of roughly 25,000 each. See 'Armée de Terre, 7e brigade blindée', Ministère des Armées, 1 August 2018, https://www.defense. gouv.fr/terre/l-armee-de-terre/le-niveau-divisionnaire/1re-division/7e-brigade-blindee; and 'Armée de Terre, Le niveau divisionnaire', Ministère des Armées, https://www.defense. gouv.fr/terre/l-armee-de-terre/le-niveau-divisionnaire.

36   During the Cold War, I developed a method to do so. See Barry R. Posen, 'Measuring the European Conventional Balance: Coping with Complexity in Threat Assessment', *International Security*, vol. 9, no. 3, Winter 1984–1985, pp. 67–70.

37   On Russian ground formations, see Grau and Bartles, *The Russian Way of War*, pp. 30–8. Russian motorised rifle divisions are estimated to have 6,500 people, brigades 3,000–4,500 people. Thus, it is not plausible that a Russian division could somehow generate the equivalent of three to four brigades' worth of combat power, regardless of

how many weapons it may possess. The propensity of Western analysts to treat the three to four subsidiary regiments of Russian divisions as equivalent to three or four brigades is difficult to fathom. The Russian army was previously so dissatisfied with its divisional formations that it converted many of them into Western-style brigades on what appears to be a one-for-one basis. Recently, the Russian army started to rebuild a few divisions but it is not clear why. The US Defense Intelligence Agency speculates that 'the re-introduction of some smaller divisions may be based more on their potential intimidation value than they are on their potential value in combat'. See US Defense Intelligence Agency, 'Russia Military Power: Building a Military to Support Great Power Aspirations', 2017, Appendix B: Russian Ground Forces, pp. 50–7, esp. p. 52, https://www.dia.mil/Portals/27/Documents/News/Military%20Power%20Publications/Russia%20Military%20Power%20Report%202017.pdf.

38 According to NATO Secretary-General Jens Stoltenberg, 'ministers also agreed on a NATO Readiness Initiative, the so-called "Four Thirties". This is not about new forces. But about increasing the readiness of the forces our nations already have. Today, Allies committed, by 2020, to having 30 mechanized battalions, 30 air squadrons and 30 combat vessels, ready to use within 30 days or less. This shows our determination to instill a culture of readiness across the Alliance.' NATO, 'Press Conference by NATO Secretary General Jens Stoltenberg Following the Meeting of the North Atlantic Council (NAC) in Defence Ministers' Session', 7 June 2018, https://www.nato.int/cps/en/natohq/opinions_155264.htm?selectedLocale=en.

39 The professional literature on urban combat is quite large. A good treatment of the problem is Gian Gentile et al., *Reimagining the Character of Urban Operations for the US Army: How the Past Can Inform the Present and Future* (Santa Monica, CA: RAND Corporation, 2017), https://www.rand.org/pubs/research_reports/RR1602.html. As with many recent treatments of the issue, the authors focus on what the offence requires to overcome the many problems inherent in urban fighting, especially against defending forces of motivated, if indifferently armed, irregular light infantry. The analysis is also strongly informed by a counter-insurgency/stability-operations perspective. One may infer from the discussion, however, that well-equipped and well-trained infantry units could make urban operations extremely costly for mechanised adversaries. In practice, modern militaries often mix and 'task-organise' mechanised and light infantry combat units for urban missions.

40 See the entries for these countries in IISS, *The Military Balance 2020*. On the eve of the Cold War's end, the army of the Federal Republic of Germany was the most capable in Europe, and Germany was assumed to be NATO's main theatre of battle. Though focused largely on the mechanised-warfare threat posed by the Warsaw Pact, of 12 German divisions ten were heavy,

one was airborne and one was geared for 'mountain' operations. See Federal Minister of Defence, 'White Paper 1985: The Situation and Development of the Federal Armed Forces', Federal Republic of Germany, pp. 191–9. See also IISS, 'Germany: Federal Republic', *The Military Balance, 1986–1987* (London: IISS, 1986), pp. 67–9, which lists the large number (70+) of reserve 'light' infantry battalions fielded by the German army at mobilisation. I infer from German practice that infantry was considered to be of some utility even against a highly mechanised threat.

41 Barrie et al., 'Defending Europe', p. 29.

42 I have tried to duplicate the IISS arithmetic and it appears that its formula yields a shortfall of 164 aircraft, not 264.

43 Even this is generous to the Russians because it includes 60 'interceptors' best suited for defence in Russian-controlled airspace. More importantly, in counting available NATO aircraft for an offensive operation, the IISS study excluded from its total many NATO aircraft reserved for defensive quick-reaction missions. The study does not explain which ones and why. See Barrie et al., 'Defending Europe', p. 30. The European Defence Agency credits EU members with a total of 2,200 combat aircraft. Most of them are also NATO members, so the IISS must assume that most European combat aircraft are unavailable for the support of NATO ground forces. See European Defence Agency, 'The Military: Key Partner in the Single European Sky', 7 March 2019, p. 14, https://www.eda.europa.eu/docs/

default-source/eda-publications/2019-eda-ses-brochure_a4---final.

44 See Barrie et al., 'Defending Europe', maps 3.4 and 3.5, pp. 31–2.

45 Simple arithmetical techniques exist for assessing the destructive potential of a given inventory of aircraft against a variety of ground targets given varying assumptions about the attrition these aircraft might suffer from air defences. See Barry R. Posen, *Inadvertent Escalation: Conventional War and Nuclear Risks* (Ithaca, NY: Cornell University Press, 1991), pp. 101–6, 219–34. For example, 'Defending Europe' credits NATO with 364 available combat aircraft. The authors imply that this is the number of aircraft ready for combat. These aircraft are assumed to be able to fly two sorties per day. In general, a payload of four effective weapons per aircraft is also a reasonable assumption. Modern air-launched weapons are deadly under ideal conditions. Some of the worst attrition against Russian ground-based air defences – 4% per sortie – occurred over Hanoi and over the Golan Heights in the 1970s. Combining the foregoing assumptions, available NATO aircraft on their first sorties could field nearly 1,400 precision-guided weapons over the battlefield in Poland. Even assuming NATO pilots missed half the time, if the Russian army were attacking with great vigour, and thus exposing themselves often, they might lose 700 armoured fighting vehicles. This is about a third of the tanks and other combat vehicles one would expect to find in the 14 Russian brigades that would presumably be available for

offensive operations. Of course, these are only potentials, and in real war, such potentials are seldom realised. The old verities of fog, friction and fear would diminish Russia's inclination to expose its ground forces to frequent aerial attack and would limit the ability of NATO aircraft to find Russian ground units. Some NATO aircraft would probably be unavailable, instead flying air-defence sorties or attacking Russian air-defence units in order to reduce the attrition they could inflict, if left unhindered, on the rest of NATO's combat aircraft. NATO air commanders would not wish to continue suffering 4% attrition per sortie, which over time would grind the air force to pieces, and would adapt their tactics accordingly. Mutual adaptations to the problems of real war would thus likely slow the pace of combat. But the arithmetic does suggest that NATO airpower could pose grave problems for a Russian ground offensive.

NATO ground forces do have significant numbers of effective shoulder-fired short-range air-defence missiles, which can give helicopters and low-flying aircraft considerable trouble.

Republican Politics and Policy After Trump

Kori Schake

Robert Pinsky has written that 'American culture as I have experienced it is so brilliantly and sometimes brutally in motion that standard models for it fail to apply'.[1] That observation holds, as well, for American politics. The American political system is tied tightly to public attitudes, and the American people are more tolerant of risk than most, so US politics tends to have wider fluctuations and sharper syncopations than that of other established democracies. American political parties have few means of enforcing discipline – the 2016 Republican nominee switched parties, having been a lifelong Democrat, and a major challenger in the Democratic primary race was unrepentantly not a Democrat. So American politics is more of a wild scrum than that in countries where party leaders control accession and have more means of penalising political apostasy. In the United States, politics, like religion, is a marketplace. While that gives charlatans greater prospects, it also seems to produce more positive experimentation and diversity than in other political systems.

The US electorate is evenly split: officially, 37% are registered Democrats, 35% registered Republicans and 28% independents. But that suggests more fluidity than voting patterns actually reflect because most self-styled independents lean strongly towards, and vote reliably for, one party. Most American voters choose to avoid political news, which tends

Kori Schake leads the foreign- and defence-policy team at the American Enterprise Institute. She is the former deputy director-general of the IISS.

Survival | vol. 62 no. 6 | December 2020–January 2021 | pp. 35–50   https://doi.org/10.1080/00396338.2020.1851082

to reinforce party alignment. Factoring in the leaners, the more accurate description of American voters is that 47% reliably vote Republican and 48% reliably vote Democratic.[2]

Only initial surveys of voter attitudes were available at publication, and those may not fully capture views of mail-in ballot voters, so conclusions can only be tentative. But some significant patterns are emerging. Party-line voters had strong and lopsided reactions in this year's election: 98% of Republicans said they'd be excited if Donald Trump were re-elected, while 96% of Democrats dreaded such an outcome. Regarding the pandemic, 92% of voters for Joseph Biden thought he would handle it better, whereas 93% of Trump supporters thought Trump would. Some 80% of Biden voters considered COVID-19 more important than the economy, while 76% of Trump voters thought the reverse. A 76% majority of Republicans were enthusiastic about how government was working, while 74% of Democrats said they were angry about it.[3]

American elections hinge on the parties ensuring that their supporters actually vote, as doing so is not compulsory, and on persuading that narrow slice of roughly 5% who do not reliably vote for a given party to cast a ballot for it. Around 159 million Americans voted in this election. Overall turnout was as advantageous to President Trump as it was to his challenger: nearly 5m Americans who didn't vote for Trump in 2016 did so in this election.[4] The rare unseating of an incumbent president was the result of Democrats' effective mobilisation in key swing states, a 20-point shift in support away from Trump on the part of independents and the defection of a small proportion of Republicans.[5]

A welcome anticlimax
The intensity of views in an extremely polarised country did not disrupt the election or produce significant violence during or after it, as many had feared might happen. While many voters experienced long lines, and there were some voting-machine outages and other technical problems, the directors of the Stanford–MIT Healthy Elections Project concluded that 'on Election Day, we saw fewer problems than in any recent election'.[6] The norms of America's secular sacrament of voting were preserved, except for

one: that of a graceful concession by the losing candidate. Trump vociferously insisted the election had been stolen and set in motion a flurry of legal challenges to the vote counts. None affected the outcome, but some may cast a pall over Republican perceptions of its legitimacy.[7]

The balancing reflex at the core of US federal-government institutions remains active in American political culture, accounting for the frequency of split-ticket voting, whereby the same voter will choose one party for president and the other party for congressional seats. Ticket splitting this election was an important element in President-elect Biden's success. Renegade Republicans succeeded in persuading a small but ultimately significant slice of their co-partisans and leaners to abandon the Republican presidential candidate, and that was enough to prevent Arizona, Michigan, Pennsylvania and Wisconsin from going for Trump. Arizona, traditionally a Republican state, shifted farthest, electing a Democratic senator as well as delivering the state's Electoral College votes to Biden. That may not prove to be a durable change in voter preference, however, since Trump's disrespect for popular senator John McCain and the endorsement of Biden by McCain's widow and former Republican senator Jeff Flake probably moved voters to spurn Trump in particular.

Some Republican factions, like the gleeful pirates of the Lincoln Project, also targeted Republican senatorial candidates who had defended the president during his impeachment trial or supported him on the campaign trail. But most Republican dissidents just gathered under the umbrella of Defending Democracy Together to endorse candidate Biden. From the mildly censorious Maine Senator Susan Collins to the sycophantic South Carolina Senator Lindsey Graham, most Republican senators were returned to office. Republicans even picked up seats in the House of Representatives and won conservative victories on ballot initiatives rejecting affirmative action and affirming labour practices of the gig economy in reliably Democratic California.[8] The 2020 election turned out to be better for Republican candidates and conservative issues than for Trump himself.

The election outcome had something for everyone. Democrats got the presidency, and flipped two reliably Republican states, Arizona and Georgia. They picked up senators in Colorado and Arizona, and forced both Georgia

Senate races to run-offs that will decide control of the Senate in January. Had the Democratic candidate in North Carolina not been enmeshed in a sex scandal, they would likely have taken that Senate seat as well. And in what may be some consolation in disguise for Biden, Republicans retained enough support in the Senate to impede a leftward lurch by progressive Democrats. Republicans held off a predicted 'blue wave' and had strong showings in state races, giving them control over redistricting that will result from the decennial census. Their success in House elections included several victories by female challengers, who appeared to win mainly by virtue of being female, and who doubled the number of Republican women in the House.[9]

Despite the great dangers Trump posed to constitutional rule and political norms in the United States, he may ultimately turn out to have been good for democracy in America. Many decry the lack of civics education there, but the Trump administration has inadvertently provided Americans with primers on presidential powers, the Emoluments Clause of the Constitution, checks and balances, and the power of the president to declare national emergencies and reallocate congressionally appropriated funds for unauthorised purposes. His norm-shattering behaviour motivated Americans to understand their own political system and use it: a higher percentage of Americans voted than in any election since 1900.

The deeper truth revealed by the 2020 election is that the only thing the American political system cannot withstand is apathy. Failure to participate is what leaves the American system vulnerable. As Thomas Jefferson wrote, 'I know of no safe depository of the ultimate power of the society but the people themselves, and if we think them not enlightened enough to exercise their control with a wholesome discretion, the remedy is not to take it from them, but to inform their discretion.'[10]

Beyond the high turnout, other hopeful signs for democracy in America surfaced during this election cycle. The foreign interference that had loomed so large in 2016 appears to have been effectively foreclosed. The National Security Agency (NSA) and the military's Cyber Command deserve a victory lap for having taken the problem seriously when national politicians either did not or responded timorously.[11] Information warfare is the emergent frontier, and the NSA worked cooperatively with allies to formulate a successful strategy of defence, and even managed to inject deterrence into the equation.

On the civil-society front, social-media companies began to take responsibility for their accelerant effects on democracy. The oceans of data they collect through users' voluntary participation are being used to push messages that have not been subject to the scrutiny of public advertising in political campaigns. They had huge effects in the 2020 campaign because so many Americans now get their news from social media. Such companies did not originate information silos – talk radio and cable television became partisan well before voters got their news from social media. But the higher perceived reliability of information when received from curated groups on Facebook or Twitter, and the speed and ease of mobilising vigilante actions, do present challenges the US political system has not been able to handle effectively. Late in the game but nonetheless significantly, Twitter and even Facebook began labelling false content and dampening algorithmic associations that encourage violence.

Money appears to have been irrelevant

Although $14 billion was spent this election cycle, money appears to have been largely irrelevant to electoral outcomes. Biden was the first candidate in history to raise a billion dollars, and Trump's penury in the cycle's waning days may have required the campaign to pull ads, but the election remained close. A full 84% of voters had decided more than a month before Election Day how they would vote. Maine's senatorial challenger, Sara Gideon, spent $70m compared to Collins's $24m, but Collins was re-elected.[12] Good old-fashioned political organising delivered the primary for Biden in South Carolina and turned Georgia blue in the general election.

In numerous instances, money was even a disadvantage. Races that drew heavy contributions from outside the relevant state, such as the challenge to Senate Majority Leader Mitch McConnell in Kentucky, were won by the candidate that did not receive them. Perhaps national attention caused some candidates to shift attention to issues of national interest; those who succeeded steadfastly focused on local issues and refused to let themselves be made into national symbols. Virginia's Danica Roem, a Democrat running in a heavily Republican district and the nation's first transgender member of Congress, was re-elected by insistently campaigning on traffic problems. Americans tend to like their politics provincial. Surveys of public attitudes consistently show that Americans dislike and distrust the federal government, but have positive views about their local government.

Some surprises

The 2020 race may also be illustrative of the challenges associated with identity politics, as a number of shibboleths have been thrown into question. Democrats have operated under the assumption that demography will vanquish the Republican Party as non-white Americans become the majority of voters. But Trump unexpectedly carried 12% of black votes and 32% of Hispanic votes.[13] Hispanic voters along the Texas border, who many expected would bridle at Trump's border wall and racism, prevented Texas from going Democratic. While we don't yet know why Texas voters in the border region elected Republican members of Congress, the mere fact they did so shatters the belief that Hispanic voters only care about so-called Hispanic issues, or think about them in the terms progressives have anticipated.

Although the candidates hardly discussed foreign policy, it did play a part in the 2020 election, if only as a continuation of domestic policy. It was widely expected that anti-communist and anti-Castro sentiment that had driven first-generation Cuban immigrants to be conservative would relax in subsequent generations; likewise the anti-communist and anti-Chávez or -Maduro sentiment for Venezuelan immigrants. Yet this was not the case, as Trump's strident policies reversing Obama's opening to Cuba, sanctioning Venezuela's oil commerce and actively supporting its opposition resonated with Cuban- and Venezuelan-Americans. They voted 71% for Trump, delivering Miami-Dade County, and probably Florida, for him.[14] They also voted a straight Republican ticket, bouncing out incumbent Democratic representatives.

Locally focused races and the political preferences of the Latino electorate are likely to inform micro-targeted politics. Politics has always been local. But the ubiquity of social media means that parties will likely struggle to sustain national messages, and that high-visibility national firebrands will reach into local races and hurt candidates from their own parties who are trying to focus on local issues.

The election did not deliver a resounding repudiation of Trump's politics or policies. In fact, specific policies were substantially irrelevant. The Republican Party did not even produce a platform. While the Democratic Party did, and the Biden campaign put out numerous detailed policy papers, none of them got much attention.

When the dancing and lawsuits are finally over, what will the election mean for Republicans? Trump's advocates have styled him a modern Andrew Jackson, America's first brazenly populist president. Jackson, like Trump, disdained the norms of comportment that defined American politics, railed against a 'corrupt establishment', advocated populist policies, indulged novel economic approaches that bankers and businesspeople warned against, refused compliance with Supreme Court rulings, and abandoned the allies that had aided American military victories. He also vituperatively contested an election he lost long after it was decided. When Jackson was asked whether he had any regrets from his time in office, he replied, 'I have only two regrets: I didn't shoot Henry Clay and I didn't hang John C. Calhoun.'[15] Trump has both the portrait and a sculpture cast of Jackson in the Oval Office. Jacksonian contrariness has been the best guide to Trump's actions, so his reflexes will probably continue to mimic Jackson's.

Whether Trump will maintain his mesmeric hold on elected Republican officials and deliver electoral outcomes is a question for the future of the Republican Party. If he does, the 2020 election may not mean its wholesale demise. The red mirage occasioned by counting rules and the Republican preference for in-person voting did not presage a blue tsunami. Suburban women established a wide gender gap, but that may be attributable to Trump specifically rather than Republican policies generally. Trump has not consigned Republicans to the status of a rump party of white supremacists, as some anguished progressives claim. Although black women voted 91% for Biden, young black men showed unexpected if still slight support for Trump, and Republican candidates did reasonably well with many minority groups. On balance, the 2020 election saw the emergence of a contemporary version the 1980s Reagan Democrats: working-class voters worried about the economy and uncomfortable with progressive social policies, coupled with a Wall Street keen on a permissive business environment.

Democrats often use the language of rights to advocate progressive social policies, characterising opposition to such policies as the infringement of rights and effectively foreclosing responsibility for balancing competing goods. For example, some Democrats refuse to acknowledge religious opposition to abortion as legitimate. Dalibor Rohac's work shows that the backlash against the EU conflating liberal political structures and norms in Central Europe may be the result of associating them with the imposition of progressive social policies in more conservative societies like Poland.[16] Something of a similar tenor may be occurring in the US. The legal, administrative and cultural foreclosure of competing visions of right has been in the ascendancy among Democrats for some time, and it costs them support. Describing Trump's supporters as deplorables or racists decreases the competitive political space. And while some of them clearly are, it's just bad politics to, as George W. Bush put it, 'judge other groups by their worst examples, while judging ourselves by our best intentions'.[17]

This Democratic tendency has left Republicans space to organise, and a multi-racial blue-collar conservatism isn't as crazy as it sounds, at least outside the earshot of Trump's loud and vituperative racism. Most voters – Republican and Democrat – are low-information voters, and care more about their own lives than sweeping ideological campaigns. The exceptions are evangelicals, who constitute 27% of the electorate and are a driving force in conservative politics on everything from Israel to Supreme Court nominations, and whose fervour could be a durable partisan advantage for Republicans unless more Democrats become comfortable with religion as a restraint on policy.[18]

Demography is also unlikely to live up to Democratic aspirations. Democrats have believed time was on their side – that Republicans would inevitably become sabre-toothed tigers in a tar pit, lashing out but unable to transcend the shrinking pool of white and rural Americans. But demography isn't destiny, especially not in an immigrant country like the United States. And adaptations brought on by the pandemic may reduce urbanisation.

In addition, Trump has shown that a compliant Congress can enable a licentious executive branch to break or circumvent diaphanous constitutional or statutory constraints. This has stoked fears that a successor could emerge with the same illiberal ambitions who provides less melodrama to activate resistance, and thereby achieve what Trump only attempted.[19] At the same time, leading Republicans' post-election claims of fraud and Trump's unwillingness to concede the election have reinforced perceptions raised by the Senate's refusing to vote on the nomination of Judge Merrick Garland to the Supreme Court in 2016 but confirming Justice Amy Coney Barrett in 2020 that the Republican Party no longer plays by the rules. This will ensure that the civil-society groups that have done so much to constrain Trump initiatives will maintain their vigilance on the Republican Party after he is gone. Biden's welcome efforts to unite the country could further reduce Republican defiance of norms and the risk of an illiberal Trump successor.

A way forward?

While Republican successes in congressional races will likely force Democrats to moderate their fringe, Republicans themselves may not become more temperate, especially if Trump remains a powerful force. The line-up of leading aspirants for the 2024 Republican presidential nomination suggests that Trump's alchemy could persist. It includes Tom Cotton, Ted Cruz, Nikki Haley, Josh Hawley, Mike Pompeo and Mike Pence. None of these people argues for a different Republican path. None of them has Trump's personal comportment, which could expand the reach of their ideas. But none of them have his ensorcelling appeal, either. Even that appeal, however, has proven to be of limited utility. Trump's willingness to say out loud what many people believe but feel can't be expressed, and a genuine knack for asking first-order questions, such as why allies don't do more to defend themselves, are keys to his unique attractiveness. Yet he lost the support of suburban women because they grew weary of his distasteful conduct, and public attitudes have significantly resisted his policy answers to those first-order questions.[20]

According to the *Wall Street Journal*, Trump's actions in the immediate aftermath of the election will strongly affect whether his appeal endures.

'Mr. Trump's legacy will be diminished greatly if his final act is a bitter refusal to accept a legitimate defeat. Republican officials will turn away, and eventually so will the American public that wants to see the election resolved.'[21] Some Republican officials already have, including former president George W. Bush, Senators Mitt Romney, Lisa Murkowski and Pat Toomey, and several governors. As of the date of publication, Trump, with more than two months still in office, had commenced an extravaganza of firings – including the secretary of defense – and his team had hinted at executive orders. The Biden administration would quickly vacate the orders, and any appointments are largely irrelevant in the waning days of an administration. But it is hard to say whether Trump's closing acts in office would remind voters of his intemperance or foster nostalgia for his reality-TV style of governance when Republicans remaining in office are engaged in tepid compromises of governance.

> Trump commenced an extravaganza of firings

It is also possible that Trump will lose his ability to rally voters and therefore politicians. He will surely offer a running critique of the Biden administration and of his Republican successors, whether by starting his own broadcast network, incessantly tweeting or calling into Fox News from his Mar-a-Lago estate. But as he loses the indemnity of office, and both federal and state jurisdictions advance investigations and prosecutions, his influence could decline. Then again, perceived persecutions could further anoint him as a cult hero. He is sure to remain focused on himself as a victim of fraud and calumny, and his personality compels him to seize attention. What remains to be seen is whether Republicans remain interested in him, or shift their gaze to politicians wielding the levers of governance.

Much will depend on whether those politicians are solving the problems voters are worried about. Half of Trump voters were from small towns or rural areas, which likely gave them different experiences of policing and COVID-19.[22] Some 88% of his voters said the George Floyd protests were a factor in their decision, and the advocacy of some Democrats to defund the police badly dented support for candidates not running in progressive districts. The 376 counties with the highest COVID-19 infection rates voted for Trump to a greater extent than places less affected.[23] But the pandemic is resurging in many of these locales, which may increase their need for government services and reduce denialism about COVID-19.

Cooperation between the federal and state governments to provide reliable public-health information, advance vaccines and distribution, and ensure funding for social services is very much in Republican interests, and not just because Republican voters are about to be disproportionately affected. Republicans want to sell conservatism to voters who need government to work for them. They won't succeed if messages for the benefit of Main Street are buried under the perception that Republicans are the party of Wall Street. Most Republican voters who favour economic reopening will not get it until the pandemic is under control. Thus, from a narrow partisan perspective, unless Republicans take a strong hand in formulating policy for COVID-19 recovery, Democrats will get the credit. Republicans are at risk of cementing the perceived truth of conservative writer P.J. O'Rourke's quip that 'Republicans are the party that says government doesn't work and then they get elected and prove it'.[24] Capable management of the pandemic would also show state governors to good effect, which is especially important when Democrats hold the White House and Congress is abysmally unpopular.

Continued legislative gridlock could well result if Republicans win the two Senate run-off elections in Georgia. But gridlock is not always bad. In a way, it is what the American system was designed to produce. America's Founding Fathers were much less concerned about government inaction than they were about the potential for a narrow but energised majority to impose its will. Gridlock is best understood not as governmental failure but as policy failure, indicating that neither party has been able to come up with an idea attractive enough to the other party's voters to enable its implementation.

Four years ago in these pages, I argued there was a successful path forward for conservative ideas after repudiating Trump policies. I still believe that's true. American institutions passed, if barely, the 'historically important test of the institutional checks and balances built into American democracy'.[25] I would very much like to be wrong in my 2016 judgement that 'Trump would rewrite what it means to be a Republican'.[26] And in fact, voting patterns in the 2020 election show an opening for Republicans to win elections and also broaden their coalition by appealing to the values of defending human dignity, expanding human potential and building a freer and safer world.

It remains true, as it was in 2016, that 'Republicans have a lot of hard work to do to reclaim the loyalty of Trump's supporters. This election has shown that Republican leaders at the national level have failed in the essential task of providing policy responses to voters' most pressing concerns.'[27] Some argue that policy didn't matter in the 2020 election, that preservation of a disappearing culture alone was the basis for voting. That may seem plausible because Trump himself is such an outsized cultural figure. But culture was not the only determinant. Many people felt they were voting to protect their lives; others ardently believed economic recovery was the urgent need. It was more a policy election than it might have appeared.

Foreign policy

The 2016 election was 'an anti-establishment moment because our choices have caused a significant slice of the electorate to lose confidence – in expertise, in the fundamental fairness of the system, and in the ability of government to make things better rather than costly, intrusive and worse'.[28] The 2020 election was an establishment moment because people want government to work, whether to manage the pandemic, defibrillate the economy or navigate world affairs. After Trump's deviation from Republican orthodoxy on key foreign-policy issues, public opinion now favours traditional Republican policies. According to survey data compiled by the Chicago Council on Global Affairs, 'after four years in office, Trump has failed to appreciably deflate public support for trade, immigration, and military alliances. Instead, the public remains largely in sync with establishment views on these core issues. U.S. leaders should recognize that they have more political space to advance and defend internationalist positions than they seem to realize.'[29]

But some Trump policies will and should persist, even after the man himself passes from political relevance. The Trump administration was right that China's commercial and military aggressiveness and unwilling-ness to adhere to the rules constraining other states merit greater concern than previous US administrations had accorded them. The US was right to try to persuade China to become a responsible stakeholder, and to identify a mutually beneficial outcome that held out the prospect of forgoing the costs of countering China and enlisting help from other countries. Indeed, that still seems to be the Trump administration's nominal objective, even though it has squandered a great deal of goodwill from other countries and hypocritically adopted some of China's mercantilist practices.

Many other elements of Trump's foreign policy should be dispensed with. The Biden administration would be wise to rapidly revise the National Security Strategy, excising all the 'America first' belligerence and substi-tuting 'effective multilateralism'. Playing team sports is America's great advantage. When the US has to do hard things, the American public likes its friends to help out. Trump was not wrong to press allies about burden-sharing. But the Biden team would be wise to pick up on Hal Brands and Zack Cooper's idea of reconceptualising burden-sharing metrics so as to de-emphasise input measures such as the percentage of GDP spent on defence and instead stress risk-sharing, which reflects the actual responsibilities that allies are shouldering.[30]

While the Trump administration translated its political objectives into a sensible defence strategy, that strategy is corrosively underfunded. It was premised on real annual increases of 3–5% in defence spending, which were allocated only in the first two Trump budgets. Defence spending has been contracting in real terms since 2018. And while skimping might not translate directly into strategic failure, it does increase the risk of losing a potential war against China, which would be the most consequential war the US had faced in the last 30 years. Beyond defence, the Trump admin-istration sought to catastrophically cut diplomacy spending, which would have made its strategy unexecutable had Congress complied. Diplomatic spending needs to increase substantially to make American diplomacy capable of doing its part.

*   *   *

Four years on, it still feels right to say that 'what is needed is a careful analysis of who Trump's supporters are, empathy for and engagement with their problems, an understanding of the issues that are motivating their rejection of establishment answers, and the building of a track record of conservative solutions'.[31] There is a strong temptation simply to reject Trump's most belligerent supporters, who seem to care only for their own rights, not the rights of others. But there is no path to conservative vibrancy or national success unless Trump's supporters and opponents alike become educated to common ground.

America and the world have survived the Trump administration, the United States' latest Jacksonian revival. Voting patterns from 2020 suggest that Republicans have an opportunity to revive the expansive coalition that brought electoral and policy success in the 1980s, and have the public support to restore bedrock conservative national-security policies. But they may miss the chance if Trump continues to dominate the Republican landscape.

Notes

1   Robert Pinsky, *Democracy, Culture, and the Voice of Poetry* (Princeton, NJ: Princeton University Press, 2005), p. 76.

2   'Poll Results: Georgia', Fox News, 3 November 2020, https://www.foxnews.com/elections/2020/general-results/voter-analysis?state=GA.

3   'National Exit Polls: How Different Groups Voted', *New York Times*, 3 November 2020, https://www.nytimes.com/interactive/2020/11/03/us/elections/exit-polls-president.html.

4   David Wasserman et al., '2020 National Popular Vote Tracker', *Cook Political Report*, https://cookpolitical.com/2020-national-popular-vote-tracker.

5   Matthew Continetti, 'America's Polarized and Divided Politics Aren't Going Anywhere', *Washington Free Beacon*, 6 November 2020, https://freebeacon.com/columns/stalemate-2020/.

6   Quoted in Nathaniel Persily and Charles Stewart III, 'The 2020 Election Meltdown that Didn't Happen, Even Amid the Covid Pandemic', *Wall Street Journal*, 6 November 2020, https://www.wsj.com/articles/the-2020-election-meltdown-that-didnt-happen-even-amid-the-covid-pandemic-11604667974. See also Michael Tanenbaum, 'Philly's Ballot-counting Livestream Video Is a Testament to Election Workers Everywhere', *Philly Voice*, 3 November 2020, https://www.phillyvoice.com/philly-ballot-counting-livestream-video-youtube-poll-workers-2020-election/.

7 The Stanford–MIT Healthy Elections Project explains that 'litigation is almost completely a product of the fact that the legislatures of Michigan, Pennsylvania and Wisconsin were reluctant to change their absentee-ballot laws to prepare for the vast expansion of mail voting during the pandemic'. Quoted in Persily and Stewart, 'The 2020 Election Meltdown that Didn't Happen, Even Amid the Covid Pandemic'.

8 Jeremy B. White, 'California Proves It's Not as Liberal as You Think', *Politico*, 5 November 2020, https://www.politico.com/states/california/story/2020/11/05/california-proves-its-not-as-liberal-as-you-think-1334485.

9 See Simone Pathe, 'Republican Women See Record-breaking Success in the House', CNN, 5 November 2020, https://edition.cnn.com/2020/11/05/politics/house-races-republican-women/index.html.

10 National Archives, 'From Thomas Jefferson to William C. Jarvis, 28 September 1820', Papers of Thomas Jefferson, Founders Online, https://founders.archives.gov/documents/Jefferson/98-01-02-1540.

11 When General Mark Milley's term as Chairman of the Joint Chiefs of Staff expires in 2022, the Biden administration might consider the architect of the NSA's work, General Paul Nakasone, as the next chairman.

12 Joshua Jamerson, Julie Bykowicz and Chad Day, '2020 Election Lesson: Trump's Coalition Proved Durable', *Wall Street Journal*, 4 November 2020, https://www.wsj.com/articles/trump-rural-coalition-proved-durable-confounded-democrats-11604536974?st=euvoniehfec8125.

13 Peter Baker and Maggie Haberman, 'Win or Lose, Trump Will Remain a Powerful and Disruptive Force', *New York Times*, 4 November 2020, https://www.nytimes.com/2020/11/04/us/politics/trump-post-presidency-influence.html.

14 See Ami Dar (@AmiDar), tweet, 4 November 2020, https://twitter.com/AmiDar/status/1324074540989878272.

15 J.L. Bell, 'Jackson on Calhoun and Clay', Boston 1775, 22 August 2016, http://boston1775.blogspot.com/2016/08/jackson-on-calhoun-and-clay.html.

16 Dalibor Rohac and Lance Kokonos, 'Poland's Culture Wars', *Foreign Policy*, 2 November 2020, https://foreignpolicy.com/2020/11/02/poland-hungary-culture-wars-abortion-russia/.

17 German Lopez, 'George W. Bush in Dallas: "Too Often We Judge Other Groups by Their Worst Examples"', *Vox*, 12 July 2016, https://www.vox.com/2016/7/12/12164176/george-bush-dallas-shooting-speech-video.

18 See 'National Exit Polls: How Different Groups Voted', *New York Times,* 3 November 2020, https://www.nytimes.com/interactive/2020/11/03/us/elections/exit-polls-president.html.

19 See Tom Nichols, 'A Large Portion of the Electorate Chose the Sociopath', *Atlantic*, 4 November 2020, https://www.theatlantic.com/ideas/archive/2020/11/large-portion-electorate-chose-sociopath/616994/.

20 See Dina Smeltz et al., 'Divided We Stand: Democrats and Republicans Diverge on US Foreign Policy',

Chicago Council on Global Affairs, 17 September 2020, https://www.thechicagocouncil.org/publication/lcc/divided-we-stand.

21 Editorial Board, 'The Presidential Endgame', *Wall Street Journal*, 6 November 2020, https://www.wsj.com/articles/the-presidential-end-game-11604706255.

22 Jamerson, Bykowicz and Day, '2020 Election Lesson: Trump's Coalition Proved Durable'.

23 Carla K. Johnson, Hannah Fingerhut and Pia Deshpande, 'Counties with Worst Virus Surges Overwhelmingly Voted Trump', Associated Press, 6 November 2020, https://apnews.com/article/counties-worst-virus-surges-voted-trump-d671a483534024b-5486715da6edb6ebf.

24 P.J. O'Rourke, *Parliament of Whores: A Lone Humorist Attempts to Explain the Entire U.S. Government* (New York: Atlantic Monthly Press, 1991), p. 19.

25 Kori Schake, 'Republican Foreign Policy After Trump', *Survival*, vol. 58, no. 5, October–November 2016, p. 34.

26 *Ibid.*, p. 35.

27 *Ibid.*, p. 36.

28 *Ibid.*

29 Jonathan Monten et al., 'Americans Want to Engage the World: The Beltway and the Public Are Closer than You Think', *Foreign Affairs*, 3 November 2020, https://www.foreignaffairs.com/articles/united-states/2020-11-03/americans-want-engage-world.

30 Hal Brands and Zack Cooper, 'After the Responsible Stakeholder, What? Debating America's China Strategy', *Texas National Security Review*, vol. 2, no. 2, February 2019, https://tnsr.org/2019/02/after-the-responsible-stakeholder-what-debating-americas-china-strategy-2/.

31 Schake, 'Republican Foreign Policy After Trump', p. 36.

America and the Illiberal Order After Trump

Michael J. Boyle

The liberal order, as we knew it, is gone. The network of institutions, rules and norms established by the United States after the Second World War has long been under siege, pressured from without by China and other rising powers, and from within by populist leaders who saw little value in it. The coronavirus pandemic has compounded these pressures and revealed that many assumptions about the liberal order were false. Global institutions such as the World Health Organization (WHO) have not proven capable of coordinating governments to respond collectively to threats, liberal-democratic states have not cooperated either inside or outside of such institutions, and the United States could not be counted on to lead others through a crisis.[1] Multinational institutions such as the United Nations appeared irrelevant as states closed their borders and chased after medical supplies with increasing desperation. The G7 and G20 both failed to come up with workable plans, while the WHO became a battleground for influence between Washington and Beijing.[2] The greatest failure, however, lay with the United States, which catastrophically failed to manage its own epidemic, much less lead others in managing theirs.[3] Against this background, any hope of a return to the previous liberal order premised on US power is now extinguished.

Michael J. Boyle is an associate professor of political science at Rutgers University–Camden and a senior fellow at the Foreign Policy Research Institute. His most recent book is *The Drone Age: How Drone Technology Will Change War and Peace* (Oxford University Press, 2020).

Survival | vol. 62 no. 6 | December 2020–January 2021 | pp. 51–76   https://doi.org/10.1080/00396338.2020.1851085

The big question is what comes next.[4] There are three broad schools of thought. The first is that the United States can recover from this crisis and restore some version of the liberal order, curtailing China's geopolitical ascent.[5] This view holds that the institutions of the liberal order are battered but fundamentally sound, and can be recast to take account of diminished American power.[6] Under the second view, China will emerge victorious from the pandemic because it has successfully controlled the virus at home, albeit with draconian measures, and will use its success and a dose of propaganda to assert an increasingly dominant status.[7] In a manner befitting its power, China will seek to dramatically revise or overturn the liberal order and elevate its own institutions. A third, more pessimistic, outlook is that the world will belong to no one and that what will follow this crisis is anarchy, closer in practice to a chaotic multipolar order than to the unipolar order that prevailed following the collapse of the Soviet Union.[8] In this scenario, the decline of the US will cripple institutions such as the IMF and the World Bank, and produce a patchwork of institutions and norms mirroring the dispersal of power and influence in a world dominated by neither Washington nor Beijing.

There is a fourth, worrying possibility: that the increasingly stark geopolitical competition between the US, Russia and China will yield not anarchy but an illiberal order, marked by strengthened regional hierarchies, the hollowing out of the institutions of the liberal order, and the spread of illiberal practices and values.[9] Under this bleak scenario, the order becomes illiberal because it reflects the character and foreign-policy practices of the leading states: Russia and China, two illiberal, authoritarian powers; and the United States, which showed signs of a slide into authoritarianism under President Donald Trump. A global struggle involving three illiberal states would induce other states to mimic their foreign-policy practices and furnish a permissive environment for the growth of authoritarianism elsewhere. This darker world would not be an inevitable consequence of China's exporting its values, but rather an outcome of the United States' abandonment of its liberal values and its decision to act more like Russia and China in the struggle for power and influence. The international order will consolidate around illiberalism so long as the three most powerful states in the system –

the United States, Russia and China – have that character. In a 2018 speech, German Foreign Minister Heiko Maas acknowledged that due to internal changes in the three most powerful states, the 'world order that we once knew, had become accustomed to and sometimes felt comfortable in – this world order no longer exists'.[10]

The consolidation of an illiberal order would be more favourable to China and Russia, and to illiberal regional powers such as Turkey and Saudi Arabia, than to the remaining liberal democracies. This presents some difficult choices for the next US administration. After the damage inflicted by the Trump administration, the world is unlikely to go back to trusting the leadership of the US and accepting its natural leadership of a liberal order.[11] At the same time, in an environment shifting to the advantage of its enemies, and with its allies increasingly weak, distrustful and divided, the US cannot afford to withdraw entirely from the world for fear of giving Russia and China opportunities to exploit. Facing the immense difficulty of either restoration or retrenchment, a Biden administration must instead engage in rapid reform of American political institutions in order to compete effectively with Russia and China and salvage, in weaker forms, the surviving institutions of the liberal order. To be successful, US foreign policy must now begin at home: the US, if it recovers, will not be able to manage a long-term ideological struggle against illiberalism unless it addresses illiberalism in its political institutions and shows that liberalism has something to say for itself in a world unforgiving of its weaknesses.

Two and a half superpowers

The days when US policymakers hoped that it was possible to work with China as a responsible stakeholder of the liberal order are over. Today, most policymakers and analysts accept that the US will be locked in a struggle against an increasingly assertive China for generations. Some have described this as the Cold War 2.0.[12] The logic behind this claim is that China is a rising power, with vast economic clout and growing military strength, and is positioning itself as a counterweight to the US. China's grey-zone operations and cyber attacks, its hostage-taking of foreign citizens and its aggressive propaganda suggest that Beijing is seeking to expand its global reach. The consequences of its harsh authoritarianism are now undeniable, from its construction of vast concentration camps for Uighurs in Xinjiang to its brutal clampdown in Hong Kong. In some ways, China's conduct seems to echo the Soviet Union's at the beginning of its advance to global power, and to imply that more clashes between the US and China are inevitable. The Cold War 2.0 analogy is also comforting to the American foreign-policy establishment in its suggestion that the US would eventually prevail without resorting to outright war.

Yet the analogy misleads more than it informs, especially concerning the role that ideology will play. Naturally, the US and China will engage in intense geopolitical competition for some time, and China will attempt to extend its global reach, as its recent economic and security agreements with Iran indicate.[13] But the ideological character of the contest is different from that of the first Cold War. China does not offer an ideology or model of government that is easily transferable to other states. Its attempts to promote the Beijing consensus as an alternative model of development has been taken up only by a relatively small number of states, many of which have used it as leverage to play Washington and Beijing off one another.[14] The ideological appeal of China is principally limited by the fact that it is pursuing a national vision of greatness, not a global project intended to make the world like China. The future that China offers is not the promised land of a world transformed by the abolition of private property, which the Soviet Union once appeared to offer, but rather one in which capitalist acquisition and wealth creation is made more efficient and less encumbered by democracy and human-rights concerns than what has been on offer from the West.

China's ideological appeal is limited

China's own mistakes have also circumscribed its ideological appeal. These include, in particular, its efforts to bully and exploit states in the developing world to give it exclusive access to natural resources. Especially under President Xi Jinping, China's assertiveness in the South China Sea has made its neighbours in Asia even more nervous. Recent border clashes with India have only reaffirmed suspicions of China's expansionist intentions and made others harden their positions. It is increasingly clear that bandwagoning with China comes with unacceptable costs. As Australian Minister of Defence Linda Reynolds has noted, 'in the grey zone, when the screws are tightened, influence becomes interference, economic cooperation becomes coercion and investment becomes entrapment'.[15] While China has traditionally feared encirclement by US allies, it has effectively encircled itself with enemies.[16] Its efforts to crush dissent, as well as its bungled attempt to hide the scale of the coronavirus outbreak, have also won it few friends in Europe and North America.

The Cold War 2.0 analogy also ignores Russia's substantial role in opposing the United States and joining China in trying to undermine the liberal order. Critics argue that Russia should not be considered a superpower along the lines of China and the United States, with Barack Obama having once dismissed Russia as little more than a 'regional power'. According to this view, its vestigial superpower status derives largely from its legacy nuclear arsenal rather than its ability to wield broad geopolitical power. It is certainly true that Russia is not comparable to China or the United States in many standard measures of power. Its economy is relatively small and quite weak, subject to price fluctuations in oil and gas revenues and plagued by stagnant incomes, growing unemployment and rising discontent. In 2019, the Russian Federation ranked 11th in the world in GDP, below India and Brazil.[17] It is also widely distrusted in its own region for its invasions of Georgia in 2008 and Ukraine in 2014.

This view, though, understates how well President Vladimir Putin plays a weak hand, developing new strengths to compensate for Russia's shortcomings. Unable to compete in raw military or economic power globally, Russia has instead positioned itself as a power broker in regions such as the Middle East, which has no dominant one.[18] This explains Russia's willingness to join the negotiations on the Iran nuclear deal, to prop up the regime of President Bashar al-Assad in Syria and to send mercenaries into Libya. In other regions, it plays the spoiler, undermining the US and its allies with covert actions that violate long-held norms, such as offering bounties to the Taliban for killing American soldiers in Afghanistan or assassinating dissidents abroad. A large element of its strategy has been exploiting institutional weaknesses in democratic states by interfering in their elections, hacking their computer systems, flooding their media with disinformation and exploiting opportunities for corruption of public officials.[19] Russia does not need to compete with the US or China in every way as long as it can use corruption, disinformation, subversion and cyber warfare to inflate its influence. By doing so, Russia can preserve its strategic independence and carve out a space for manoeuvre amid two giants with global ambitions.

If Russia were just an obstructionist power – albeit a nuclear-armed one – it would still be possible to dismiss it as half a superpower. But since 2014 Russia has developed a stronger relationship with China that amplifies Moscow's power and influence. By casting them as US rivals but also minimising their potency, American foreign policy has helped to drive Russia and China closer together in an uneasy strategic partnership, creating a bloc of two powerful authoritarian states opposed to American power.[20] The Trump administration's National Security Strategy rightly describes Russia and China as strategic rivals that together wish to 'shape a world antithetical to US values and interests'.[21] But it also portrays both countries as having little impact outside their regions and underestimates the seriousness of their attack on the liberal order. Secretary of State Mike Pompeo's calls for a 'new alliance of democracies' to balance China comes too late and ignores the role Russia plays in bolstering China.[22] Their partnership does not resolve all differences: Russian and Chinese interests are not always aligned, and geopolitical competition between them is regular and ongoing. But they are in accord about the undesirability of the liberal order and the advantages that would flow from working in concert to overturn it. To that end, practical Sino-Russian cooperation has increased in terms of joint military exercises and cooperation on missile defences. In 2019, trade between the two exceeded $100 billion for the first time, and today China is Russia's largest trading partner and Russia is China's largest oil supplier.[23] Their relationship, which Putin himself describes as 'alliance-like', has some fissures, but also sufficient grounding against the liberal order to keep them aligned against the United States.[24]

An illiberal order

Although neither country can sell its own government as a model for others in the way that the Soviet Union once did, together they are making a different kind of ideological argument for replacing the liberal order with an illiberal one. Their case comprises three overlapping critiques of the liberal order. Firstly, Russia has led an attack on the efforts by the United States to sidestep the restrictions on the use of force in the UN Charter and to engage in regime change. Russia's rhetorical strategy is to present itself as a defender of 'Charter liberalism', specifically existing institutions such as the UN and international law, and to call for a return to first principles in their application, especially concerning the injunction against the use of force other than for self-defence.[25] Like China, it positions itself as a defender of sovereign rights of recognised states regardless of their human-rights records. The underlying idea is to reinforce the UN Charter's restrictions on the use of force and to articulate a norm of neo-Westphalian sovereignty that will restrain the US from using military force to overthrow governments the way it did in Iraq in 2003 and Libya in 2011.[26] Russia in this way seeks to stake out the moral high ground, appearing to support a fairer and more rules-based world order and the restraint of an overbearing rival. Russian arguments against US interventionism are flagrantly hypocritical, as Russia itself has intervened in Georgia, Ukraine and Syria without UN approval. But the Russian position has still resonated with China and many rising powers, including Brazil, India and South Africa, which are protective of their sovereign rights due to long legacies of imperialism and embrace the norm of non-intervention as a way of guarding against US intervention in their affairs.

Secondly, for over 20 years Russia and China have advocated a return to a multipolar order, sharing the baseline view that a world with a less dominant US and a diffusion of power to regions is consistent with their interests.[27] In 2007, speaking in Munich, Putin argued that unipolarity was inherently dangerous because it encouraged the US to behave recklessly and would eventually destroy it from within.[28] On balance, China has remained more ambiguous, hinting at various points that it would accept a unipolar order, or at least one with a more equitable relationship between the US and China. But an underlying theme of its arguments since 1992 has been a call for a multipolar world that restrains any one country from pursuing 'gunboat diplomacy'.[29] Although it has shied away from directly targeting the US by name, it has consistently called for a 'democratization of international relations' and an effective end to unipolarity.[30] For more than a decade, China has positioned itself as a partner of 'newly emerging powers' in the developing world in hopes that their gradual development will foster a multipolar order.[31] At a minimum, it demands that non-Western countries have a greater say in setting rules and norms of the international order than they did in the US-dominated one.

> *Putin has called liberalism 'obsolete'*

Thirdly, Russia and China are repudiating liberalism at home and abroad, and rejecting the laissez-faire free trade traditionally associated with globalisation.[32] They depict liberalism as an ideology of weakness, enfeebling states already strained by the forces of globalisation and allowing their societies to be infected by pernicious outside influences. Putin has argued that liberalism is 'obsolete', urged its rejection at home and sought to repel American proselytising abroad.[33] China is redoubling its efforts to extend its 'discourse power' against the West, and includes several core values of liberalism – such as constitutionalism, civil society and universal values – among its 'seven perils'.[34] The underlying argument – that liberalism fails at home to deal with the causes of societal disorder – implies that global institutions premised on Lockean liberalism, such as the United Nations, might also fare poorly against transnational threats and the effects of hyper-globalisation, especially the rapid movement of capital flows and people. If liberalism is falling apart at home, the reasoning also goes, then international institutions premised on its ethos may no longer be fit for purpose. Russia and China couple these arguments with covert efforts to illustrate the weaknesses of liberal governments by means of disinformation and election-hacking, as well as killing or imprisoning dissidents, spies and journalists.[35]

The call for a return to respecting sovereignty norms, a fairer multipolar order and a rejection of liberalism as an organising principle in politics constitutes an attack on what John Mearsheimer has described as the 'thick' version of the liberal-international order.[36] This version, in operation from 1990 to 2019, involved a bipartisan effort to transform the order from one constrained by the boundaries of state sovereignty into something more ambitious and progressive.[37] One result was that respect for democracy and human rights became a condition of entry for many institutions of the liberal order. The West, under American leadership, wanted to spread liberal democracy around the world and to recast the order itself as truly international, based on a normative consensus in support of human rights and the responsibility of states to adhere to specific standards of liberal political and economic governance.[38]

It is this thick version of the liberal order that China and Russia reject and seek to replace. Beyond that, their arguments articulate an alternative order favourable to their interests and established by instilling illiberal values in governments around the world. The quid pro quo is the expansion of their freedom of action for stronger norms against intervention and in support of repressing domestic enemies. This deal is attractive to governments nervous about unchecked American power and alarmed about the degree to which successive US administrations have swept international law aside and forcibly overthrown governments. The reassertion of the right of non-interference would end what is perceived as the United States' exclusive prerogative, as the presumptively 'indispensable power', to undertake humanitarian intervention, regime change and other selective uses of force.

With the US restrained, Russia and China would enjoy a permissive environment for establishing informal hierarchies in their immediate regions and extending their influence outward through illiberal means.[39] Consistent with their preferences for a neo-Westphalian conception of sovereignty, inter-state war of the old kind – declared, formal and conducted by recognised armies – and overt regime change would be rare. But beneath those thresholds, Russia and China would be free to play dirty and to extend their influence by penetrating, influencing and weakening the political systems of other governments through subversion, disinformation, corruption and hacking. What will change is not the tactics – these are not new – but rather their scope and the frequency of their use, particularly against the remaining liberal democracies and liberal institutions, as both Russia and China reassert their regional dominance and probe the limits of their geopolitical reach.

In this illiberal order, the contest for influence would become particularly bitter with respect to the character of institutions, with the traditional ones of the liberal order coming under the greatest pressure. As the examples of the Shanghai Cooperation Organisation, the Asian Development Bank and the Asian Infrastructure Investment Bank show, China and Russia are developing these regional institutions alongside existing US-led ones in order to weaken them and enmesh other countries in a deeper economic relationship with Moscow and Beijing. The idea is to afford these countries greater access to capital while limiting their freedom to seek other trading partners. By way of China's Belt and Road Initiative, development would be advanced through preferential deals, but with multiple choke points built in to give China leverage against participants that might later object to their terms. These institutions weaken US leverage and the patronage networks that left many governments in the developing world beholden to Washington.[40] Within traditional institutions of the liberal order, such as the World Trade Organization and the WHO, Russia and China employ coalitions of illiberal states to stymie US initiatives, particularly in the area of human rights. Witness the duelling letters sent in 2019 to the UN Human Rights Council over China's detention programme in Xinjiang: 22 liberal democracies (excluding the US) signed a condemnatory letter, while 37 authoritarian and illiberal states signed a supportive one.[41] Russia, China and their supporters will continue to mount other efforts to change the character of these organisations, such as changing vote allocations and influencing committee appointments.

Accompanying the shift to an illiberal order will be the worldwide diffusion of illiberal values. Freed from respect for democracy and human rights as a precondition of joining and benefiting from global institutions, other states could indulge in illiberal governance at home, cracking down on dissidents, rigging elections and persecuting minorities, all under the guise of protecting sovereignty. Underwritten by Russian and Chinese power, and supported by norms prioritising sovereign prerogatives, governments could impose trade restrictions to withstand some of the negative effects of globalisation while celebrating exemplary economic and cultural nationalism. Liberal commitments to democracy and human rights would no longer impede governments from restricting global trade and finance, or immigration flows, on the pretext of surviving in a world made turbulent by the rapid movement of people, ideas and capital.

The shift towards illiberalism was already evident in the pre-pandemic world and is likely to accelerate thereafter. According to Freedom House, 2020 was the 14th straight year of decline in global freedom, with 64 countries having experienced some deterioration in the strength of their democracy.[42] With support from Russia and China, authoritarian governments and populist right-wing movements are finding common cause. As Bruce Jones and Torrey Taussig have written, 'worryingly for the Western institutions in which they operate, illiberal actors across the West and beyond at times appear to be forging a loose "nationalist international", with shared disdain for liberal domestic and multilateral arrangements'.[43] Transnational links, now in evidence among right-wing parties worldwide, have opened up space for Russia or China to intervene, offering assistance ranging from overt endorsement to covert support for elements aligned with their interests.

Both China and Russia present a vision of the world attractive to governments weary of fighting the coronavirus. It prioritises a neo-Westphalian approach to sovereignty, insisting on strong governments against threats that move easily across borders. It offers tight control over immigration and the use of digital surveillance to control unseen risks from within their populations. To a world increasingly worried about dispersed and congested supply lines, an illiberal order stresses self-reliance against the evils of globalisation and justifies closing borders to people and goods in the name of economic and cultural nationalism. It rejects global institutions based on shaky US leadership in favour of less demanding regional institutions. In a world that has been reminded of the need for capable, insulated governments against unpredictable perils, an illiberal order, even at a steep price, might seem attractive.

Illiberal America

The democratic decay of the United States itself has lent momentum to the development of an illiberal order. Much of the blame rests with Trump, who was elected as the American embodiment of the illiberal values espoused by an increasingly reactionary Republican Party. But Trump is a symptom as well as a cause, given that many drivers of democratic decay in the US – the influence of money in its politics, gerrymandering and a hyper-partisan media – long predate his entry into politics. Even so, political and social polarisation has now reached levels in the US not seen since Reconstruction.[44] Authoritarian instincts, particularly among Republican voters, have grown.[45] Since the emergence of the Tea Party, the Republican Party has drifted farther to the right than most of its European counterparts, making US politics largely a contest between a centrist party and a far-right one.[46] Corruption under Trump has soared, with the US ranking 23rd out of 180 countries on Transparency International's 2019 index.[47] Democratic norms that have traditionally restrained the political parties have been shattered, and Republicans have sought to use any lever of power necessary to stack institutions such as the federal judiciary to their advantage.[48]

Corruption under Trump has soared

As a result, American institutions are growing more dysfunctional. Polarisation has hobbled the effectiveness of the US Congress in conducting effective oversight of presidential actions.[49] Appointments to major positions in the executive and judicial branches are routinely held up by Republican Senate leaders for political gain. Relations between the executive and the legislative branches are increasingly rancorous, with each side denying the legitimacy of the other to act in various domains, including foreign policy.[50] Due to Republican obstructionism, Congress often cannot pass an annual budget and must resort to last-minute emergency appropriations.[51] This has increased doubt about the ability of the US government to honour its debt, which in April 2020, before the full effect of the pandemic was known, was estimated to be a cumulative $24 trillion.[52]

The election of Donald Trump marked an important change in American foreign policy. Despite efforts to explain him through the Jacksonian tradition,

Trump represents something different: an attempt to extend American dominance through predominantly illiberal means.[53] Trump's foreign policy is not isolationist, and despite various glosses on 'America First', it does not articulate a radically new foreign policy.[54] Instead, it echoes many of the presumptions of his predecessors – in particular, that the US is the leader of a unipolar order, that alliances and institutions are useless without it, that it can use force as needed. What is different with Trump is the centrality of illiberalism to his thinking. He praises the illiberal elements of George W. Bush's policy – for example, preventive war, torture and extraordinary rendition – and amplifies them with new ones borrowed from authoritarian governments. His endorsement of crackdowns on dissidents worldwide and his willingness to solicit bribes for policy changes are closer to the behaviour of Russia and China than to that of any Republican predecessors. Such emulation has made the boasts of a new 'swagger' in American foreign policy all the more pathetic, because under Trump the US has become more of a value-taker from authoritarians than a global value-maker.

The influence of illiberalism in Trump's foreign policy can be seen in his approach to democratic allies and authoritarian rivals. Many critics have noted that he effectively reversed the traditional pattern of supporting friendly democracies and isolating authoritarian rivals. He treats long-standing allies such as Canada, France and the United Kingdom as if they have accepted a subordinate status in a hierarchy dominated by the United States. When Trump threatens firm allies like Germany for their failure to 'pay' for their defence, he belittles them as though they were mere appendages of American power. In adopting an entirely transactional approach to alliances, he echoes his predecessors' discomforts about burden-sharing without making any conscientious effort to persuade allies to increase their commitments. Thus, Trump's behaviour erodes the hierarchical element of the liberal order, abandoning the procedures and atmospherics of consent that rendered it tolerable and disregarding the autonomy and preferences of other states, much as authoritarian great powers like China have treated their tributary states.

Trump has also shown far greater contempt for established institutions than his predecessors have done. Granted, many presidents have sidelined the UN and other multilateral institutions when they have stood in the way of American objectives, and when expeditious have sought to extend American influence through such institutions. Trump, however, has tried to hold them hostage to American demands by denying their legitimacy, threatening their funding or withdrawing from them outright. His approach derives from the illiberal presumption that dominant states call all the shots all the time. Trump sees value in international institutions only insofar as they act in accord with and amplify American power.[55]

Finally, Trump's conduct appeared to mimic the illiberalism of Russia, China and other authoritarian states in his celebration of nationalism and naked self-interest. Some have described Trump's foreign policy as 'illiberal hegemony' because it abandoned efforts to spread democracy.[56] Trump did not accept the traditional liberal presupposition that a state's regime type is relevant to its foreign-policy orientation, according no special status to democracies or the US itself. In 2017, President Trump remarked in a CNN interview that 'there are a lot of killers. You think our country's so innocent?'[57] Implicitly, Trump's foreign policy emphasised an organic conception of the nation and defended any actions to protect it as natural and inevitable. This explains Trump's call for a 'great awakening of nations, for the revival of their spirits, their pride, their people and their patriotism'.[58] A corollary was that, as one of his advisers remarked, liberal internationalism was 'well past the point of diminishing returns' and that states should act unashamedly in the interest of their nation.[59] This is more than just cold-blooded realism; in Trump's hands, it amounts to a licence to do whatever is needed to protect the dominant group, including restrictions on immigration or crackdowns on minorities. Trump's denial of liberal norms in favour of a chauvinistic conception of the nation also was at the root of US Secretary of State Pompeo's making the validity of human rights conditional on their alignment with foundational American beliefs.[60] This redefinition places the US closer to China and other illiberal states, many of which have rejected universal definitions of human rights on the same grounds.

While illiberalism has manifested itself during previous administrations, only with Trump did it become the central thrust of US foreign policy. It has diminished America's reputation but also its power, for as Hannah

Arendt long ago noted, power diminishes when it is used for domination. Its gravest effect has been on the liberal order. Shredding norms and institutions, denigrating the value of international public goods and celebrating America's unilateral military power, Trump offered little incentive for states to accede to a thick liberal order that grants exceptional privileges to the United States.[61] In effect, he allowed the mask to slip, advertising the liberal order's brutality but offering few reasons to accept its continuance.

The case for reform

The United States' descent into illiberalism and the growing assertiveness of Russia and China are yielding an illiberal order distinguished by renewed efforts to establish regional hierarchies, the weakening and supplanting of US-led global institutions, and the propagation of illiberal values. These changes are resetting the ways in which states compete, as evidenced by the increase in scope and frequency of tactics such as cyber warfare, subversion and disinformation, designed to sow discord in democratic political systems.[62] Over time, the rules, norms and institutions that marked the liberal order will atrophy and give way to ones that formally protect state sovereignty but turn a blind eye to subversion.

For the United States, already marked by deep dysfunction and an illiberal Republican Party, such a world presents a dangerous temptation. The country could continue to drift in an illiberal direction, becoming more like Russia and China in the contest for global influence as it ceases to uphold and defend existing institutions. Doing so might yield some short-term benefits: an unconstrained US could shake down allies for greater burden-sharing and more advantageous trade deals, manipulate global institutions and – as it often did in the Cold War – underwrite authoritarian and illiberal governments to advance its own interests. Such measures might allow it to compete with Russia and China effectively, but at the cost of consolidating the illiberal order, fracturing alliances, permanently disabling many global institutions and squandering whatever moral legitimacy the US still possesses.

The obvious alternative is to attempt to return to the status quo ante and restore the liberal order that existed during the Obama administration, as

Joe Biden has pledged to do. This policy of restoration is naturally attractive, as it casts Trump as an aberration and allows the US to reclaim the mantle of world leadership. But it is not clear that durable restoration is possible. Many allies have come to distrust the US due to its erratic policies and contemptuous behaviour. Given the current levels of domestic political polarisation and institutional dysfunction, there is also no reason to believe that a future Republican president would not repudiate many of the policies of a restorationist Biden administration. The breakdown of the Cold War-era bipartisan strategic consensus has reduced the United States' capacity to maintain a stable and predictable foreign policy.[63] The prescription for remedying US foreign policy probably cannot be just more US leadership.[64]

Retrenchment carries risks

Another option would be for the US to retrench, scaling back its military commitments abroad in the hopes of reallocating resources to domestic policy. There are powerful arguments for this approach. The Pentagon budget is bloated with enormous waste while healthcare, education and infrastructure remain chronically underfunded. The US military interventions in Afghanistan and Iraq have cost $6.4trn, to little if any strategic advantage.[65] There is a growing consensus in Washington that continued immersion in the Middle East would produce diminishing returns.[66] The pursuit of hegemony and the defence of the liberal order has led the US to incur high political and economic costs while allowing other threats, such as climate change, to grow.[67]

A strategy of retrenchment, however, also carries risks. In regions like Europe and Asia, it could signal to Russia and China that US alliances are vulnerable. US allies, in turn, would have fewer reasons to honour US leadership and join coalitions when needed. Retrenchment would thus create permissive conditions for the regional hierarchies that Russia and China are seeking to establish and allow them to expand their reach outwards, accelerating rather than restraining the development of an illiberal order.[68] It might also cripple some of the key global institutions, thus undercutting the ability of the United States to manage transnational threats such as climate change and nuclear proliferation.[69]

Neither restoration nor retrenchment would halt or reverse the emergence of an illiberal order without the reform of America's own illiberalism. Its urgent foreign-policy challenge is at least partially ideological: to prove that liberal democracy can compete in an increasingly illiberal world. For this, domestic institutional reforms are required. First, however, the Biden administration needs to stop the current bleeding at the international level. To do so, it should immediately seek to reassure allies in Europe and Asia of its military support and guarantees, and reaffirm commitments to institutions such as the WHO and to various existing trade deals. In particular, it should renegotiate the Trans-Pacific Partnership, as Biden has pledged to do. More broadly, the US should advocate a 'flexible coordinator' model of international collective action rather than presumptively defaulting to American leadership in all areas. Such a model would allow allies greater diplomatic autonomy and leverage over a particular issue. A post-Trump foreign policy must forsake the default assumption that the US retains *primus inter pares* rank over all issues and decisions, and go beyond the atmospherics of consent to provide genuine issue ownership for allies. Doing so would set the US apart from Russia and China as a liberal-international steward. Such an approach would not forsake American power – the US would still enjoy military superiority and political influence – but would rather apply it so as to enable flexible and adaptive coalitions of partners to take the lead over different issues.

In addition, the United States should recast its approach to Russia and China. Neither is a suitable or willing US ally, and their long-term goal – an illiberal order conducive to their geopolitical expansion – is not in the US interest. This does not mean that the US should be unrelentingly hostile to them, which would only drive them closer together. Cooperation over common threats like climate change is possible, and should be pursued. But cooperation with Moscow or Beijing will not happen until both recognise that the US is no longer on the defensive and is capable of reasserting itself after experiencing what Putin has described as a 'deep internal crisis'.[70] One way to signal this reassertion is to make Russia and China pay a larger, more public cost for interference in US elections and attempts to subvert American democracy. To do so, it goes almost without saying that the White

House cannot publicly deny the reality of such efforts or task the US intelligence community's leadership to downplay them, as Trump has done. Nor can it merely treat such attacks as garden-variety aspects of spycraft. Instead, it must confront them as overt security threats. More muscular retaliatory policies could include sanctions on governments or individuals, trade penalties, the limitation of access to US banks and covert reprisal.[71]

With these policy adjustments made, the Biden administration can turn to the paramount element of a reoriented US foreign policy: domestic reform. There are many areas in pressing need of it, including healthcare, economic inequality, education and policing. From a foreign-policy perspective, however, the most profound and urgent need is to fix the institutions of democratic governance itself. Much as the civil-rights movement in the 1960s galvanised Americans to believe that the US had a fixable if flawed political system, sustained efforts to fix American institutions today would renew faith in the United States and give other countries a reason to join it in opposing the consolidation of an illiberal order. To this end, the Biden administration should seek the swift passage of a new Voting Rights Act, named after the late US congressman John Lewis, which would address the racial discrimination that underlies voter suppression, especially in poor and minority areas.[72] It should also back statehood for both Washington DC and Puerto Rico, thus changing the Electoral College map in a way that will compel the Republican Party to stop catering to a minority of white voters and abandon the illiberalism embraced by the party during the Trump years.

In addition, Congress should tighten US laws against corruption to reduce foreign influence in the US political process. In addition to diminishing public trust, an American political system penetrated by foreign powers can lower the confidence of allies and partners in shared intelligence and jointly undertaken action, and impel them to distance themselves from the United States. The Biden administration needs to propose legislation to close the loopholes opened by the US Supreme Court's *Citizens United* decision that allow money to pour into the US system through corporations.[73] It also needs to tighten regulations on lobbying for foreign entities and close the revolving door through which US national-security officials can capitalise on their experience and connections to lobby for other governments. Cutting off these pathways of corporate and foreign influence in American politics will boost faith in the integrity of the political system and thwart efforts by Russia, China and other illiberal states to influence policy outcomes.

A difficult third step for a Biden administration would involve rolling back the vast executive powers that the White House has accumulated. Presidents are generally and perhaps understandably loath to shrink the powers of the office, but now it is necessary. An over-endowed executive branch – and, in particular, tolerance for the profligate use of the executive order – is the primary reason that Trump has been able to inflict so much damage on the American polity over the past four years. He is not unique: both George W. Bush and Obama relied heavily on executive orders to govern in the face of a deadlocked Congress. Like many authoritarians, however, Trump has inordinately relied on special powers deriving from national emergencies to enact policies that Congress would never have approved. According to the Brennan Center for Justice, the president can now invoke 136 statutory emergency powers, many of which are obscure and have rarely been used.[74] The fact that the US government is substantially ruled by decree, with each president imposing or repealing previous executive orders, makes the government less predictable and credible to allies. It also allows illiberal policies to flourish when someone like Trump is elected. If Biden wants to enhance the democratic credibility of the United States abroad, efforts to abolish some emergency powers, to strengthen the oversight powers of Congress and to reduce the sweeping executive powers of the presidency are necessary.

*   *   *

It seems counter-intuitive that in a time of great danger US foreign policy must begin at home. It also seems jarring that to meet the challenge of illiberalism the US needs to limit the powers of the executive branch. But the hard reality of the post-Trump moment is that an illiberal order is coalescing around the preferences of Russia and China. Liberalism is failing at home and abroad. Addressing this requires admitting that the unipolar moment is over and that a 'thick' liberal order is out of reach. But it does not mean abandoning liberalism or pretending that there is no ideological dimension to the threat. While not succumbing to the temptation of behaving as if it faces a second cold war, the US must toughen its line against the efforts of Russia and China to sow discord in democratic governments while also urgently fixing its own political institutions. A foreign policy of reform is the best way to rise to the threat and to show a fearful world that liberalism is not a defunct value system.

Notes

1 See Richard Haass, 'The Pandemic Will Accelerate History Rather than Reshape It', *Foreign Affairs*, 7 April 2020, https://www.foreignaffairs.com/articles/united-states/2020-04-07/pandemic-will-accelerate-history-rather-reshape-it.

2 See Stewart Patrick, 'When the System Fails: COVID-19 and the Costs of Global Dysfunction', *Foreign Affairs*, vol. 99, no. 4, July/August 2020, pp. 40–50.

3 See Fintan O'Toole, 'Donald Trump Has Destroyed the Country He Promised to Make Great Again', *Irish Times*, 25 April 2020, https://www.irishtimes.com/opinion/fintan-o-toole-donald-trump-has-destroyed-the-country-he-promised-to-make-great-again-1.4235928?mode=sample&auth-failed=1&pw-origin=https%3A%2F%2Fwww.irishtimes.com%2Fopinion%2Ffintan-o-toole-donald-trump-has-destroyed-the-country-he-promised-to-make-great-again-1.4235928.

4 See Colin H. Kahl and Ariana Berengaut, 'Aftershocks: The Coronavirus Pandemic and the New World Disorder', War on the Rocks, 10 April 2020, https://warontherocks.com/2020/04/aftershocks-the-coronavirus-pandemic-and-the-new-world-disorder/; and Thomas J. Wright, 'Stretching the International Order to Its Breaking Point', *Atlantic*, 4 April 2020, https://www.theatlantic.com/ideas/archive/2020/04/pandemic-lasts-18-months-will-change-geopolitics-good/609445/.

5 See Daniel Deudney and G. John Ikenberry, 'Liberal World: The Resilient Order', *Foreign Affairs*, vol. 97, no. 4, July/August 2018, pp. 16–24; G. John Ikenberry, 'The End of the Liberal International Order?' *International Affairs*, vol. 94, no. 1, January 2018, pp. 7–23; and G. John Ikenberry, 'The Illusion of Geopolitics: The Enduring Power of the Liberal Order', *Foreign Affairs*, vol. 93, no. 3, May/June 2014, pp. 80–90.

6 See G. John Ikenberry, 'The Next Liberal Order', *Foreign Affairs*, vol. 99, no. 4, July/August 2020, pp. 133–42; and Jake Sullivan, 'The World After Trump', *Foreign Affairs*, vol. 97, no. 2, March/April 2018, pp. 10–19.

7 See Kurt M. Campbell and Rush Doshi, 'The Coronavirus Could Reshape Global Order', *Foreign Affairs*, 18 March 2020, https://

www.foreignaffairs.com/articles/
china/2020-03-18/coronavirus-could-
reshape-global-order; Michael Green
and Evan S. Medeiros, 'The Pandemic
Won't Make China the World's
Leader', *Foreign Affairs*, 15 April 2020,
https://www.foreignaffairs.com/
articles/united-states/2020-04-15/
pandemic-wont-make-china-worlds-
leader; and Mira Rapp-Hooper,
'China, America, and the International
Order after the Pandemic', War on
the Rocks, 24 March 2020, https://
warontherocks.com/2020/03/
china-america-and-the-international-
order-after-the-pandemic/.

8   See Alexander Cooley and Daniel
    H. Nexon, 'How Hegemony Ends:
    The Unraveling of American Power',
    Foreign Affairs, vol. 99, no. 4, July/
    August 2020, pp. 143–56; and Kevin
    Rudd, 'The Coming Post-COVID
    Anarchy', *Foreign Affairs*, 6 May 2020,
    https://www.foreignaffairs.com/
    articles/united-states/2020-05-06/
    coming-post-covid-anarchy.

9   See Michael J. Boyle, 'The Coming
    Illiberal Order', *Survival*, vol. 58, no. 2,
    April–May 2016, pp. 35–66.

10 Speech by Foreign Minister Heiko
    Maas, 'Courage to Stand Up for
    Europe – #EuropeUnited', 13 June
    2018, https://www.auswaertiges-
    amt.de/en/newsroom/news/
    maas-europeunited/2106528.

11 See Keren Yarhi-Milo, 'After
    Credibility: American Foreign Policy
    in the Trump Era', *Foreign Affairs*,
    vol. 97, no. 1, January/February 2018,
    pp. 68–77.

12 See Steven Lee Myers and Paul Mozur,
    'Caught in "Ideological Spiral", U.S.
    and China Drift Towards Cold War',

New York Times, 14 July 2020, https://
www.nytimes.com/2020/07/14/world/
asia/cold-war-china-us.html; Graham
Allison, *Destined for War? Can America
and China Escape Thucydides's Trap?*
(New York: Houghton Mifflin, 2017);
Walter Russell Mead, 'Americans
Aren't Ready for Cold War II', *Wall
Street Journal*, 10 June 2019; and Yuen
Foong Khong, 'The US, China and the
Cold War Analogy', *China International
Strategy Review*, vol. 1, no. 2, February
2020, pp. 223–37.

13 See Farnaz Fassihi and Steven
    Lee Myers, 'Defying US, China
    and Iran Near Trade and Military
    Partnership', *New York Times*, 11
    July 2020, https://www.nytimes.
    com/2020/07/11/world/asia/china-
    iran-trade-military-deal.html.

14 See Stefan Halper, *The Beijing
    Consensus: How China's Authoritarian
    Model Will Dominate the 21st Century*
    (New York: Basic Books, 2010); and
    Joshua Cooper Ramo, *The Beijing
    Consensus* (London: Foreign Policy
    Centre, 2004). For a critique, see Scott
    Kennedy, 'The Myth of the Beijing
    Consensus', *Journal of Contemporary
    China*, no. 65, April 2010, pp. 461–77.

15 Australian Government, Department
    of Defence, 'Remarks of Senator the
    Hon Linda Reynolds CSC, Minister of
    Defence, at the USAsia Pacific Centre',
    6 July 2020, https://www.minister.
    defence.gov.au/minister/lreynolds/
    speeches/usasia-pacific-centre.

16 On China's encirclement fears,
    see Felix K. Chang, 'China's
    Encirclement Concerns', Foreign
    Policy Research Institute, 24 June
    2016, https://www.fpri.org/2016/06/
    chinas-encirclement-concerns/.

17   Based on GDP data from the World Bank, https://data.worldbank.org/indicator/NY.GDP.MKTP.CD?most_recent_value_desc=true.

18   Dmitiry Frolovskiy, 'What Putin Really Wants in Syria', *Foreign Policy*, 1 February 2019, https://foreignpolicy.com/2019/02/01/what-putin-really-wants-in-syria-russia-assad-strategy-kremlin/.

19   See Philip Zelikow et al., 'The Rise of Strategic Corruption', *Foreign Affairs*, vol. 99, no. 4, July/August 2020, pp. 107–20; and Dominic Tierney, 'Russia's Strength Is Its Weakness', *Atlantic*, 21 July 2018, https://www.theatlantic.com/international/archive/2018/07/russia-strength-in-weakness/565787/.

20   See Tom O'Connor, 'Russia and China Seek No "Military Alliance", Instead a "Strategic Partnership" of the Most Powerful Kind', *Newsweek*, 20 December 2019, https://www.newsweek.com/russia-china-no-alliance-powerful-partnership-1478556; and Dmitri Trenin, 'China, Russia and the United States Contest a New World Order', Carnegie Moscow Center, 7 May 2019, https://carnegie.ru/2019/05/07/china-russia-and-united-states-contest-new-world-order-pub-79078.

21   White House, 'The National Security Strategy of the United States of America', December 2017, p. 25, https://www.whitehouse.gov/wp-content/uploads/2017/12/NSS-Final-12-18-2017-0905.pdf.

22   Secretary of State Mike Pompeo, 'Communist China and the Free World's Future', speech at the Richard Nixon Presidential Library and Museum, 23 July 2020, https://www.state.gov/communist-china-and-the-free-worlds-future/.

23   Christopher Weidacher Hsiung, 'The Emergence of a Sino-Russian Economic Partnership in the Arctic?', Arctic Institute, 19 May 2020, https://www.thearcticinstitute.org/emergence-sino-russian-economic-partnership-arctic/.

24   Quoted in Jacob Stokes and Julianne Smith, 'Facing Down the Sino-Russian Entente', *Washington Quarterly*, vol. 43, no. 2, Summer 2020, pp. 137–56; and Dmitri Trenin, 'Russia Analyst: China and Russia Are Partners, Not Quite Allies', *Defense News*, 2 December 2019, https://www.defensenews.com/outlook/2019/12/02/russia-analyst-china-and-russia-are-partners-but-not-quite-allies/.

25   See Anne L. Clunan, 'Russia and the Liberal World Order', *Ethics and International Affairs*, vol. 32, no. 1, Spring 2018, pp. 45–59.

26   See Boyle, 'The Coming Illiberal Order'.

27   'China–Russia: Joint Declaration on a Multipolar Order and the Establishment of a New International Order', *International Legal Materials*, vol. 36, no. 4, February 1997, pp. 986–9.

28   Vladimir Putin, speech at the 43rd Munich Conference on Security Policy, 10 February 2007, http://en.kremlin.ru/events/president/transcripts/24034.

29   China's foreign ministry used the term 'gunboat diplomacy' in a statement quoted in Susan Turner, 'Russia, China and a Multipolar World Order: The Danger in the Undefined', *Asian Perspective*, vol. 33, no. 1, 2009, p. 168.

30 Turner, 'Russia, China and a Multipolar World Order', pp. 168–9.

31 Joshua Eisenman and Eric Heginbotham, 'Building a More "Democratic" and "Multipolar" World: China's Strategic Engagement with Developing Countries', *China Review*, vol. 19, no. 4, November 2019, pp. 55–83.

32 See O'Connor, 'Russia and China Seek No "Military Alliance", Instead a "Strategic Partnership" of the Most Powerful Kind'.

33 Helier Cheung, 'Is Putin Right? Is Liberalism Really Obsolete?', BBC News, 28 June 2019, https://www.bbc.co.uk/news/world-europe-48798875.

34 See 'How Much Is a Hardline Party Directive Shaping China's Current Political Climate?', China File, 8 November 2013, https://www.chinafile.com/document-9-chinafile-translation; and Nadège Rolland, 'China's Vision for a New World Order', NBR Special Report No. 83, National Bureau of Asian Research, 27 January 2020.

35 See Elias Groll, 'A Brief History of Attempted Russian Assassinations by Poison', *Foreign Policy*, 9 March 2018.

36 John Mearsheimer, 'Bound to Fail: The Rise and Fall of the Liberal International Order', *International Security*, vol. 43, no. 4, Spring 2019, p. 23.

37 See Charles L. Glaser, 'A Flawed Framework: Why the Liberal International Order Concept Is Misguided', *International Security*, vol. 43, no. 4, Spring 2019, p. 53.

38 See Mearsheimer, 'Bound to Fail', p. 23.

39 See Graham Allison, 'The New Spheres of Influence', *Foreign Affairs*, vol. 99, no. 2, March/April 2020, pp. 30–40.

40 Mearsheimer, 'Bound to Fail', p. 23.

41 Catherine Putz, 'Which Countries are For and Against China's Xinjiang Policies?', *Diplomat*, 15 July 2019, https://thediplomat.com/2019/07/which-countries-are-for-or-against-chinas-xinjiang-policies/.

42 See Sarah Repucci, 'A Leaderless Struggle for Democracy', Freedom in the World 2020, Freedom House, https://freedomhouse.org/report/freedom-world/2020/leaderless-struggle-democracy.

43 Bruce Jones and Torrey Taussig, 'Democracy and Disorder: The Struggle for Influence in the New Geopolitics', Brookings Institution, February 2019, https://www.brookings.edu/wp-content/uploads/2019/02/FP_20190226_democracy_report_WEB.pdf.

44 See Shanto Iyengar et al., 'The Origins and Consequences of Affective Polarization in the United States', *Annual Review of Political Science*, vol. 22, 2019, pp. 129–46.

45 See Amanda Taub, 'The Rise of American Authoritarianism', *Vox*, 1 March 2016.

46 See Sahil Chinoy, 'What Happened to America's Political Center of Gravity?', *New York Times*, 26 June 2019, https://www.nytimes.com/interactive/2019/06/26/opinion/sunday/republican-platform-far-right.html.

47 Transparency International, country data, 2019, https://www.transparency.org/en/countries/united-states.

48 See Steven Levitsky and Daniel Ziblatt, *How Democracies Die: What History Reveals About Our Future* (New

York: Crown, 2018).

49 See Thomas Mann and Norman Ornstein, *It's Even Worse than It Looks: How the American Constitutional System Collided with the New Politics of Extremism* (New York: Basic Books, 2012).

50 See Juan Linz, 'The Perils of Presidentialism', *Journal of Democracy*, vol. 1, no. 1, Winter 1990, pp. 50–69.

51 See Sarah Binder, 'The Dysfunctional Congress', *Annual Review of Political Science*, vol. 18, 2015, pp. 85–101.

52 The estimate is from 'The National Debt Explained', Investopedia, 23 September 2020 (update), https://www.investopedia.com/updates/usa-national-debt/.

53 On Trump and the Jacksonian tradition, see Taesuh Cha, 'The Return of Jacksonianism: The International Implications of the Trump Phenomenon', *Washington Quarterly*, vol. 39, no. 4, Winter 2016–17, pp. 83–97; Michael Clarke and Anthony Ricketts, 'Donald Trump and American Foreign Policy: The Return of the Jacksonian Tradition', *Comparative Strategy*, vol. 36, no. 4, November 2017, pp. 366–79; Walter Russell Mead, 'The Jacksonian Tradition and American Foreign Policy', *National Interest*, no. 58, Winter 1999–2000, pp. 5–29; and Thomas Wright, 'Trump Takes Allies Back to 19th Century Global Order', Brookings Institution, 3 March 2017, https://www.brookings.edu/blog/order-from-chaos/2017/03/21/trump-takes-allies-back-to-19th-century-global-order/.

54 See Michael C. Desch, 'America's Liberal Illiberalism: The Ideological Roots of Overreaction in American Foreign Policy', *International Security*, vol. 32, no. 3, Winter 2007/2008, pp. 7–43.

55 The Trump administration has adopted essentially the same view of US executive departments and administrative agencies, co-opting and subverting them to preclude them from pursuing policies at all inconsistent with administration policy preferences and, in many cases, Trump's personal and political interests. See Mann and Ornstein, *It's Even Worse than It Looks*.

56 Barry Posen, 'The Rise of Illiberal Hegemony', *Foreign Affairs*, vol. 97, no. 2, March/April 2018, pp. 20–7.

57 Sophie Tatum, 'Trump Defends Putin: "You Think Our Country Is So Innocent?"', CNN, 6 February 2017, https://edition.cnn.com/2017/02/04/politics/donald-trump-vladimir-putin/index.html.

58 Tracy Wilkinson and Noah Bierman, 'In First UN speech, Trump Derides Kim Jong Un as "Rocket Man" and Threatens to "Totally Destroy" North Korea', *Los Angeles Times*, 19 September 2017, https://www.latimes.com/nation/la-fg-trump-un-speech-20170919-story.html.

59 Michael Anton, 'The Trump Doctrine', *Foreign Policy*, Spring 2019, p. 46.

60 Pranshu Verma, 'Pompeo Says Human Rights Policy Must Prioritize Property Rights and Religion', *New York Times*, 16 July 2020, https://www.nytimes.com/2020/07/16/us/politics/pompeo-human-rights-policy.html.

61 See Patrick Porter, 'A World Imagined: Nostalgia and the Liberal Order', Policy Analysis No. 843, CATO Institute, 5 June 2018, p. 10, https://

www.cato.org/sites/cato.org/files/
pubs/pdf/pa-843.pdf.

62 See Henrik Breitenbauch and Niels
Byrjalsen, 'Subversion, Statecraft and
Liberal Democracy', *Survival*, vol. 61, no.
4, August–September 2019, pp. 31–41.

63 See Kenneth A. Schultz, 'Perils of
Polarization for US Foreign Policy',
Washington Quarterly, vol. 40, no. 4,
Winter 2017–18, pp. 19–21.

64 See William Burns, 'The United States
Needs a New Foreign Policy', *Atlantic*,
14 July 2020, availabe at https://
carnegieendowment.org/2020/07/14/
united-states-needs-new-foreign-
policy-pub-82295.

65 Neta Crawford, 'United States
Budgetary Costs and Obligations
of Post-9/11 Wars Through FY2020:
$6.4 Trillion', Watson Institute for
International and Public Affairs,
Brown University, 13 November 2019,
https://watson.brown.edu/costsofwar/
files/cow/imce/papers/2019/
US%20Budgetary%20Costs%20
of%20Wars%20November%20
2019.pdf?utm_source=Daily%20
on%20Defense%20(2019%20
TEMPLATE)_11/15/2019&utm_
medium=email&utm_
campaign=WEX_Daily%20on%20
Defense&rid=84648.

66 See Steven Simon and Jonathan
Stevenson, 'The End of Pax
Americana', *Foreign Affairs*, vol. 94, no.
6, November/December 2015, pp. 2–10.

67 See Stephen Wertheim, 'The Price of
Primacy: Why America Shouldn't

Dominate the World', *Foreign
Affairs*, 10 February 2020, https://
www.foreignaffairs.com/articles/
afghanistan/2020-02-10/price-primacy.

68 See Thomas J. Wright, 'The Folly of
Retrenchment', *Foreign Affairs*, vol. 99,
no. 2, March/April 2020, pp. 10–18.

69 See Burns, 'The United States Needs a
New Foreign Policy'.

70 Andrew Higgins, 'Putin Says US Is
in "Deep Internal Crisis"', *New York
Times*, 14 June 2020, https://www.
nytimes.com/2020/06/14/world/
europe/putin-interview-united-
states.html.

71 See Breitenbauch and Byrjalsen,
'Subversion, Statecraft and Liberal
Democracy'.

72 Luke Broadwater, 'After Death of John
Lewis, Democrats Renew Push for
Voting Rights Law', *New York Times*,
21 July 2020, https://www.nytimes.
com/2020/07/21/us/john-lewis-voting-
rights-act.html.

73 Michael Sozan, 'Ending Foreign-
influenced Corporate Spending in
US Elections', Center for American
Progress, 21 November 2019, https://
www.americanprogress.org/issues/
democracy/reports/2019/11/21/477466/
ending-foreign-influenced-corporate-
spending-u-s-elections/.

74 'A Guide to Emergency Powers and
Their Use', Brennan Center for Justice,
24 April 2020 (updated), https://
www.brennancenter.org/our-work/
research-reports/guide-emergency-
powers-and-their-use.

A New Concert? Diplomacy for a Chaotic World

Pamela Aall, Chester A. Crocker and Fen Osler Hampson

Diplomacy is vital for global stability and order, and has historically played a central role in the policies of states and international institutions. Not long ago there were plentiful examples of diplomatic successes in peacemaking and conflict management.[1] But the practice of peacemaking is not thriving today. Despite strong demand for international cooperation and diplomatic initiatives, evidence from Cameroon, the China–India border regions, the Koreas, Libya, the Sahel, the South China Sea, Syria, Ukraine and Venezuela indicates that the supply is lacking.

Why has diplomatic traction become so difficult to establish? One reason is that national decision-makers and other key participants in global politics operate in a more complicated universe than before. Elements of a legacy liberal order may endure, but a unipolar world has yielded to a multipolar one, and the global agenda has become much larger and more complex. Since we do not know where the international order is headed, it is necessary to prepare for a number of possibilities, to keep options open, and to avoid easy assumptions about 'hidden hands' and self-correcting mechanisms. A range of new challenges requires a careful rethink about how diplomacy is organised and practised. There is no single 'right' approach to the conduct of diplomacy in these troubled times.

Pamela Aall is senior advisor for conflict prevention and management at the US Institute of Peace and teaches at American University. **Chester A. Crocker** is Schlesinger Professor of strategic studies at Georgetown University. A former diplomat, he chaired the board of the US Institute of Peace for many years. **Fen Osler Hampson** is Chancellor's Professor at Carleton University in Ottawa and president of the World Refugee & Migration Council.

Survival | vol. 62 no. 6 | December 2020–January 2021 | pp. 77–94   https://doi.org/10.1080/00396338.2020.1851087

States are currently employing a variety of familiar diplomatic practices to project power in pursuit of national interests, to achieve stability in unsettled zones and to improve governance in fragile or transitional societies. These practices tend to fall into one of three distinct silos. Power diplomacy is generally deployed in geopolitical rivalries, using deterrence, containment, alliance-building and other competitive instruments backed by coercive power. US–China and US–Russia relations illustrate this pattern. Stabilisation diplomacy as practised by the African Union, France and the United States in the Sahel, for example, aims at de-escalating conflict and preventing its spread through instruments such as peacekeeping, military assistance, intelligence-sharing and containment of jihadist militants. Governance diplomacy involves intrusive efforts to reorder internal governance arrangements within states; it can also take the form of initiatives that inculcate new norms, rules and principles directed at advancing human rights and democracy. Relevant examples include current efforts by European Union members in Belarus, as well as US and allied efforts at nation-building in Iraq and Afghanistan, and United Nations-sponsored engagements in East Timor, Liberia and Kosovo. These three silos sometimes overlap, as in Afghanistan and Iraq, but are not typically integrated into a coherent strategic framework. This is problematic because none of them, by itself, is up to the task of strengthening security in troubled regions, or organising cooperative ventures around shared problems such as climate stress and pandemics.

In keeping with Robert Gates's call for a rediscovery of the 'remarkable symphony of American power',[2] we are proposing a new variety of 'concert' diplomacy to bring together states and institutions with different ideologies, values and domestic systems. In this new form of diplomacy, differing entities will cooperate in specific fields of common interest with the general goal of maintaining global order, drawing upon legal, political and institutional tools – as well as power tools – to do so. Non-state participants may also be included. Just as symphonic concerts feature many instruments and a conductor, concert diplomacy will require a range of tools and leaders capable of guiding their use.

The scope and ambition of such concert diplomacy would depend on the problem at hand. In the cases of preventing nuclear war and geopolitical conflict, the great powers themselves would have to be the drivers of the concert. But there cannot be a single concert to address every item on the global agenda. The centre of gravity on regional issues will vary by region, while the drivers of concert diplomacy on functional issues could include a range of state, inter-state and non-state actors. The idea is to foster greater use of informal, minilateral constellations of relevant actors – not to replace or compete with today's formal institutions of global governance, but to operate alongside them.

Competing views about the future of diplomacy

Discussion of the kinds of diplomacy that will be needed to manage the evolution of the international system tends to posit a binary choice between a ruthlessly competitive, Cold War-style diplomacy of containment and deterrence on the one hand, and a return to the 1990s heyday of liberal internationalism – when diplomacy was focused on inculcating new norms and systems of governance – on the other. Infused in both visions of world order is nostalgia for a bygone era.

Realists who argue that the rise of China and the resurgence of Russia in its 'near abroad' are signalling a return to great-power politics privilege a form of diplomacy that is at once competitive and defensive, and centred on a renewed emphasis on alliance management and developing clear spheres of influence. The underlying premise of their argument is that the economic and military rise of China, coupled with the relative decline of the United States, is creating systemic instability, with a growing risk of direct military confrontation as China challenges US dominance in the Asia-Pacific.[3]

According to Graham Allison, the pattern of rivalry that is emerging between China and the United States is a familiar one going back centuries to the days of Athenian rule in the eastern Mediterranean, as documented by Thucydides in his account of the Peloponnesian wars and the rivalry between Athens and Sparta.[4] Allison believes that the diplomatic statecraft required to manage contemporary great-power entanglements mandates the careful nurturing of US alliances in Europe and the Indo-Pacific as key elements of an effective containment and deterrence strategy. Economic statecraft will also have a role to play in enhancing America's relative power

by penalising China with steep tariffs and other punitive economic measures when it undermines the rules and norms of international trade.

Realists have different views about the threat that Russia poses to international order. Whereas some believe that Russia has embarked on a quest
for status and has defensive intentions in its regional sphere of influence,
others argue that its intentions are less benign and that President Vladimir
Putin's true quest is to resurrect the Soviet Union's Cold War status and
boundaries. Both camps agree that, given Russia's economic weakness, it
has had to embrace various forms of hybrid warfare, including cyber attacks,
to promote its interests.

Realists are also divided in their views about the main strategic and
diplomatic challenges posed by resurgent great-power rivalries. Whereas
'offensive' realists, like Allison, focus on changing power balances and the
importance of establishing clear spheres of influence via strong economic and
military partnerships to check Chinese and Russian expansion, 'defensive'
realists are more concerned about managing the risks of any strategic mis-
calculation and avoiding unnecessary provocations in an uncertain world
where domestic, populist pressures and nationalism are in the ascendancy.[5]
These pressures are especially evident in authoritarian states such as China
and Russia, where they threaten the primacy of ruling elites who, in turn,
are appealing to atavistic, nationalist sentiments in order to retain power.

Liberal internationalists interpret the evolution of diplomacy in the
twenty-first century very differently, believing that the proliferation of
regional and global institutions in a deeply complex, hyper-interdependent
world heightens the prospects for cooperation among states and a stable
international order, even with the weakening of US hegemony.[6] Under
this scenario, diplomacy will continue to focus on the strengthening of
governance institutions while simultaneously consolidating the foundations
of democracy in various corners of the globe through peacebuilding,
economic assistance, democratic development and the promotion of human
rights. A vast constellation of states, civil-society groups, non-governmental
organisations (NGOs) and international organisations are key agents of
institutional transformation in the liberal understanding of governance
diplomacy.[7] Some observers argue that regional organisations are likely to

play an increasingly important role, much as the EU has done to promote economic and political cooperation, democracy and integration among its members.[8] In the liberal paradigm of international order, the deepening web of 'complex interdependence' spun by the globalisation of trade and investment, which now includes China as a major player in global value chains and investment flows, will further reduce the incentives for armed conflict. Yet such assessments cannot overlook the lasting damage that US President Donald Trump's weakening of the World Trade Organization and his renegade tariff wars as part of his 'America First' campaign are causing to the international system.

Diplomacy in a changing world

Nostalgic ruminations about the health of the liberal-international order in the second half of the last century, and its purported 'decline' in this century, overlook the fact that international institutions, such as the UN Security Council, struggled with (and often were hamstrung by) great-power rivalries during much of the Cold War. A brief moment of nation-building, peacemaking, democracy promotion and regional stabilisation in the 1990s was underpinned by a transitory unipolar moment.[9] American dominance of the international system with the collapse of the former Soviet Union and China's own relative weakness and isolation following the Tiananmen Square massacre in 1989 meant that there were no real challengers to the leadership of the US and its Western allies. Certain types of diplomatic practice emerged that are not replicable today.

For example, the regionalised peace process in the Balkans in the 1990s, which culminated in successful negotiations at Dayton, Ohio, was orchestrated and led by the United States with European support, and featured a series of calibrated diplomatic interventions backed by the judicious use of NATO's military power against Serbia (which had no material external allies) to 'ripen' the conditions for a negotiated agreement. Reflecting on the outcome of those negotiations, US mediator Richard Holbrooke wrote that Serbia's leaders 'were headstrong, given to grandiose statements and theatre, but they were essentially bullies. Only force, or its credible threat, worked with them.'[10]

Similarly, the road to the peace conference in Madrid in October 1991 that facilitated the Oslo peace process and subsequent negotiations between Arabs and Israelis was paved by US power and the victory of the US-led coalition in the First Gulf War. As in the case of Dayton, US diplomacy succeeded in accelerating the peace process not just because the US was determined to reach a deal but because, as then-secretary of state James Baker noted, 'the defeat of Iraq created a new geostrategic dynamic in support of peace', which was combined with what Baker described as US 'willingness to act as a neutral broker and tell difficult truths to both sides'.[11]

The Good Friday Agreement that was reached in Belfast, Northern Ireland, in April 1998 offers a somewhat different set of lessons about the role of diplomacy in ending violent conflict and promoting the development of new governance arrangements. Throughout the 1970s and 1980s, violence in Northern Ireland thwarted repeated efforts to end hostilities through negotiations. However, in the 1990s the peace process was renewed and 'internationalised', not just through the engagement of other actors to support and lead the peace process, but also through the taming of transnational non-state groups and interests which had sustained the conflict. The efforts of the external mediation teams led by former US senator George Mitchell, former Finnish prime minister Harri Holkeri and Canadian general John de Chastelain were critical to the process. A European Community framework offered powerful incentives for a negotiated deal. Again, the US played a catalytic role in building the process and supporting it.[12]

As these and many other cases illustrate, the US was central to peace and conflict diplomacy during the 1990s. It was able to exercise its influence on a global scale because it had no real opposition. The liberal, rules-based order it sought to promote depended heavily on this unipolar moment. Similarly, Cold War diplomacy, with its spheres of influence, depended on a bipolar world order. Today, structural changes in the international system have been redefining the relationships among powerful states, international organisations, local government and civil society. The emergence of powerful non-state actors, transformative communication technologies and global threats to planetary survival, as well as the heightened salience of domestic politics in the conduct of foreign policy, mean that the kind of diplomacy practised during the Cold War, and in the unipolar moment that succeeded it, is no longer practical or possible.

Peacemaking led by one dominant power, as at Dayton, for example, is an unrealistic prospect, except in the case of conflicts that have not attracted the interest of other major powers, or that lie within the unchallenged sphere of influence (or sphere of interest) of a single power. Outside these spheres, peacemaking and conflict management are likely to fall to international and regional organisations, and to non-official actors, in keeping with another structural shift that has matured during the last 20-odd years involving the role that regional organisations play in world affairs. Once relegated to second-tier status, regional bodies now confer legitimacy, and often play gatekeeping and norm-enforcing roles, in order to constrain global actors and set the terms of UN intervention. They may sometimes receive low-key support from major or regional powers if they decide to construct a case-specific 'group of friends', or a more broadly focused concert of states that perceive a common interest in cooperating rather than exporting their rivalries.[13]

Regional bodies now confer legitimacy

Among the major powers themselves, evidence of direct rivalries appears to be increasing, most notably in Eastern Europe, around China's 'first island chain', and between China and India. Polarisation and power diplomacy connected with these geopolitical contests raise the risk of actual conflict, a prospect that should remind American and Chinese leaders that they need to be able to collaborate in some areas and to develop clear rules of the road to avoid armed confrontation – and with it the prospect of a nuclear exchange.[14] In the case of US–Russian relations, Thomas Graham and Dmitri Trenin have argued in this journal that while any kind of partnership is out of the question, a more realistic goal is 'competition conducted with a measure of mutual restraint, leavened by cooperation on some transnational challenges', including regional ordering in the Arctic, the Middle East and Eastern Europe. The fact of 'polycentrism', they conclude, points to the need for multilateral frameworks that include both official and non-official experts.[15]

To this picture should be added the breakdown of any semblance of harmony or coherence within the greater Middle East, where confrontation between Iran and its Sunni neighbours is only one source of tension. Regional competition between Turkey and Qatar on the one hand, and Egypt, Saudi Arabia and the United Arab Emirates (UAE) on the other, is also playing out in the eastern Mediterranean, Libya and the Red Sea/Horn of Africa. Regional power struggles such as these are complicating initiatives by global actors, while dramatically increasing regional powers' resort to interventions and proxy-war tactics that are aggravating local internal conflicts. Perhaps nowhere else is the need for a new concert diplomacy more evident, even as Bahrain's and the UAE's recognition of Israel signals a historic shift in the diplomatic stance of some Arab states.

Rounding out these structural problems are two interrelated obstacles to peacemaking and conflict management: the splintering of local political authority into competing factions, and the growing inability of external actors to influence events in target countries. Without some degree of alignment between the interests and incentives of global, regional and local actors, diplomatic leverage is difficult to exert.[16] This is particularly problematic in light of the proliferation of non-state armed groups, whose flourishing undercuts the making and maintaining of peace and undermines government itself, without providing alternative negotiating partners for peacemakers.[17] Engaging such groups is a tall order for local and regional governments, to say nothing of more distant powers. It seems probable that only a new form of diplomacy, operating at multiple geographic and societal levels, will suffice to manage such situations.[18]

It should also be acknowledged that peacemaking and conflict management have become less of a priority for powerful states. Since 9/11, the US and other Western-oriented security exporters have shifted their focus to counter-terrorism and averting the destabilising consequences of state fragility. Concerns about the consequences of state fragility have led to the prioritisation of the goal of stability and the use of security instruments to deal with militant movements in ungoverned spaces. However, this short-sighted approach rarely produces the kinds of sustained diplomatic initiatives that were necessary to bring peace to Aceh, Colombia and

Nepal, and to wind down the Sudanese civil war. Support for negotiated and mediated political settlements is very much a normative – and not just a security – undertaking.[19]

In addition, transnational problems such as weapons proliferation, piracy, human trafficking and terrorism will require cooperative efforts among diverse parties to overcome.[20] This is nothing new – serious challenges to peace and security have often demanded new alliances, new institutions and new tools. The Second World War gave rise to the UN and the European Coal and Steel Community. The superpower confrontation of the Cold War produced formal alliances that continue to influence international politics. The end of the Cold War provided a strong boost to non-military tools of conflict management, including negotiation, mediation, facilitation, capacity-building and interactive conflict resolution. Joseph Nye has argued that these sometimes surprising outcomes must be replicated in coping with pandemics, climate change and economic instability, as well as a host of technology-driven risks and possibilities for which no rules of the road or shared mechanisms currently exist.[21] Even countries that can appear hostile to collaborative diplomacy stand to benefit from such an approach. China's importance to the global economy and its shared interest in combatting climate change mean that it has overlapping interests, and not just strategic rivalries, with other countries. Russia too has shared interests with other countries such as avoiding nuclear war, supporting strategic stability (both at home and in neighbouring regions) and energy cooperation.[22]

Towards a new diplomatic concert

Concert diplomacy is based on the premise that states and institutions with differing values and systems may nonetheless cooperate to achieve certain goals, such as maintaining global or regional order, or warding off common threats, such as nuclear war or climate change. The word 'concert' became associated with international politics in the 1800s, when Austria, France, Great Britain, Prussia and Russia joined together in the Concert of Europe, an arrangement that brought peace to Europe for much of the century. That peace did not come about because the members of the concert held similar values or visions of the European future. They did, however, respect each other's territorial sovereignty and core interests, and share the goals of jointly managing European security, maintaining existing boundaries and calming the continent's political turmoil. It was a conservative response to the liberal ideas that emerged in the aftermath of the French Revolution, and had as its guiding principle the preservation of the status quo. Above all, it was based on what Kyle Lascurettes calls 'loose process norms' – that is, informal institutionalisation – and regular meetings to address the issues of the day.[23] Legend has it that the arrangement got its name because the delegates attended a concert together and thought that the metaphor of musical collaboration suited their own efforts. The earliest meanings of the word 'concert' may also have incorporated a sense of contestation as well as cooperation, indicating an agreement born of debate and rivalry. The Concert of Europe reflected that meaning as well. Achieving it was not necessarily a harmonious process, but depended on a respectful balancing act among its five members and their strong national interests.

Concert diplomacy in the twenty-first century, like its nineteenth-century predecessor, would incorporate regularised procedures and meetings, and a shared commitment to seeking consensus outcomes.[24] In terms of the management of great-power relations, the twenty-first-century version would operate similarly to the nineteenth-century concert, but at a global level. All of today's major powers would be included, even those which are not – but arguably should be – permanent members of the UN Security Council. But unlike the nineteenth-century version, the new concert would also feature multiple formats, operating on a global scale for some issues, at a regional level for others and on a functional basis for specific challenges such as pandemics. It would bring together different types of entities, and not just major powers, to solve problems and achieve common ends.

Maintaining the status quo would probably not be one of those ends. Instead, the goal might be to devise and monitor a peace process, much as a group of states and NGOs did to facilitate peace negotiations between the government of the Philippines and the Moro Islamic Liberation Front between 2001 and 2014 (and sporadically since then). It might be to address a common threat, as in the collaboration among states, international associations and private corporations to fight piracy off the coast of Somalia in the early 2000s. It might be to fight disease in countries beset by conflict, as with the international response to the Ebola virus in the 2010s.[25] These examples demonstrate that a variety of actors can share an interest in promoting certain values, identifying and fixing problems, responding to the risk of military escalation or cyber threats, or defending common goods, such as economic development, global health and environmental protection.

Governance diplomacy as it has been practised for the last 30 years is unlikely to be a major feature of concert diplomacy for a number of reasons. One is that major donors are diluting their insistence on governance standards.[26] China's interest in promoting the stability of incumbent governments and its growing influence over UN peacekeeping operations mean that the governance dimensions of such operations are likely to be scaled back.[27] At the same time, many countries in places like Africa and the

Governance diplomacy will be more narrowly focused

Middle East are increasingly resistant to external pressures to embark on major governance reforms because they fear losing or upsetting a delicate domestic political balance. In addition, many are less dependent on Western donors than before, and less inclined to embrace Western values, which are no longer regarded as universal. As Stephen Krasner notes, this does not mean that promoting good governance will stop altogether, but that governance diplomacy will be more narrowly focused on specific problems such as combatting corruption.[28]

Twenty-first-century concert diplomacy promises to be a much more fluid and variegated process than the nineteenth-century version. While the Concert of Europe might have dimly anticipated the EU, it was founded to protect its members' national sovereignty rather than to negotiate a power-sharing arrangement with a central authority. The new concert diplomacy, on the other hand, must embrace a diverse set of participants and tolerate a variety of political systems. It would bring together unlike institutions, including international organisations, regional organisations, NGOs, civil society and even, on occasion, the private sector.

Finally, unlike earlier concert diplomacy, the contemporary version would not demand that all its members focus on the same topics. Concerts may be informal and temporary, tied to the resolution of a specific problem. They may be longer term and sealed by contracts, but with low-bar exit clauses. The principal feature all these configurations would share is the practice of diplomacy by states and other actors that see the advantage of collaboration in reducing the risks of conflict, and of working out procedures to manage international challenges.

Already, traces of nascent concert diplomacy are emerging in certain fields, as in the use of the non-proliferation regime as the basis for negotiating the Joint Comprehensive Plan of Action (JCPOA) with Iran; the intelligence cooperation of the Five Eyes alliance; the intergovernmental Financial Action Task Force that counters terrorist financing and money laundering; the multi-dimensional Colombian peace process which engaged many different actors, including Colombian civil society; and the Rapid Response Mechanism within the G7 that collaborates on information-sharing to deal with cyber threats to democratic political processes. Such collaboration can extend to parties that may disagree on almost all other fronts. Graham and Trenin, for instance, have identified a range of low-hanging fruit for US–Russian cooperative endeavours that could become the core of a broadened diplomacy to foster restraint and enhance security in various sensitive regions.[29]

Conflicts in need of concerts

Many contemporary situations cry out for a concert-diplomacy approach. A case in point is the turmoil in the Red Sea–Horn of Africa region. A humanitarian and security crisis is gradually emerging at this African–Middle Eastern crossroads due to a combination of weak or transitioning states (Djibouti, Eritrea, Ethiopia, Sudan); ongoing conflicts in Somalia, South Sudan and Yemen; the export of Middle Eastern rivalries into the Horn through the acquisition of bases and the use of proxies; and a lack of coherent engagement by major powers that instead compete with each other in pursuit of exclusive bilateral links with regional actors. Egypt, the UAE, Saudi Arabia, Turkey and Qatar have all made attempts to carve out spheres of influence in the Horn, the latter two working to oppose the former three in a pattern that parallels their competitive behaviour in North Africa and the eastern Mediterranean. Conflict over water rights (Ethiopia–Sudan–Egypt), religion, inter-ethnic relations, inter-generational divides and control of rents in a region characterised by unaccountable governance is creating plenty of tinder for conflagrations.[30]

While it is evident to virtually everyone – major powers, regional powers, counter-terrorism allies, global shipping interests, humanitarian NGOs – that heightened local turmoil should be avoided, there is also a notable absence of leaders prepared to deploy the region's diplomats and envoys in a collective effort. The answer is not for major powers to compete for illusory domination of the area, but rather for them to explore means of bridging the core interests of the region's key actors, including those of the Horn's Arab and Turkish neighbours. A functioning concert initiative would focus on developmental priorities, support African and Asian mechanisms for negotiating differences, work with Arab-African capitals to help contain threats to maritime security and place constraints on the use of proxies to destabilise neighbours.

Elsewhere, concert diplomacy might help to take a hot crisis off the boil. The sudden escalation in September 2020 of the Nagorno-Karabakh crisis between Armenia and Azerbaijan is a case in point. Since 1992, after the last hot war in the area, the Organisation for Security and Cooperation in Europe (OSCE) has been the lead agency in seeking to manage the conflict, through the mechanism of the Minsk Group co-chaired by France, Russia and the US.[31] While this effort was generally successful in quelling the violence and achieved some limited breakthroughs, for nearly 30 years the sides remained entrenched in zero-sum positions about the future of the Nagorno-Karabakh enclave and several surrounding districts.

As a result, popular attitudes in Azerbaijan and Armenia were deeply hostile to the opposing side. It was clear that any compromise deal between Yerevan and Baku (the sides met on a number of occasions) would meet the resistance of their populations' deeply entrenched nationalist views. The extreme antipathy within Nagorno-Karabakh to a settlement involving any compromise – and the strong support from Armenian diaspora communities in France, the US and elsewhere – was another obstacle to peace.

The situation changed in November 2020 as Azerbaijan's superior military strength allowed it to regain lost territory. Russia, as the dominant neighbour of both sides and the diplomatic and military ally of Armenia, then stepped in to broker a ceasefire and political agreement that confirmed Azerbaijan's gains. The interpositioning of Russian peacekeepers served to freeze the conflict and solidify the new situation on the ground. Russia acted outside of the Minsk Group process to achieve this end, but unlike 30 years ago, it was not possible simply to impose a ceasefire on the parties. Azerbaijan's military advantage and Turkey's active participation as Azerbaijan's ally changed the balance of power in the region. The involvement of both Russia and Turkey, which are already on opposite sides in Libya and Syria, created another source of tension between Moscow and Ankara.

As of this writing, it seems that the violence has stopped, at least for the moment. It also seems that the OSCE concert process, which had some success in keeping talks going, has been sidelined by the direct participants, including Russia and Turkey. However, despite the ceasefire agreement, this conflict is far from resolved and would benefit from a redoubled effort on the OSCE's part. To be effective, this revitalised concert needs to strengthen its leadership and political will, and bring in allies (perhaps the co-chairs' Security Council colleagues) to the OSCE/Minsk process. An expanded concert would also bring Turkey – the other key conflict party – into the high-level discussions to hammer out a long-term plan. Importantly, the effort needs to go beyond the formal process to engage the hardened attitudes among citizens, and would benefit from further initiatives to prepare them for peace, a challenge that the EU and the Minsk Group have begun to address.[32]

*   *   *

A new form of concert diplomacy will be critical in responding to the COVID-19 pandemic and other transnational threats.[33] Neither a ruthless, Cold War-style competition nor the liberal internationalism of the 1990s is a credible alternative. Even at the height of the Cold War, the former was too risky and was gradually set aside in favour of negotiated terms of coexistence. Likewise, there was plenty of power-based realism during the heyday of unipolar liberalism as even its chief proponents sometimes ignored their own rules.[34] Powerful states adopted a mix-and-match approach, deploying power diplomacy, stabilisation diplomacy and governance diplomacy depending on the circumstances and their interests.

This kind of à la carte decision-making, which tends to exploit short-term advantages without regard to dangerous precedents and unintended consequences, seems increasingly unsuited to contemporary challenges. If a race to the bottom is to be avoided in turbulent conflict zones such as the greater Middle East and eastern Mediterranean, a new form of regional diplomacy will be needed. A regional security regime is probably beyond reach, but a process of periodic consultation among global and regional leaders on a well-defined agenda is not. Such a concept might build upon the annual IISS-sponsored Manama Dialogue, moving beyond scripted conference presentations to a focused, working-group format.[35] Similarly, if the global response to migration crises or disease outbreaks is to improve from today's ramshackle free-for-all, leaders will need to make diplomatic efforts to develop operational regimes and rules that can be implemented. The European Commission's new Pact on Migration and Asylum is an example of an attempt to strike the right balance between a fair sharing of responsibility and European solidarity. However, it will take catalytic leadership to translate professed commitments into genuine actions.

Other examples of purposeful and successful concert-style diplomatic initiatives can be found, but the demand for and supply of such initiatives are badly out of balance, and the imbalance is getting worse. The solution we have proposed points to the need for more informal and flexible diplomatic responses at various levels in order to prevent and manage potential conflict. The UN system could actually be strengthened if major powers worked alongside it to hammer out understandings and build consensus, as was done in the case of the JCPOA negotiations and earlier in the anti-personnel-landmines treaty via the Ottawa Process. This sort of thinking has proven its worth in instances of counter-terrorism collaboration. It needs to be applied more broadly in helping build rules of the road, confidence-building mechanisms and regimes of mutual restraint anywhere that powerful states risk bumping into each other. Today's challenges require joint and flexible responses; the responding actors and institutions need the ability to operate in diverse places and to use a broad range of tools in support of diplomatic objectives. The critical missing factor is leadership networks, a modern interpretation of the relationships that enabled the nineteenth-century European concert to function. Human agency is required to initiate a diplomatic process, move it forward and keep it focused. This is not the work of a single leader or government. It requires a convergence of incentivised individuals with the necessary mandate and political will to get things done.

Acknowledgements

We would like to thank Ross Harrison and Allan Rock for comments on an earlier draft of this article.

Notes

[1] Examples include the reunification of Germany (1990), the Comprehensive Cambodian Peace Agreements (1991), the Dayton Peace Agreement (1995), the Good Friday Agreement (1998), the Accra Comprehensive Peace Agreement (2003), the Comprehensive Peace Agreement for Sudan (2005), the agreement that ended the Aceh conflict (2005), the Comprehensive Peace Accord for Nepal (2006), the New START Agreement between the US and Russia (2010) and the Final Agreement that ended the conflict in Colombia (2016).

[2] Robert Gates, 'The Overmilitarization of American Foreign Policy', *Foreign Affairs*, vol. 99, no. 4, July–August 2020.

[3] See Robert Kagan, 'China's Dangerous Taiwan Temptation', Brookings Institution, 20 August 2020.

[4] See Graham Allison, 'Thucydides's Trap Has Been Sprung in the Pacific', *Financial Times*, 12 August 2012; Graham Allison, *Destined for War: Can America and China Escape Thucydides's Trap?* (Boston, MA: Houghton Mifflin Harcourt, 2017); and Graham Allison, 'The Myth of the Liberal Order: From Historical Accident to Conventional Wisdom', *Foreign Affairs*, July–August 2018.

[5] The classic statements of defensive realism are Robert Jervis, *Perception and Misperception in International Politics* (Princeton, NJ: Princeton University Press, 1976); and Robert Jervis, 'Cooperation Under the Security Dilemma', *World Politics*, vol. 30, no. 2, January 1978, pp. 167–214.

[6] See John G. Ikenberry, 'Liberal Internationalism 3.0: America and the Dilemmas of Liberal World Order', *Perspectives on Politics*, vol. 7, no. 1, March 2009, pp. 71–87; and John G. Ikenberry, 'The End of the Liberal International Order?', *International Affairs*, vol. 94, no. 1,

January 2018, pp. 7–23.

7   See Daniele Archibugi, *The Global Commonwealth of Citizens: Toward Cosmopolitan Democracy* (Princeton, NJ: Princeton University Press, 2008); Richard Perle, 'Democracies of the World, Unite', *American Interest*, vol. 2, no. 3, January/February 2007; and John G. Ikenberry and Anne-Marie Slaughter, 'Forging a World Under Liberty and Law: US National Security in the 21st Century', Princeton Project Papers, Woodrow Wilson School of International Affairs, Princeton University, 27 September 2006.

8   See, for example, Peter Wallensteen, *Regional Organizations and Peacemaking: Challengers to the UN?* (London: Routledge, 2014).

9   See Fen Osler Hampson and David Malone (eds), *From Reaction to Conflict Prevention: Opportunities for the UN System* (Boulder, CO: Lynne Rienner Publishers and the International Peace Institute, 2002); Fen Osler Hampson, *Nurturing Peace: Why Peace Settlements Succeed or Fail* (Washington DC: US Institute of Peace Press, 1996); Lise Morjé Howard and Alexandra Stark, 'How Civil Wars End: The International System, Norms, and the Role of External Actors', *International Security*, vol. 42, no. 3, Winter 2017–18, pp. 127–71; and Stephen John Stedman, Donald Rothchild and Elizabeth Cousens (eds), *Ending Civil Wars: The Implementation of Peace Agreements* (Boulder, CO: Lynne Rienner Publishers for the International Peace Institute and Center for International Security and Cooperation, Stanford University, 2003).

10   Richard Holbrooke, 'The Road to Sarajevo', in Chester A. Crocker, Fen Osler Hampson and Pamela Aall (eds), *Herding Cats: Multiparty Mediation in a Complex World* (Washington DC: US Institute of Peace Press, 1999), p. 343.

11   James A. Baker III, 'The Road to Madrid', in *ibid.*, p. 204.

12   See Paul Arthur, 'Multiparty Mediation in Northern Ireland', in *ibid.*, p. 485.

13   See Teresa Whitfield, *Friends Indeed? The United Nations, Groups of Friends, and the Resolution of Conflict* (Washington DC: US Institute of Peace Press, 2007).

14   See Joseph S. Nye, Jr, 'Perspectives for a China Strategy', *Prism*, vol. 8, no. 4, June 2020, pp. 121–31.

15   Thomas Graham and Dmitri Trenin, 'Towards a New Model for US–Russian Relations', *Survival*, vol. 62, no. 4, August–September 2020, p. 126.

16   See Saadia Touval and I. William Zartman, 'International Mediation in the Post-Cold War Era', in Chester A. Crocker, Fen Osler Hampson and Pamela Aall (eds), *Turbulent Peace: The Challenges of Managing International Conflict* (Washington DC: US Institute of Peace Press, 2001).

17   See IISS, *The Armed Conflict Survey 2020* (Abingdon: Routledge for the IISS, 2020), pp. 14–18.

18   See Teresa Whitfield, 'Mediating in a Complex World', Centre for Humanitarian Dialogue, July 2019.

19   See Howard and Stark, 'How Civil Wars End'.

20   See Chester A. Crocker, Fen Osler Hampson and Pamela Aall (eds), *Diplomacy and the Future of World Order* (Washington DC: Georgetown

University Press, forthcoming in 2021).

21 Nye, 'Perspectives for a China Strategy'.

22 See, for example, Evan R. Sankey, 'Reconsidering Spheres of Influence', *Survival*, vol. 62, no. 2, April–May 2020, pp. 37–47, in which the author argues for 'spheres of restraint' to secure great-power interests without violating small countries' sovereignty.

23 See Kyle Lascurettes, *The Concert of Europe and Great-power Governance Today* (Santa Monica, CA: RAND Corporation, 2017), p. 18.

24 See *ibid*. For an in-depth study of how the concert functioned and its impact as an institution, see Jennifer Mitzen, *Power in Concert: The Nineteenth-century Origins of Global Governance* (Chicago, IL: University of Chicago Press, 2013).

25 Concert diplomacy may also be supported by research projects that encourage a concert-like collaboration on developing practices for conflict management and peacebuilding. One example of this is the Private–Public Partnership on Peacebuilding (Px4), an initiative by the Carnegie Corporation and the Norwegian Ministry of Foreign Affairs, which requires its grantees to work across borders in joint research projects on peace.

26 See Vanda Brown, Harold Trinkunas and Shadi Hamid, *Militants, Criminals, and Warlords: The Challenge of Local Governance in an Age of Disorder* (Washington DC: Brookings Institution Press, 2017).

27 See Lise Howard, 'The Future of UN Peacekeeping and the Rise of China', in Crocker, Hampson and Aall (eds), *Diplomacy and the Future of World Order*.

28 Stephen D. Krasner, 'Learning to Live with Despots: The Limits of Democracy Promotion', *Foreign Affairs*, vol. 99, no. 2, March/April 2020, pp. 49–55.

29 Graham and Trenin, 'Towards a New Model for US–Russian Relations'.

30 This set of issues is discussed in detail in 'Final Report and Recommendations of the Senior Study Group on Peace and Security in the Red Sea Arena', forthcoming from US Institute of Peace Press. Chester Crocker was a member of the study group.

31 Additional Minsk Group members are Belarus, Finland, Germany, Italy, Sweden and Turkey, as well as Armenia and Azerbaijan.

32 See 'Press Statement by the Co-chairs of the OSCE Minsk Group', 16 January 2019, https://www.osce.org/minsk-group/409220; and the work of the European Partnership for the Peaceful Settlement of the Conflict over Nagorno-Karabakh, available at https://epnk.org. The latter organisation, a European civil-society consortium, is itself another concert arrangement in support of peacemaking in this conflict.

33 See François Heisbourg, 'From Wuhan to the World: How the Pandemic Will Reshape Geopolitics', *Survival*, vol. 62, no. 3, June–July 2020, pp. 7–24.

34 See Patrick Porter, 'A World Imagined: Nostalgia and Liberal Order', Cato Institute, *Policy Analysis*, no. 843, June 2018.

35 For details on the proceedings of the IISS Manama Dialogue, see https://www.iiss.org/events/manama-dialogue/manama-dialogue-2020.

Joe Biden's Post-transatlantic Moment

Fabrice Pothier

Transatlantic relations have always had their share of tensions and crises, but the Trump era has injected them with a level of toxicity unmatched since the Suez crisis in 1956. Beyond US President Donald Trump's intemperate tweets lay a fiercely ideological stance against the very idea of European integration. The European Union and NATO have been its prime targets, and he has singled out European leaders who embody today's Europe – first and foremost German Chancellor Angela Merkel – for criticism. The Trump administration's vocal enthusiasm for Brexit also reflects a deeply anti-European mindset.

The Trump administration's few constructive transatlantic moves, such as the US contributions to NATO's military deterrent, hardly offset the larger damage. The dependence of some Central European states – especially Germany – on US deterrence and security assurances remains palpable. Mentally, however, Europeans have started to look towards a future in which America is less central to their strategic calculations. The idea of European strategic autonomy is no longer the exotic preserve of think-tankers; it is central to the European agenda, even if a concrete strategy for achieving it has not yet been formulated.

This post-transatlantic moment presents President-elect Joe Biden with the opportunity to shape a more mature and balanced relationship. Each side, however, will have to overcome its own biases and be willing to invest energy in more than just legacy issues.

Fabrice Pothier is IISS Consulting Senior Fellow for Defence Policy and Strategy. He is also Chief Strategy Officer at Rasmussen Global and co-founder of the Transatlantic Commission on Election Integrity.

Survival | vol. 62 no. 6 | December 2020–January 2021 | pp. 95–102   https://doi.org/0.1080/00396338.2020.1851088

The Biden administration's positions

The Biden team has signalled that the US is back as a reliable global power. For Europe, to make good on this claim the US will have to end Trump's ambiguous, and ultimately corrosive, posture on NATO by reaffirming an unconditional US commitment to European security. The allies' approach to Russia will gain in coherence, even if sour differences on matters such as Nord Stream II will remain. How a Biden administration will handle the announced reductions in the US troop presence in Germany will be an important test. Notwithstanding the upbeat messaging, the Biden administration could continue to lean hard on European allies to do and spend more, as Barack Obama did. But the friendly tone that they anticipate will make all the difference. It is also clear that the economic shock of the COVID-19 pandemic has reduced both the significance and the urgency of the 2%-of-GDP defence-spending goal. With respect to the broader European neighbourhood, including Eastern Europe and the Middle East, a diplomatically more active US administration is likely. But this will not automatically translate into greater engagement on the ground, especially on military matters. Biden shares with Trump – and a large majority of the American public – strong resistance to US military involvement abroad. As vice president, Biden argued against a US troop surge in Afghanistan. His policy advisers' consistent refrain of working through alliances such as NATO can also be read as a greater willingness to delegate or outsource more of the heavy lifting to allies, including European ones.

NATO, however, is unlikely to be the main focus of Biden's transatlantic agenda. The centre of gravity of transatlantic cooperation has shifted towards the EU. While the original US–EU priority was trade relations, over the last 20 years security issues, including intelligence cooperation, sanctions, cyber, data protection and arms control, have gained importance. Here too some repair work will be needed. The most striking symbolic move would be for the United States to rejoin the Joint Comprehensive Plan of Action (JCPOA) – the Iran nuclear deal – as the Biden team has indicated it could do, but this is a fraught proposition. How exactly his administration would re-engage with Iran remains unclear, and it will depend to some extent on congressional attitudes. Moreover, the Iranians themselves are unlikely to assess that returning to the status quo ante, in light of the economic damage caused by the Trump administration's maximum-pressure strategy, is enough. Given that French President Emmanuel Macron has made saving the JCPOA his signature foreign-policy issue, France could be a key player in fashioning an expanded transatlantic approach to re-engagement with Iran.

On the trade front, the Biden administration is expected to remove irritants – mainly US tariffs on some European products and companies – that have impaired the US–EU relationship under Trump. Yet a substantially more fruitful trade agenda with the EU, including revisiting the failed Transatlantic Trade and Investment Partnership, seems far from certain. Politics on the two sides of the Atlantic appear too far apart to support an ambitious regulatory alignment, especially on sensitive matters like food standards. Both trading blocs have also grown more protectionist, even if some EU officials like to describe its stance merely as better defending trade interests. Biden's proposal of a 'Buy America Act', while a fairly typical campaign promise and not a new idea, might be an early sign of difficult times ahead for transatlantic trade relations. A narrower trade agreement on some key (and less sensitive) sectors is possible, though the Democratic Party's record of trade scepticism leaves room for doubt.

Past those important confidence-building steps, climate will most likely be the paramount transatlantic issue for the US under Biden. He announced during his presidential campaign that the US would rejoin the Paris climate agreement on day one of his presidency. Apart from powerfully signifying American re-engagement on an existential global issue, this would reduce the EU's reliance on China as a global partner. It would also enable the US and the EU to exert more pressure on China and India – two economies that are critical to reducing global carbon emissions. In addition, the United States' return to the global climate fold could also create opportunities for new joint initiatives, such as developing a carbon border tax. The EU is committed to this initiative, and increasingly in practical need of it to finance the €750 billion Next Generation EU fund for post-pandemic economic recovery. European Commission insiders recognise the complexity of implementing a carbon border tax on 'dirty' imports like steel products.

And the political challenge the EU will face in the World Trade Organization (WTO), especially from big exporters like China, will be formidable. But should the Biden administration follow through on the Democratic Party's pledge to support a similar 'carbon adjustment fee' in the US, an EU carbon tax could become more feasible.[1]

Dealing with China

A crucial question is whether and how the Biden administration can work with Europe in addressing China's growing global ambition. The new Washington consensus on China – a mixture of containment and decoupling – will likely persist as one of few points of bipartisan agreement in the new administration, as suggested by Speaker of the House Nancy Pelosi's hawkish tone on China. While Biden himself may tilt towards the more traditional policy of engagement, he has already shifted his position closer to that of the Trump administration. The difference will be mainly one of nuance. China will remain the United States' primary economic and military competitor, but the Biden administration is likely to adopt a less abrasive stance towards regional US allies and a less maximalist one towards China itself.

In fact, Biden's relatively moderate approach to China is likely to converge on the tougher European one that has emerged over the last few years: hard on economic and political differences but committed to maintaining dialogue and cooperation in selected areas, such as climate. Some marked transatlantic differences may remain, including a more open US policy towards Taiwan versus the EU's policy of discretion. Biden will also inherit a trade war with China, which he will find hard to de-escalate – though he might try – without significant concessions from Beijing. In the WTO, better transatlantic coordination could emerge to exert pressure on China on issues such as subsidies and fair market access. But given the limited enthusiasm of the US Congress for multilateral institutions, the EU and European leaders should not count too heavily on this eventuality.

Regarding China, the US and Europe would do well to focus on key issues rather than multilateral institutions. One issue would be global environmental development standards. Both the US and the EU have struggled to come up with compelling alternatives to China's Belt and Road Initiative

(BRI). Even though the BRI has not been an unalloyed success for Beijing, it remains the most attractive geostrategic initiative on offer. The EU's Connectivity Strategy, which seeks to set higher standards for the development of key countries and regions, is well intentioned but lacks a critical mass of concrete projects, consisting mainly of a rule book as opposed to China's chequebook. The US-led Indo-Pacific Corridor makes equal sense, but due to the ideological profile of the Trump administration has failed to rally allies and partners sufficient to turn it into a viable alternative to the BRI. Under the Biden administration, the US could join forces with the EU with an eye to forging such an alternative. For example, African countries with large deposits of critical raw materials often find themselves compelled to export them to China, which refines them and reaps far greater profits. The US and EU could devise plans for funding the targeted development – to include processing capacity and green export corridors – of countries and regions that are rich in raw materials essential for powering green and digital transitions, but that lack the resources and expertise to maximise gains from their utilisation. Such an initiative would establish a firm geopolitical presence while helping developing countries to move up the value chain and the US and EU to reduce their reliance on China.

Global governance

A similar approach could guide the US and the EU on critical technologies. Even if 5G has now become the rallying cry, given that most 5G licences will be issued by early 2021, the focus arguably should lie elsewhere. One of the most critical areas is data flow. Today's global trade is reliant on the transmission of data pertaining to services – and, increasingly, physical goods – from one country to another. Yet no global norms exist as to how companies and governments should share and store data. There are some ad hoc, bilateral standards, including a data-adequacy agreement between the EU and Japan as part of the free-trade agreement signed a year ago. Singapore is developing a minilateral framework with partners including Chile and Australia on data adequacy. Last year, Abe Shinzo, then the Japanese prime minister, proposed that a free-data-flow initiative be undertaken by the G7 countries. Some EU member states were enthusiastic, but the Trump administration was not. EU–US cooperation on data exchange has historically been difficult, the July 2020 judgment by the European Court of Justice invalidating the Safe Harbour agreement to transfer personal data from the EU to the US being the latest episode. A recent draft EU strategy would bar third-country access to the EU's industrial data.[2] Along with improved transatlantic mood music, efforts by the Chinese government and leading Chinese tech companies to set the agenda for global data flow could prompt less US and EU parochialism and closer US–EU cooperation on digital issues, including global norms for data flow. But the EU will need to resist the temptation to salve its inferiority complex in the digital sector with overregulation. In turn, the Biden administration and the US Congress will need to chart a clearer regulatory path.

Another potentially ripe area for American and European cooperation is what in essence defines them: democracy. Biden and some of his close advisers have explicitly called for democracies to work better together, starting with strengthening their own fundamentals.[3] Biden and his team routinely mention money laundering and 'dark money' – that is, foreign funds flowing into Western markets and financial institutions to illicitly buy commercial and political influence – as one of the liberal-international system's starkest weaknesses. How far the US and the EU will be willing to go to address the vulnerabilities to foreign money in their financial systems will be an important test of the vigour of post-Trump transatlantic relations. The UK will be a critical player given its still-central role in the global financial system, and its upcoming chairmanship of the G7 could present a rich opportunity to address the problem. While the need to attract foreign investment during a recession will be a countervailing factor, both the Biden administration and European leaders should retain strong motivations to lay the groundwork for more effective practical cooperation on dark money and strategic corruption.

*   *   *

The Biden administration's foreign policy will have important elements of continuity and particularly strong domestic drivers, just as those of its predecessors did. Biden is inheriting a country with deep social and economic fissures. His stated top priority will be to facilitate the United States' recovery from the COVID-19 pandemic. Unlike Trump's 'America First' imperative, Biden's domestic focus will not dictate insularity or transactionalism. But it will mean that the administration will take pains to ensure that US foreign-policy priorities are clearly and carefully aligned with the interests of the US middle class. Climate is one such priority given the growing concern among Americans in that group – most of them Democratic voters – about the impact of climate change. A hard-headed trade agenda, geared to US jobs and competitiveness, will also be salient. As noted, Biden is likely to bring more finesse to relations with China, and to restrain US military engagement. Given that the Republican Party appears likely to retain a slim majority in the Senate and will have a slightly larger minority in the House of Representatives, Biden's room for manoeuvre in foreign policy will be limited.

Increasingly confident about defining its power on its own terms, Europe has finally moved on from waiting for the United States. This is true, with few exceptions, even for the German political class. The EU likes to define itself as a global multilateral and regulatory power. But a sense of European exceptionalism could stand in the way of a new kind of partnership with the United States. Many opportunities for cooperation will arise outside traditional multilateral contexts. The EU will have to strike the right balance between imposing its regulations and working with the US and other like-minded countries to set global norms. Instead of immediately urging the new US administration to fix global and regional issues, European leaders might start by asking the new US president what they can do to help him address some of his daunting domestic challenges. If the last four years have taught Europe and the rest of the world anything, it is that when the US succumbs to populist fever, the rest of the world falls sick.

Notes

[1] Democratic National Committee, 'Combating the Climate Crisis and Pursuing Environmental Justice', 2020 Democratic Platform, https://democrats.org/where-we-stand/party-platform/combating-the-climate-crisis-and-pursuing-environmental-justice/.

2   See Samuel Stolton, 'Data Sharing Services Must Be "Established in the EU," Leaked Regulation Reveals', Euractiv, 30 October 2020, https://www.euractiv.com/section/digital/news/data-sharing-services-must-be-established-in-the-eu-leaked-regulation-reveals./

3   The author co-founded the Transatlantic Commission on Election Integrity, of which Biden was a member from 2018 to 2019.

Brexit, Scotland and the UN Security Council

Norman Dombey

In autumn 2020, the United Kingdom was in a perilous position. COVID-19 infection rates were ratcheting up, and the UK was the only European country besides Belgium with a per capita death rate from the coronavirus among the ten highest in the world. Its pandemic-induced economic recession was also one of the worst in the G7. Under cover of this crisis, Conservative advocates of an extremely hard Brexit appeared to be in control of government policy. British membership of the European Union had ended officially on 31 January 2020, but on the ground Brexit would only arrive with the end of a transition period on 31 December 2020. Despite the public-health and economic emergencies, British Prime Minister Boris Johnson refused to consider an extension of that transition. Yet there remained wide differences between UK and EU negotiators about the shape of a future trading relationship. A potential 'no-deal' Brexit loomed – which, for some hardliners, may have been the idea all along.

Even if a deal is reached, the Johnson government has steered for a much harder Brexit than the one generally presented in the 2016 referendum debate. That hard Brexit could have baleful second-order consequences, including the break-up of the United Kingdom. Scotland's overwhelmingly pro-EU voters, unhappy that they have been pulled out of Europe against their will, increasingly favour a second referendum on

Norman Dombey is a professor emeritus of theoretical physics at the University of Sussex. He has written extensively on nuclear proliferation and participated in related diplomatic efforts, including international Pugwash conferences.

Survival | vol. 62 no. 6 | December 2020–January 2021 | pp. 103–112   https://doi.org/10.1080/00396338.2020.1851089

Scottish independence. Public-opinion polling indicates that, if such a referendum were held now, independence would prevail.[1] While it is not entirely clear how Scottish nationalists would force Westminster to grant a second referendum, there is a reasonable view that Scottish demands for one could not be put off forever. And if Scotland became independent, difficulties could arise for Britain and its world role.

According to Ptolemy, the British Isles constitute two large islands together with several smaller islands. He called the larger of the two islands Megalos Brettanias, or Great Britain, while the smaller of the two he called Hibernia, now Ireland. Great Britain is thus a geographical name for the large island comprising the mainland parts of England, Scotland and Wales, together with nearby small islands. Therefore the United Kingdom of Great Britain and Northern Ireland will be no more after Scottish independence, just as its predecessor, the United Kingdom of Great Britain and Ireland, was no more following Irish independence. The two new states would probably be called the United Kingdom of England, Wales and Northern Ireland and the Kingdom of Scotland. Both states would presumably wish to be members of the United Nations and England–Wales–Northern Ireland would hope to be recognised as the successor to the present UK in the UN and as a permanent member of the UN Security Council. England–Wales–Northern Ireland would also hope to be recognised as a nuclear-weapons state under the Nuclear Non-Proliferation Treaty (NPT).

In 2012, on the eve of the last referendum for Scottish independence, former prime minister John Major warned that a rump England–Wales–Northern Ireland would struggle to keep its position as a permanent member of the Security Council.[2] Many analysts have dismissed such doomsaying, pointing to precedents such as Russia's preservation of Security Council status after the break-up of the Soviet Union.[3] And the United Nations Association–UK and UK parliamentary researchers have assessed that England–Wales–Northern Ireland would probably retain the UK's seat after Scottish independence assuming that it was a matter for the Security Council to decide. This may be too sanguine. The issue could turn on broader international politics if the decision rested with the General Assembly rather than the Security Council, and this appears to be a distinct possibility.

The Soviet-Russian precedent

On 21 December 1991, representatives of the republics of Armenia, Azerbaijan, Belarus, Kazakhstan, Kyrgyzstan, Moldova, Russia, Tajikistan, Turkmenistan, Ukraine and Uzbekistan agreed at Alma-Ata in Kazakhstan to the dissolution of the USSR and the foundation of the Commonwealth of Independent States.[4] Russia agreed that it would take responsibility for the Soviet Union's international obligations. This was broadly welcomed in the West, but an urgent problem emerged.

The Soviet Union possessed thousands of nuclear weapons distributed throughout its republics – Belarus, Kazakhstan, Russia and Ukraine in particular. Article I of the NPT specified that signatory nuclear-weapons states such as the Soviet Union could not transfer nuclear weapons to any other state.[5] It was extremely important to international security that the control of these weapons continue to be centralised so that they remained in just one state; this would also help prevent nuclear weapons or nuclear materials from being sold or otherwise transferred to putative rogue states such as Saddam Hussein's Iraq or Muammar Gadhafi's Libya. The United States and its allies determined that the best way of achieving this was to ensure that the weapons and missiles were under Russia's control and sited within Russia, the largest former Soviet republic, and that the weapons in other republics were transferred as soon as possible to Russia. Boris Yeltsin, the president of the Russian Federation, agreed.

The Soviet ambassador to the UN then sent to the UN secretary-general a letter from Yeltsin, which stated that

> the membership of the Union of Soviet Socialist Republics in the United Nations, including the Security Council and all other organs and organizations of the United Nations system, is being continued by the Russian Federation (RSFSR) with the support of the countries of the Commonwealth of Independent States. In this connection, I request that the name 'Russian Federation' should be used in the United Nations in place of the name 'the Union of Soviet Socialist Republics'. The Russian Federation maintains full responsibility for all the rights and obligations of the USSR under the Charter of the United Nations, including the financial

obligations. I request that you consider this letter as confirmation of the
credentials to represent the Russian Federation in United Nations organs
for all the persons currently holding the credentials of representatives of
the USSR to the United Nations.[6]

The secretary-general circulated Yeltsin's letter to all UN member states –
effectively, the General Assembly – inviting objections. None were received,
so Yeltsin represented Russia at the next UN Security Council meeting
on 31 January 1992. If there had been no dissolution agreement by the
Commonwealth of Independent States stating that Russia should take the
USSR's place in the UN and its agencies that was subsequently approved by
the UN, Russia would have been just one of several new successor states and
might not have been able to take the USSR's place as a permanent member of
the Security Council. Or, at least, had it tried it could have been challenged.

The five permanent members of the Security Council (P5), as defined
by Article 23 of the UN Charter, are also the five nuclear-weapons states
recognised by the NPT. There is no logical connection between the P5
and the nuclear-weapons states: the UN Charter was signed in June 1945,
before the military forces of any state possessed nuclear weapons.[7] Article
IX of the NPT defines a nuclear-weapons state as 'one which has manufactured and exploded a nuclear weapon or other nuclear explosive device
prior to 1 January 1967'. So Russia could well have not been recognised as a
nuclear-weapons state for NPT purposes, as the Russian Federation was not
recognised as a state prior to that date.

The Yeltsin letter was construed to allow Russia to take the USSR's place
as a member of the P5 and as a nuclear-weapons state. The other route would
have been to amend the UN Charter and the NPT. To amend either is very
difficult. Amendment of the Charter requires agreement of the P5 and two-
thirds of the members of the General Assembly; those who agree must also
separately ratify the amendment under their own domestic procedures before
the amendment comes into force. Amendment of the NPT requires agreement
of all nuclear-weapons states, all 35 members of the Board of Governors of the
International Atomic Energy Agency and a majority of NPT signatories; those
who agree must then ratify the amendment before it comes into force.

The UN Charter specifies that 'the Republic of China, France, the Union of Soviet Socialist Republics, the United Kingdom of Great Britain and Northern Ireland, and the United States of America shall be permanent members of the Security Council'. If a Scottish majority votes to leave the United Kingdom, the geographical composition of 'Great Britain' and therefore the 'United Kingdom' will have changed from what was contemplated in June 1945. Without a compelling reason on a par with international nuclear security, it may take more than a letter from Boris Johnson to secure the rump UK's place as a permanent member of the Security Council.

To follow Russian precedent, both England–Wales–Northern Ireland and Scotland would first have to agree on a package of measures on the division of assets including embassies; on procedures for the use of sterling in Scotland; and on the siting of the *Trident* submarine force currently based in Scotland, among other issues. This agreement would allow Scotland to support England–Wales–Northern Ireland in its application to be recognised as the successor state to the current UK among the P5. Scotland would thus enjoy considerable leverage in such a negotiation. It could, for example, insist that the *Trident* base be moved from Scotland to an England–Wales–Northern Ireland port after an appropriate period of transition.

The Yeltsin letter suggests that, whatever the ultimate disposition, it would be largely political as opposed to legal.[8] Suppose the England–Wales–Northern Ireland–Scotland negotiation were successful. Scotland would then write a joint letter with England–Wales–Northern Ireland to the UN secretary-general requesting consideration of the letter as confirmation of the credentials to represent England–Wales–Northern Ireland in United Nations organs for all the persons currently holding the credentials of representatives of the UK to the UN, and that the name 'United Kingdom of England, Wales and Northern Ireland' should be used by the United Nations in place of the name 'United Kingdom of Great Britain and Northern Ireland'. In that case, the secretary-general would surely follow the precedent of the dissolution of the Soviet Union and circulate the letter to all member states to ask if any state objected to the arrangement.

This time, unlike in 1991, there would almost certainly be objections. Russia and China could well object in order to further diminish British political influence. Brazil, India, Indonesia, Nigeria and others would likely protest because they could not see why England–Wales–Northern Ireland, a small European state the size of Cuba with a population of around 60 million, should be a member of the P5 given that each of them is much larger in both size and population. Even some European states may object, as they are fed up with the British after Brexit and with British bad faith in the subsequent negotiations.

What happens then? As Yeltsin understood – but did not have to face, since his proposal drew no objections – contested UN succession arrangements are referred to the Credentials Committee of the General Assembly, which consists of nine members and has always included China, Russia and the US.[9] The committee, in turn, recommends a course of action to the General Assembly. If there were any objection to England–Wales–Northern Ireland and Scotland's request for the representatives of England–Wales–Northern Ireland to replace the representatives of the UK in the UN and its agencies, the Credentials Committee would recommend a course of action to the General Assembly, which would then put it to a vote. If the General Assembly decided that the matter were important, Article 18 of the UN Charter would require that a two-thirds majority of the General Assembly approve of the disposition proposed by England–Wales–Northern Ireland and Scotland. If not, only a simple majority would be needed.

Other cases

For a contested transition, China's situation furnishes the most germane precedent. The Republic of China under Chiang Kai-shek was overthrown by the forces of Mao Zedong and the People's Liberation Army in 1949. Resolution 1668, passed by the General Assembly in December 1961, decided that the question of the representation of 'a founder member who is named in the Charter of the United Nations' was an important question in the case of China.[10] Thus, a two-thirds majority was required to replace the Republic of China with the People's Republic of China in the UN and on the Security Council. In October 1971, the General Assembly achieved such a majority, passing Resolution 2758, stating that 'the representatives of the People's Republic of China are the only lawful representatives of China to the United Nations and the People's Republic of China is one of the five permanent members of the Security Council'.[11]

Cambodia's political transition in the 1970s is also instructive. After Vietnam overthrew the Khmer Rouge government of what was then called Kampuchea and led by the genocidal Pol Pot, the Vietnam-backed Heng Samrin government was established. The United States, China and other states refused to recognise it. In September 1979, the Soviet Union sponsored a motion to replace the representatives of Kampuchea, which included members of the Khmer Rouge, with representatives of the new government. The Credentials Committee recommended no change on a vote of six to three.[12] That recommendation then went to the General Assembly, which decided by a vote of 71 to 35 that Kampuchea should continue to be represented at the United Nations.[13] A two-thirds majority was obtained, although there was no need for one as the General Assembly had not resolved that the matter was important.

If a new version of Resolution 1668 were put to the General Assembly, stating again that the question of the representation of a founder member who is named in the Charter of the United Nations is an important question, and this resolution passed, it is unlikely that England–Wales–Northern Ireland would be able to achieve the two-thirds majority required to occupy the UK's seat in the P5 given the likely objections of the BRICS countries (Brazil, Russia, India, China and South Africa) and like-minded members. If the matter were not deemed important, England–Wales–Northern Ireland would seem more likely to be able to muster a simple majority and thus take the present UK's place on the Security Council.

Alternatively, England–Wales–Northern Ireland could elect not to follow the Russian example and instead simply notify the UN secretary-general that henceforth it will take the UK's place at the UN and make the legal case that it is entitled to do so. But this would not change much. The secretary-general would still likely circulate the letter to all UN members and ask for objections. Even if he or she did not, any member state could object. If any did, then the matter would go to the Credentials Committee for advice, leading to a vote in the General Assembly.

England–Wales–Northern Ireland's third option is to do nothing. This course of inaction finds its most solid support in the case of France and Algeria. When Algeria became independent after the Évian Accords with France in 1962, France did not have to reapply to the UN to be a member and it retained its permanent seat on the Security Council. As François Heisbourg recounts, 'France forwarded no request to the UN in any of its guises, and indeed volunteered no information at all. It just stood pat and assumed that nothing had basically changed.'[14] It is possible, certainly, that England–Wales–Northern Ireland could succeed with the same inert approach. Scotland, like Algeria, would simply apply for UN membership as a new state, with no one raising a question of the current UK's changed status. But times have changed. In the 1950s and 1960s, decolonisation was a principal objective of the UN, backed by a strong African and Asian bloc, the United States and the Soviet Union. Algerian independence was seen as a salutary case of decolonisation, not as the destabilising break-up of France.

*   *   *

The Soviet and Chinese precedents strongly suggest that the General Assembly, not the Security Council, would decide. Accordingly, no one state would have a veto, and the General Assembly's decision would be acutely political. As Nigel White, a specialist in public international law, has admonished the House of Commons, 'international law on succession of states is limited and contested and, while UN precedents on membership in such situations provide some clarity, the law in this area is largely a product of practice and, in any such unstructured legal system, new precedents may well emerge as the political context changes'.[15]

Jonathan Powell said of Brexit that 'this Trumpian "great new deal" will not just take Britain out of the EU, but may also mark the end of the union, leaving a Little Englander government ruling a Little England'.[16] In the event of Scottish independence precipitated by a hard Brexit, Little England could lose the UK's seat on the Security Council.

Acknowledgements

The author would like to thank François Heisbourg, Adam Roberts and Adam Thomson for their tutorials on United Nations procedures.

Notes

1   See, for example, Chris Curtis, 'Scottish Independence: Yes Leads by 53% to 47%', YouGov, 12 August 2020, https://yougov.co.uk/topics/politics/articles-reports/2020/08/12/scottish-independence-yes-leads-53-47; and Adam Forrest, 'Scottish Independence: New Poll Shows Record Support for Secession', *Independent*, 20 August 2020, https://www.independent.co.uk/news/uk/politics/scottish-independence-poll-indyref2-record-high-sturgeon-snp-a9677891.html.

2   Nicholas Watt, Libby Brooks and Patrick Wintour, 'Scottish Independence Would Be Disastrous for All UK, Warns John Major', *Guardian*, 10 September 2014, https://www.theguardian.com/politics/2014/sep/10/scottish-independence-referendum-trident-defence-uk-john-major.

3   See, for example, UNA–UK, 'What Would Happen to the UK's Seat at the UN Security Council if Scotland Were to Become Independent?', 30 August 2017, https://www.una.org.uk/news/what-would-happen-uk%E2%80%99s-seat-un-security-council-if-scotland-were-become-independent; and Arabella Lang, 'Brexit and the UN Security Council', Briefing Paper no. 7597, House of Commons Library, 19 May 2016, https://researchbriefings.parliament.uk/ResearchBriefing/Summary/CBP-7597.

4   'The ALMA–ATA Declaration', 21 December 1992, http://www.operationspaix.net/DATA/DOCUMENT/3825~v~Declaration_d_Alma-Ata.pdf.

5   UN Office for Disarmament Affairs, 'Treaty on the Non-Proliferation of Nuclear Weapons (NPT)', https://www.un.org/disarmament/wmd/nuclear/npt/.

6   Yehuda Z. Blum, 'Russia Takes Over the Soviet Union's Seat at the United Nations', *European Journal of International Law*, vol. 3, no. 2, 1992, pp. 354–61.

7   The United States' Manhattan Project, of course, had long been under way, but the *Trinity* test did not occur until 16 July 1945.

8   I must thank two former diplomats who represented the UK and France at the UN and who gave me lessons about UN procedures and in particular the importance of the Credentials Committee of the General Assembly.

9   See *The GA Handbook: A Practical Guide to the UN General Assembly* (New York: Permanent Mission of Switzerland to the United Nations, 2017), https://www.eda.admin.ch/dam/mission-new-york/en/documents/UN_GA__Final.pdf.

10 UN General Assembly, Resolution 1668, 16th Session, UN Documents, p. 66, https://undocs.org/en/A/RES/1668(XVI).

11 UN General Assembly, Resolution
    2758, 26th Session, UN Documents,
    p. 2, https://undocs.org/en/A/
    RES/2758(XXVI).

12 Lee Lescaze, 'Pol Pot Wins
    First Round in UN Battle for
    Representation', *Washington Post*, 20
    September 1979.

13 Bernard Rossiter, 'UN Assembly,
    Rebuffing Soviet, Seats Cambodia
    Regime of Pol Pot', *New York Times*, 22
    September 1979.

14 François Heisbourg, email
    correspondence.

15 'HC 643: The Foreign Policy
    Implications of and for a Separate
    Scotland', written evidence submit-
    ted by Professor Nigel White, School
    of Law, University of Nottingham,
    to the Foreign Affairs Committee of
    the House of Commons, 16 October
    2012, https://publications.parliament.
    uk/pa/cm201213/cmselect/cmfaff/
    writev/643/m14.htm.

16 Jonathan Powell, 'Boris Johnson's
    Brexit Deal Brings a United
    Ireland Closer', *Financial Times*, 19
    October 2019, https://www.ft.com/
    content/08ae76c2-f197-11e9-a55a-
    30afa498db1b.

Why We Need More Diverse Central Bankers

Erik Jones

US Federal Reserve Chairman Jerome 'Jay' Powell opened a window on the central bank's new monetary-policy strategy in August 2020 by stressing that he was focused on the Fed's 'core constituency, the American people'.[1] A few days later, the Dutch central-bank governor, Klaas Knot, gave a speech in Amsterdam to underscore that the job of the central-banking community is 'to manage the risks that normal people have to face'.[2] This was no coincidence. Both men were responding to a call made in 2019 by the Australian central-bank governor Philip Lowe for monetary policymakers to 'talk in stories people can connect with'.[3] If former Fed chair Alan Greenspan could once pride himself on being incomprehensible, that time is over. Central bankers need to be understood – and quickly.

The splendid isolation of monetary policymakers has ended, because 'the people' are no longer happy with central bankers who seem only to care about the financial community.[4] They are also unhappy with central bankers who seem to act outside of political control. In May 2020, the German Constitutional Court challenged the way the European Central Bank (ECB) takes its decisions without political oversight.[5] The court accused the German federal government of failing in its duties to protect the German people by not paying closer attention to how the ECB works. That ruling was a wake-up call.

Erik Jones is Professor of European Studies at the Paul H. Nitze School of Advanced International Studies (SAIS), Johns Hopkins University; Senior Research Associate at the Istituto per gli Studi di Politica Internazionale in Milan; and a contributing editor to *Survival*. An earlier version of this essay appeared on Politics and Strategy: The Survival Editors' Blog on 29 September 2020.

Survival | vol. 62 no. 6 | December 2020–January 2021 | pp. 113–121   https://doi.org/10.1080/00396338.2020.1851091

Central banks have a legitimacy problem. They are too important to be left out of the democratic conversation and too complex to be included.[6] There is nothing new about this dilemma. Arguments about the excessive power that central banks can wield are as old as central banks themselves. Indeed, such arguments explain why the United States tried to live without a central bank for much of the nineteenth century and part of the twentieth century. That 'national banking' period nearly ended in disaster.[7] But if we cannot learn to live without central banks, we had better learn to live with them. That means striking a new balance in central banking between politics and economics. The best way to do that will be to start recruiting more diverse – and representative – central bankers.

Central banks are necessary
The long period during which the United States did not have a central bank came to an end shortly after the 1907 financial crisis. The big financial institutions of the day narrowly saved the US economy from collapse, but the bankers realised they could not play that role forever. Hence, they insisted that the federal government create a central bank for the US. The Federal Reserve System in place today is the result. The Great Depression of the 1930s showed the wisdom of that decision, even if the Fed did not cover itself with glory at the start of the crisis. By the end of the Second World War, just about every country had a central bank of sorts – and most of those were publicly controlled.

Public control turned out to be a mixed blessing. Central banks are complicated. They look like banks, accepting deposits and lending money, but their influence over how the economy works operates on many different levels and through a variety of different channels: financial, economic and psychological. Central banks create money, set interest rates, influence exchange rates and play an important role in making sure that commercial banks do not take on excessive risks. Doing all this at the same time means juggling complex trade-offs between inflation and unemployment, financial stability and investment.

These trade-offs are politically important. The essence of politics is making decisions about who gets what, when, where and how. Democratic politics rests on the idea that politicians as decision-makers are acting on behalf of the electorate. Alas, politicians tend to be poor at matching the activities of central banks with the desires of democratic electorates. During the 1960s and 1970s, for example, politicians instructed central banks to lower interest rates and stimulate the economy; the result was both more inflation and higher unemployment. Nobody voted for this kind of stagflation. That is why economists made the case for central banks to have 'political independence': politicians could set the broad objectives, but the central bankers would have control over how they achieved those goals, setting interest rates and other instruments without political interference.

Crises are not normal

The argument for letting central bankers work without political interference makes a lot of sense in normal times. So long as the politicians can agree on the broad objectives and the experts can agree on how to use central-banking instruments, people working in financial markets can predict what central bankers are going to do under most circumstances. This means that central bankers can shape market expectations in ways that will deliver the kind of performance that voters expect. In other words, politically independent central banks can deliver on the promises made by democratically elected politicians.

Unfortunately, the influence of central banks expands even further in times of crisis. This is a design feature, not a bug. Recall that in 1907 the US had no central bank; in the 1930s it did. Central banks exist to ensure that banks (and often also governments) have access to money in times of distress. In the last crisis, central banks were the 'only game in town' – to quote Egyptian fund manager, analyst and commentator Mohamed El-Erian, who used the phrase because no other policymakers outside of central banks appeared either willing or equipped to respond to the crisis in an effective manner.[8] During the current crisis brought on by the novel-coronavirus pandemic – a worse crisis than the last one – central banks are necessary just to keep the game going. Central banks everywhere are doing things they have never done before and on an unprecedented scale, and yet even this may not be enough without help from other policymakers – particularly those who can lower taxes and spend more money.

The justification for allowing central bankers to use their monetary-policy instruments independently is harder to make in moments of crisis.[9] The trade-offs that arise when central banks play an emergency role become more obvious and more important insofar as central bankers often have to decide which commercial banks are allowed to continue and which need to be wound up. Worse, if the crisis is severe enough and if the conditions are unfamiliar – which is an accurate description of both the last crisis and the current one – central bankers may find themselves working beyond their expertise. As they experiment with new policies, they create winners and losers across society with no guarantee that the policies will work to achieve some predetermined political objective.

The last crisis is a good illustration of this dramatic expansion at work, something that central bankers would be the first to admit.[10] As Lowe put it in his speech, central bankers need to 'tell stories about the trade-offs [they] face and how [they] are managing those trade-offs'.[11] The purpose of Knot's speech in Amsterdam was to remind listeners that 'the work of central bankers has a direct influence on your life and on everyone else's'.[12] Powell took care in his own speech to emphasise the importance of hearing directly from the American people about 'how their everyday lives are affected by our policies'.[13]

The huge growth in the balance sheets of the major central banks is further proof that something out of the ordinary has happened. Central banks bought government bonds, commercial paper, mortgages and more complex securities to ensure that banks (and often also governments) had access to money; such actions were a boon to the people who held those assets but came at a cost for people who relied on the interest from their savings.

Of course, the trade-offs faced by central bankers are more complex than they may appear. People who complain about the low rate of interest on their savings would probably not prefer that their bank fail, their job disappear or their country's economy collapse. The point is simply that when the experts start experimenting, the case for making central banks 'politically independent' gets weaker. Politicians are no better at using central banks to achieve political objectives in crisis situations than they are in normal times, but the advantage of entrusting experts with the awesome powers that central banks can wield is less compelling. Unlike bankers, politicians at least have the virtue of having been elected.

The trouble with speaking to the people

Central bankers were quick to recognise this dilemma during the last crisis.[14] Devising a solution was more difficult. Adopting a fixed rule for central bankers to follow was not a viable option because every crisis is different, even if the inevitability of crisis remains the same. Worse, the performance of the economy between crises has been changing as well. Rates of output and productivity growth are slower, as is the pace of inflation. Interest rates are also lower. The relationship between unemployment and prices has changed as well. Market participants are growing used to these new circumstances and resetting their expectations to match. The result is an increase in the demands on central bankers paired with a reduction in their room for manoeuvre.

Central bankers have realised that they are politically exposed. Because they are unelected, they have no natural constituents or supporters. Politicians can raise expectations about what central bankers can accomplish and then hide from the consequences when the policies fail. When that happens, the political independence of central bankers is a vulnerability, not a strength. The criticism central bankers faced in some countries during the last crisis was withering; many were forced from office, and some, like Panicos Demetriades in Cyprus, left under threat of violence.[15]

Because of this, central bankers have looked for ways to connect both to politicians – in ways that require them to accept greater responsibility for economic performance, particularly in moments of crisis – and to the electorate – to help citizens understand what central banks can and cannot accomplish.[16] Unfortunately, this kind of connection can be difficult to establish, because 'the people' are not the only ones who listen when central bankers speak. Financial-market participants are listening as well, and often become confused by new messages – with important consequences for economic performance.

A clear illustration of this sort of confusion comes from Europe. ECB President Christine Lagarde is a staunch proponent of Lowe's way of thinking about how central banks should connect with the public. Inadvertently, however, she demonstrated the pitfalls of plain speaking in March 2020, just as the coronavirus pandemic was sweeping across Europe. Lagarde responded to a question about whether the ECB's policies benefit one government over another by insisting that picking winners and losers is not the central bank's responsibility. From a narrative perspective, Lagarde's response was correct. But financial-market participants heard something different, reacting to the possibility that the ECB would not put a floor under Italian bond prices – even though doing so was necessary for European monetary policy to function. Within a week, the ECB had to commit €750 billion in new purchases to correct that impression, an amount that has since grown to €1.35 trillion.[17]

The US Federal Reserve took a different approach. Rather than telling stories, the Fed went on a listening tour. This is the strategy that Powell talked about in his August speech. He explained that the Fed learned a lot about the importance of employment for the lives of ordinary people. The bank also learned about the diminished risk of inflation. This kind of anecdotal evidence reinforced the message Fed economists had derived from their models and statistical analysis. As a result, the Fed now believes it should promote employment more aggressively as a 'broad-based and inclusive goal'.[18]

Here again, the challenge of plain speaking became apparent. Whether the Fed's new phrasing of its objectives will result in greater effectiveness or broader support for monetary policy remains to be seen; meanwhile, the impact of the speech on financial markets was immediate, with the dollar weakening against other major currencies. This currency movement may wind up benefiting the Fed, but only at the expense of central banks in other countries. Indeed, voices around the ECB are already expressing concern that a strengthening of the euro against the dollar could complicate efforts to stabilise the European recovery from the economic consequences of the novel coronavirus. As Lagarde tried to explain away this problem during a 10 September press conference on monetary policy, the confusion only got worse.[19]

What else can they do?

Plain speaking is no guarantee that a central bank will find popular support. When central bankers disagree, plain speaking may even make the legitimacy crisis of a central bank worse. This is a constant source of concern in Europe among those countries that have adopted the euro as a common currency. As Martin Feldstein warned shortly before the euro was created, divisions over monetary policy could undermine popular support for Europe's common currency.[20] Implicit in that warning is an awareness that even political independence does not mean the experts will agree.

A recent speech by German Bundesbank President Jens Weidmann is a good illustration.[21] The ECB spent most of the spring and early summer stressing that it would do whatever it takes to stabilise the European economy. That coordinated media campaign quickly repaired the damage from Lagarde's March press conference, and even papered over the threat posed by the German Constitutional Court's ruling in May. As summer faded into autumn, the ECB appeared to be usefully united around the extraordinary support it was providing to the European economy. Weidmann's speech drew that unity into question by suggesting that the ECB may have reached the limits of what it can accomplish, particularly with large-scale asset purchases. Now everyone is wondering when the divisions will re-emerge among Europe's monetary policymakers, and what impact that will have on the European recovery.

There is no easy way to resolve this dilemma. Giving politicians stronger political oversight over central banks is not going to result in better policymaking. Central banks are still too powerful and too complicated to entrust to non-experts. Speaking in stories is not going to connect central banks to the people either, particularly when those stories send bad signals to markets. We have already ruled out the idea of rules, because it is hard to imagine a rule for all occasions. But if central banks cannot be subjected to stronger political oversight, or receive comprehensive instructions in advance, or talk their way into the hearts and minds of the people without creating confusion, there seem to be few other ways that this necessary institution can be made to appear more legitimate in the eyes of the electorate.

Perhaps the best way forward is to focus on the central bankers themselves. By picking experts who connect with the people, institutions as a whole might be made more representative. In that sense, central bankers should perhaps be treated less like members of a homogeneous expert community and more like judicial appointments – particularly given that they tend to disagree on matters of importance. The challenge is to broaden the pool of candidates with the necessary skills to work effectively as central bankers. This may be easier in Europe than elsewhere, given the large number of countries that use the common currency. But diversifying the pool of qualified central bankers will be no less important in other territories where the legitimacy of central banks is in doubt.

Notes

[1] Jerome H. Powell, 'New Economic Challenges and the Fed's Monetary Policy Review', speech delivered at the 'Navigating the Decade Ahead: Implications for Monetary Policy' symposium, Jackson Hole, WY, 27 August 2020, https://www.federalreserve.gov/newsevents/speech/powell20200827a.htm.

[2] Klaas Knot, '"Samen sterker uit de crisis": Hoe we Europa weerbaarder, welvarender en duurzamer kunnen maken', 1 September 2020, https://www.dnb.nl/binaries/HJ%20Schoo-lezing_Klaas%20Knot%201%20september%202020_tcm46-389991.pdf.

[3] Philip Lowe, 'Remarks at Jackson Hole Symposium', speech delivered at the 'Challenges for Monetary Policy' symposium, Jackson Hole, WY, 25 August 2019, https://www.bis.org/review/r190826a.htm.

[4] See Lawrence R. Jacobs and Desmond King, Fed Power: How Finance Wins (Oxford: Oxford University Press, 2016).

[5] Bundesverfassungsgericht, 'Judgment of the Second Senate of 5 May 2020', https://www.bundesverfassungsgericht.de/SharedDocs/Entscheidungen/EN/2020/05/rs20200505_2bvr085915en.html;jsessionid=0B344920AAC119F0AF7449D39EAAEBCB.1_cid392.

[6] See Annelise Riles, Financial Citizenship: Experts, Publics and the Politics of Central Banking (Ithaca, NY: Cornell University Press, 2018).

[7] See Gary B. Gorton and Ellis W. Tallman, Fighting Financial Crises: Learning from the Past (Chicago, IL: University of Chicago Press, 2018).

[8] Mohamed A. El-Erian, The Only Game in Town: Central Banks, Instability, and Avoiding the Next Collapse (New York: Random House, 2016).

[9] See Erik Jones and Matthias Matthijs, 'Beyond Central Bank Independence: Rethinking Technocratic Legitimacy in Monetary Affairs', Journal of Democracy, vol. 30, no. 2, 2019, pp. 127–41.

[10] See Paul Tucker, Unelected Power: The

Quest for Legitimacy in Central Banking and the Regulatory State (Princeton, NJ: Princeton University Press, 2018).

[11] Lowe, 'Remarks at Jackson Hole Symposium'.

[12] Knot, '"Samen sterker uit de crisis"'.

[13] Powell, 'New Economic Challenges and the Fed's Monetary Policy Review'.

[14] See Erik Jones, 'Do Central Bankers Dream of Political Union? From Epistemic Community to Common Identity', *Comparative European Politics*, vol. 17, no. 4, 2019, pp. 530–47.

[15] See Panicos Demetriades, *Central Bank Independence and the Future of the Euro* (London: Agenda Publishing, 2019).

[16] See Jones, 'Do Central Bankers Dream of Political Union?'.

[17] Erik Jones, 'COVID-19 and the EU Economy: Try Again, Fail Better', *Survival*, vol. 62, no. 4, August–September 2020, pp. 84–5.

[18] Powell, 'New Economic Challenges and the Fed's Monetary Policy Review'.

[19] European Central Bank, 'Press Conference', Frankfurt am Main, 10 September 2020, https://www.ecb.europa.eu/press/pressconf/2020/html/ecb.is200910~5c43e3a591.en.html.

[20] Martin Feldstein, 'EMU and International Conflict', *Foreign Affairs*, vol. 76, no. 6, November–December 1997, pp. 60–73.

[21] Jens Weidmann, 'Calling on the Government', speech delivered at the Übersee-Club Hamburg, 2 September 2020, https://www.bis.org/review/r200904a.pdf.

Noteworthy

The US election

'Congressman John Lewis, before his passing, wrote: "Democracy is not a state. It is an act."
And what he meant was that America's democracy is not guaranteed. It is only as strong
as our willingness to fight for it, to guard it and never take it for granted. And protecting
our democracy takes struggle. It takes sacrifice. There is joy in it and there is progress.
Because "We the People" have the power to build a better future. And when our very
democracy was on the ballot in this election, with the very soul of America at stake, and
the world watching, you ushered in a new day for America.'

Kamala Harris speaks on 7 November 2020 as vice president-elect of the United States.[1]

'My fellow Americans, the people of this nation have spoken. They have delivered us a
clear victory. A convincing victory. A victory for "We the People." We have won with the
most votes ever cast for a presidential ticket in the history of this nation – 74 million. I am
humbled by the trust and confidence you have placed in me. I pledge to be a president
who seeks not to divide, but to unify. Who doesn't see red and blue states, but a United
States. And who will work with all my heart to win the confidence of the whole people.
For that is what America is about: the people. And that is what our administration will be
about. I sought this office to restore the soul of America. To rebuild the backbone of the
nation – the middle class. To make America respected around the world again and to unite
us here at home. It is the honour of my lifetime that so many millions of Americans have
voted for this vision. And now the work of making this vision real is the task of our time.
[…]
To those who voted for President Trump, I understand your disappointment tonight. I've
lost a couple of elections myself. But now, let's give each other a chance. It's time to put
away the harsh rhetoric. To lower the temperature. To see each other again. To listen to
each other again. To make progress, we must stop treating our opponents as our enemy.
We are not enemies. We are Americans. The Bible tells us that to everything there is a
season – a time to build, a time to reap, a time to sow. And a time to heal. This is the time
to heal in America.
[…]
Americans have called on us to marshal the forces of decency and the forces of fairness. To
marshal the forces of science and the forces of hope in the great battles of our time. The
battle to control the virus. The battle to build prosperity. The battle to secure your family's
healthcare. The battle to achieve racial justice and root out systemic racism in this country.
The battle to save the climate. The battle to restore decency, defend democracy, and give
everybody in this country a fair shot. Our work begins with getting Covid under control.
We cannot repair the economy, restore our vitality, or relish life's most precious moments
– hugging a grandchild, birthdays, weddings, graduations, all the moments that matter
most to us – until we get this virus under control.
[…]

Survival | vol. 62 no. 6 | December 2020–January 2021 | pp. 122–124   https://doi.org/10.1080/00396338.2020.1851095

Tonight, the whole world is watching America. I believe at our best America is a beacon for the globe. And we lead not by the example of our power, but by the power of our example. I've always believed we can define America in one word: possibilities. That in America everyone should be given the opportunity to go as far as their dreams and God-given ability will take them. You see, I believe in the possibility of this country. We're always looking ahead. Ahead to an America that's freer and more just. Ahead to an America that creates jobs with dignity and respect. Ahead to an America that cures disease – like cancer and Alzheimer's. Ahead to an America that never leaves anyone behind. Ahead to an America that never gives up, never gives in. This is a great nation. And we are a good people. This is the United States of America.'

Joseph R. Biden, Jr, delivers his acceptance speech after being elected the 46th president of the United States.[2]

'We all know why Joe Biden is rushing to falsely pose as the winner, and why his media allies are trying so hard to help him: they don't want the truth to be exposed. The simple fact is this election is far from over.

[…]

Beginning Monday, our campaign will start prosecuting our case in court to ensure election laws are fully upheld and the rightful winner is seated … [The Biden campaign] wants ballots counted even if they are fraudulent, manufactured, or cast by ineligible or deceased voters.

[…]

So what is Biden hiding? I will not rest until the American People have the honest vote count they deserve and that Democracy demands.'

US President Donald Trump issues a written statement in response to the election results.[3]

Our system can accommodate even ill feeling, and it has. Our second president, John Adams, famously left Washington in 1801 before Thomas Jefferson was sworn in as the third. Closer to our own time, although Herbert Hoover attended Franklin D. Roosevelt's inauguration in 1933, their mutual dislike had hardened so much that few if any words were spoken between the two men during the ceremonial ride to the Capitol.

The critical point is that Adams and Hoover accepted the outcome of the elections they lost. In Adams's case, enmity turned to friendship: Adams and Jefferson later grew so close that as Adams lay on his deathbed on July 4, 1826, ignorant of Jefferson's death on the very same day five hours earlier, he comforted himself with the words, "Thomas Jefferson survives." By contrast, Hoover and Roosevelt never repaired their relationship. No matter. Good feeling between political adversaries isn't necessary to permit our system to function; acceptance of results is.

Former US attorneys general Eric Holder, Jr (Barack Obama administration), and Michael Mukasey (George W. Bush administration) write in the Washington Post *on 3 November 2020, date of the US presidential election.[4]*

Sources

1 Matt Stevens, 'Read Kamala Harris's Vice President-elect Acceptance Speech', *New York Times*, 8 November 2020, https://www.nytimes.com/article/watch-kamala-harris-speech-video-transcript.html.

2 Matt Stevens, 'Read Joe Biden's President-elect Acceptance Speech: Full Transcript', *New York Times*, 9 November 2020, https://www.nytimes.com/article/biden-speech-transcript.html?action=click&module=RelatedLinks&pgtype=Article.

3 'Text of Statement from U.S. President Donald Trump', CTV News, 7 November 2020, https://www.ctvnews.ca/world/america-votes/text-of-statement-from-u-s-president-donald-trump-1.5179222.

4 Erik H. Holder, Jr, and Michael B. Mukasey, 'If You Can't Think of Anything Worse than the Other Side Winning, Imagine This', *Washington Post*, 2 November 2020, https://www.washingtonpost.com/opinions/2020/11/02/eric-holder-michael-mukasey-accepting-election-results/.

Preventing the Next Social-media Genocide

Daniel Byman and Aditi Joshi

In 2018, Facebook posts appeared on more than 1,000 accounts, including those of pop stars, a military hero and a beauty queen, comparing Myanmar's Rohingya Muslim minority to animals for having committed rapes against members of the country's Buddhist majority. The posts warned that the Rohingya were jihadists preparing to strike, and displayed pictures of their victims' corpses. The source of these lies was Myanmar's military, which set up numerous false accounts, posted incendiary material and fake news about the Rohingya, trolled critics and riled up the Buddhist majority.[1] Thousands of Muslims would die in the ensuing violence, including many children. Mass rape was common. Almost 700,000 Rohingya fled in terror, creating a refugee crisis in neighbouring Bangladesh.[2] After initially ignoring the crisis, Facebook later admitted that it 'can and should do more'.[3] Meanwhile, a human-rights-impact assessment commissioned by the company warned that state infringements of human rights in Myanmar were likely to increase.[4]

Despite efforts to enhance the safety of social-media platforms after what happened in Myanmar, events in India in 2020 demonstrated that online vitriol continues to produce real-world violence. Politicians belonging to the ruling Bharatiya Janata Party (BJP), a Hindu nationalist party, have posted incendiary content targeting Muslims online. One politician, T. Raja Singh,

Daniel Byman is a professor in the School of Foreign Service at Georgetown University and a senior fellow at the Center for Middle East Policy at the Brookings Institution. **Aditi Joshi** is a research analyst at the Center for Security and Emerging Technology, and a student at Georgetown University studying Science, Technology and International Affairs, and French.

Survival | vol. 62 no. 6 | December 2020–January 2021 | pp. 125–152   https://doi.org/10.1080/00396338.2020.1851097

was accused of violating Facebook's hate-speech rules by calling Muslims traitors, threatening to raze mosques and saying that Muslim immigrants should be shot. He posted a photo of himself promoting the extrajudicial killing of Muslims and claiming they should be 'slaughtered'.[5] Singh was not alone; other politicians posted content accusing Muslims of intentionally spreading the novel coronavirus and marrying Hindu women as part of a 'love jihad'.[6] Facebook employees identified this and similar content as hate speech and warned that, given the growing religious tensions in India and the country's history of communal conflict, such rhetoric could lead to real-world violence. Indeed, when Kapil Mishra, another lawmaker, uploaded a video to Facebook warning that his supporters would 'clear' protesters against a citizenship bill excluding Muslims, deadly rioting ensued that killed dozens of people, most of them Muslims. Yet Ankhi Das, Facebook's top lobbying executive in India, told the company's staff that applying hate-speech rules to BJP politicians 'would damage the company's business prospects in the country', an important market for Facebook.[7] Three officials found in violation of hate-speech rules, including one whose account was suspended on Twitter, maintain active Facebook accounts. The company only took down some posts when called out by the *Wall Street Journal*.[8]

Rumours led to riots and pogroms

In some cases, governments have taken action themselves to address the dangers that social media can pose. In 2019, after a horrific set of terrorist attacks against Christian sites in Sri Lanka during the Easter holiday killed 259 people, the government shut down Facebook, Instagram, YouTube and other popular sites. Colombo feared that hate speech and misinformation would inflame religious tensions further, leading to a spiral of mob violence. These fears were not idle. A year before, anti-Muslim rumours had spread on Facebook, leading to riots and pogroms.[9] Non-profits had repeatedly warned Facebook that posts were contributing to increasing tensions between ethnic and religious groups. Even so, Facebook failed to respond. For example, the company took six days to respond to a reported post saying 'Kill all the Muslim babies without sparing even an infant', and ultimately did not take it down.[10]

Yet the Sri Lankan case also demonstrates how useful social media can be in a crisis. Facebook and other platforms can help aid organisations, concerned foreign governments and domestic public-service agencies to learn more about the crisis, assist refugees and coordinate the overall response. During the 2018 riots in Sri Lanka, a well-known public commentator tweeted about the distribution of dry rations in an area affected by violence and was retweeted hundreds of times. Grassroots content promoting religious harmony and non-violence, as well as appeals by celebrities to stop the violence, also went viral. Prominent, non-political social-media accounts documented the violence and allowed witnesses and victims to tell their stories.[11]

Sri Lanka also demonstrated that, in places where state-controlled, traditional media outlets lack the public's trust, social media can play a vital role in providing essential information.[12] During the 2019 Easter attacks, the news of the attacks and their locations spread on Facebook and Twitter before breaking on television.[13] Even when reports became more widespread, social media provided news from independent sources, such as the respected BBC Sinhala reporter Azzam Ameen, that were not subject to the same government pressure and censorship as the traditional media.[14] The internet ban also revealed the importance of a functional social media for contacting friends and family in areas affected by violence, and for signalling one's own safety.[15] In times of high tension, social media might also play a role in organising protests and dissent, perhaps limiting chaos.

In Myanmar, Sri Lanka and other divided societies where tensions are high, social-media companies and those who seek to improve the safety of the internet face a dilemma. Clearly, the platforms' ability to cheaply reach large numbers of users can bring communities together, nurture commerce and serve as a vital lifeline during crises. At the same time, those seeking to foment hate, including brutal governments, can exploit social-media services with potentially lethal consequences.

Although these consequences can be particularly severe where governments lead the charge, debates about content moderation tend to focus on the social-media use of jihadists, neo-Nazis and other substate groups and individuals. Social-media companies have come a long way in addressing the online activities of violent hate organisations, recognising that their own laissez-faire response was increasingly untenable. Since 2015, Twitter, Facebook and other platforms have aggressively targeted jihadists and even made progress combatting white supremacists.[16] They have also sought to reduce the spread of dangerous disinformation about topics such as COVID-19 and the protests that followed the killing of George Floyd by Minneapolis police on 25 May.[17] Even critics of Facebook and other platforms have acknowledged that important steps have been taken.[18]

When it comes to state actions, however, the responses of social-media companies are often halting and unclear. Government officials and state-media organs can be responsible, either openly or secretly, for several kinds of dangerous content. At the most extreme are specific operational instructions concerning whom to kill and when to do so. More general calls for attacks on specific communities or individuals can also be made. Yet explicit calls like these are less common than more nebulous forms of hate speech that demonise identifiable communities without directly inciting violence. Lt-Gen. (Retd) Michael Flynn, who briefly served as US President Donald Trump's national security advisor, once tweeted that 'Fear of Muslims is RATIONAL' and called on his followers to retweet him.[19] By itself, the tweet contained no invitation to violence. But hostile statements by leaders can be interpreted by the public as a script for action. In Germany, researchers found a correlation between anti-refugee Facebook posts by the far-right Alternative for Germany party and violence against refugees.[20] In an already combustible situation, hateful rhetoric can serve as a match.

When protests over Floyd's killing rocked America in May and June 2020, President Trump warned on social media that 'when the looting starts, the shooting starts'. Twitter labelled the president's remarks with a warning that declared, 'This Tweet violated the Twitter Rules about glorifying violence'.[21] Facebook allowed the message to stay up without interference, deeming it inherently newsworthy because it came from a politician. This led to considerable criticism, with a Facebook civil-rights audit declaring that the company's policy effectively created a separate set of rules for politicians and 'privilege[d] certain voices over less powerful' ones.[22] The episode highlighted an important question: what should social-media companies do when governments use them to promote hate and violence?

How states abuse social media

Governments and establishment voices have long used communications technologies to whip up hate. In the lead-up to the Rwandan genocide, Radio Télévision Libre des Mille Collines broadcast a steady stream of venom toward Tutsis and moderate Hutus, helping to initiate a genocide that killed almost a million people.[23] In the United States, the 1921 Tulsa race massacre was triggered by an incendiary newspaper article in the *Tulsa Tribune* headlined 'Nab Negro for Attacking Girl in an Elevator', which was accompanied by an editorial titled 'To Lynch Negro Tonight'. The article called for the slaying of a (likely innocent) black man arrested for allegedly attacking a white elevator operator. Inspired by the article, a white mob demanded that the sheriff turn him over. When the sheriff refused, the mob burned and destroyed businesses and homes in a prosperous African-American business district spanning 40 blocks, killing as many as 300 people.[24]

Today, social-media platforms often play the role that traditional broadcast and print media once did, but with special features that present new opportunities. For example, social-media companies are more likely to enjoy natural monopolies. Part of the reason to be on Facebook is that so many other people are on Facebook – the value of the network grows with each user, enabling each individual to enjoy more connections. (In contrast, if the *New York Times*' subscription rate doubles, this does not directly benefit the individual user.) Thus, it is often better for the consumer if a social-media company dominates the information space. A state that can access and exploit one of these natural monopolies can reach a large audience and overwhelm other sources of information.

Indeed, in some countries, platforms like Facebook *are* the internet. As technology expert Ian Bogost contends, for many in the developing world, 'being online just means using Facebook or WhatsApp'.[25] Through its 'Free Basics' programme, which offers a wide range of services at an affordable price in more than 60 countries, Facebook is often the only means that citizens have to access the internet.[26] In Myanmar, Facebook has 20m users, almost half the population.[27] Because of this market dominance and public penetration, information presented on Facebook has a tremendous impact, particularly as the platform prioritises its own services (such as Messenger) and status updates, while providing limited access to other communication platforms or to local content.[28]

Social media also makes it easier to disseminate personalised propaganda. Companies such as Facebook and YouTube are constantly collecting user data, allowing advertisers to micro-target their users to better sell products. Politicians do this too, pitching different advertisements and appeals based on individuals' preferences. Content can reach users who are interested in or likely to believe certain information while avoiding dissenters, thereby reducing any refutation of rumours. In extreme cases, states can exploit this micro-targeting to generate more effective calls for the use of violence.

Because many social-media platforms have no gatekeepers, it is possible for a small number of individuals to quickly spread ideas to others, who will also pass them on. Unverified accounts, managed by internet 'trolls', can promote a false idea with little accountability. With their superior access to resources, states can be especially dangerous in hiring and creating 'troll farms' that allow for the monopolisation of information and dialogue on the internet.[29] Given that repeated exposure to a rumour strengthens its believability and the likelihood of its being recalled and used to inform individual opinion, a capacity to publish numerous posts on different platforms from multiple accounts represents a cheap and powerful way to reinforce rumours.[30] In addition, more mainstream media often draw on social-media voices and respond to the ideas they put forward, amplifying their effects.[31] Once begun, rumours are hard to counter. Even when credible sources later disavow them, the initial misinformation tends to retain power.[32] In this way, regimes in countries as diverse as Azerbaijan, Bahrain and Guatemala have provided deliberate misinformation on political opponents or groups that they deemed disloyal.[33] Such information can range from false charges of paedophilia to simply misstating opponents' political positions on a large scale and in convincing terms, undermining trust in legitimate political processes.

At times, the regime's role may be to pass on, or at least not to counter, panicked rumours. In a crisis, information is often in short supply, and at-risk individuals will seek out whatever information is available.[34] In such cases, the regime may not itself be generating the dangerous information, but may be tacitly endorsing it, or simply not using its powers to stop it. Rumours fuel violence, which is itself interpreted by rumours.[35]

Such government actions, or deliberate inactions, can have a range of dangerous consequences. Most importantly, they can create an environment conducive to killing. Individuals who have been encouraged to fear their neighbours are more likely to heed the call of demagogues to strike back in supposed revenge, or to pre-empt what has been described as a looming threat. In addition, toxic information may generate refugee flows, as fearful populations learn about real or made-up violence against their co-ethnics or co-religionists in other parts of a country and begin to fear for their own safety. When leaders themselves are raising the temperature, it is no surprise that things boil over.

Challenges of moderating state messages

In seeking to counter the exploitation of the internet by dangerous states, social-media companies face a variety of challenges. Some are technical, some are business-related and still others are knotty political dilemmas.

Technical challenges

Finding a technical fix to the problem of bad content is difficult, and at times impossible, even for companies like Facebook that have started to devote considerable resources to the problem. Much of the misinformation put out by states does not take the form of false images (though the quality of 'deep-fakes' is getting better and better) but rather constitutes false claims and statements presented out of context. Take, for instance, the state-sponsored trolling of journalists in Turkey. When Nevşin Mengü, a former television correspondent for CNN Türk, covered an unfolding coup attempt in Turkey in July 2016, she noted, during the largely pro-government broadcast, that continued Justice and Development Party rule did pose some dangers to democracy. She also questioned the motives of some of the protesters. These brief comments triggered a state-sponsored trolling attack against Mengü during which out-of-context quotations, tweets and clips from former interviews circulated online and painted her as a coup supporter. Reactions to the misleading content included accusations of treason, calls for her to be hanged, and threats of rape and murder. Mengü also faced the possibility that the rumours of her being a coup supporter would lead to severe legal charges being brought against her.[36] Notably, the content that launched the campaign, which included genuine video excerpts, was tweeted from an existing pro-Justice and Development Party account and shared by established pro-government journalists before being picked up by high-profile politicians, the larger Twitter user base and government-linked bots. As a result, even a highly tuned technical response aimed at detecting signs of false or misleading content, such as deepfakes or fake accounts, would have struggled to stop this campaign.

Companies became dependent on automated tools

Meanwhile, an inability among social-media companies to carefully consider the context of user posts has sometimes caused useful content to be taken down.[37] In 2016, citing a violation of community standards, Facebook temporarily removed Black Lives Matter activist Shaun King from its platform for posting a screenshot of an email he had received containing expletives and racial slurs, even though his intent was clearly to expose racism, not promote it.[38] It was unclear if an algorithm or a human content moderator had originally taken down the post. In 2020, in the midst of the COVID-19 pandemic, Facebook sent human content moderators home on paid leave as it struggled to figure out how to conduct sensitive work remotely.[39] Yet the pandemic, as well as growing civil unrest and increased hate speech online, necessitated an active response to misinformation and borderline content. Facebook shifted some responsibility to full-time employees but, like peer companies including Twitter and Google, became increasingly dependent on automated technological tools to remove content.[40] Facebook CEO Mark Zuckerberg warned that technological tools would make less nuanced decisions than humans, which ultimately proved true. The shift to content moderation dominated by software revealed the likelihood of over-removal, for instance in the case of Syrian journalist Mohammed Asakra, whose Facebook posts documenting injustice in the country suddenly disappeared, leaving human-rights advocates around the world in the dark. Likewise, news articles and health information regarding the pandemic ended up being scrubbed from the internet.[41]

This and other episodes demonstrate the importance of a substantial human role in determining whether content is appropriate, even where technical tools drawing on artificial intelligence (AI) are available. Several social-media companies appear to have learned this lesson. YouTube's policy to reduce recommendations of certain controversial or misleading videos on its platform uses machine-learning algorithms in the first instance to decide what videos to flag, after which humans are given the task of watching the videos and providing feedback based on certain guidelines.[42] The algorithm can then make decisions based on what it has 'learned' about what humans find controversial or disturbing. At Facebook, humans help train AI tools to recognise certain types of content, such as terrorist messages or content related to self-harm, so that it can be taken down.[43] Facebook's algorithms have also gotten better at identifying more nuanced content, such as hate speech, before it is reported by users. Human moderators play an essential role in reviewing content flagged by algorithms and handling appeals to content takedowns. However, it is not clear how accurate these systems are. If they allow even a low percentage of hate speech to slip through, this will still represent a high volume of content.

Further complicating the process, Facebook's global policy for hate speech tries, appropriately, to take the local context into consideration, demanding that moderators have an understanding of relevant political and cultural factors when evaluating posts.[44] Yet even at the best of times, the type and volume of content take a toll on the company's human moderators, creating staffing challenges as moderators leave their jobs or are fired for not following stringent rules.[45] Furthermore, in small markets, major social-media companies can struggle to find staff with relevant language abilities. In Myanmar, the reporting system was in English, which few locals spoke.[46] Some staff were forced to rely on Google Translate or other imprecise tools to make sense of dangerous content. To its credit, Facebook hired 100 moderators for Myanmar after the violence there, but none of them can live in that country due to safety concerns, making their task more difficult.

Moreover, many of them have portfolios comprising multiple Asian countries, meaning they are unable to focus solely on Myanmar.[47]

Commercial challenges

In addition to these technical challenges, censoring or otherwise punishing government officials – for instance, by denying access to their accounts – is a good way to be excluded from key markets. Facebook, YouTube and other major platforms are continually seeking to expand around the world, but must work with governments to do so. Government approval or licencing is often necessary for companies to operate, and governments can also create favourable or unfavourable regulatory conditions that may boost one company over another, or otherwise alter the marketplace.

Because governments can take larger-scale and more immediate action than non-state actors against companies that act against state interests, companies face the prospect of a backlash should they seek to limit government messages. In the United States, for example, after Twitter placed warning labels on President Trump's tweets claiming that mail-in voting leads to voter fraud, the president threatened to revoke legal protections that facilitate social-media companies' operations in the US.[48] The country's independent legal systems and robust private-sector protections rendered these threats largely toothless, but the case highlights the dangers in countries where governments may have greater political reach. When Facebook refused to increase the removal of anti-government content in Vietnam, state-owned telecommunications companies took the company's local servers offline, causing the website to become slow, unstable and more difficult to use. Because Vietnam is one of Facebook's largest markets in Asia, the company eventually acquiesced to the government's censorship demands.[49]

Strong states with large economies are in a particularly powerful position, and many will not tolerate companies that inhibit their ability to influence their populations. Facebook is banned in China due to the country's severe restrictions on content. However, Chinese companies can still buy advertising space on Facebook to be seen by foreign audiences – indeed, China is Facebook's second-largest advertising market after the United States –

and Facebook is hoping to expand its role in helping Chinese companies advertise and otherwise reach beyond China to sell their products.[50] To do so, it will need to bear in mind that China does not hesitate to use access to its market to punish companies (and states) that enable criticism of the country.[51] Allowing any content related to China's mistreatment of Muslim minorities, for example, would incur Beijing's wrath.

Political challenges

One possible approach to dealing with undesirable content online would be to simply make it inaccessible, either by suppressing it in a targeted way, or by more broadly limiting access to entire internet platforms. Yet this is an approach that can cause as many problems as it solves. Many states regularly shut down the internet in the name of public security and, in so doing, silence dissidents, protests by ethnic and religious minorities, and other forms of legitimate dissent. A global coalition focused on ending internet shutdowns, the #KeepItOn campaign, warns that public safety, national security and fake news are often invoked to justify internet shutdowns, but regime fears related to protests, instability and elections are often the true reasons.[52] For example, the Sudanese government instituted an internet shutdown and intermittently blocked access to social media from December 2018 to February 2019 following nationwide protests. Violence ensued, with government forces killing 60 peaceful protesters and arresting hundreds more during one 11-day period in December.[53] Even after president Omar al-Bashir resigned, the government tried to combat continued protests by shutting down the internet and mobile services. In June 2019, security forces violently cracked down on a sit-in in Khartoum, killing more than 100 civilians, as the regime increasingly shut off communication throughout the country.[54] Other countries that regularly shut down the internet using public safety as an excuse include Afghanistan, Egypt, Iran, Pakistan, Turkey and Zimbabwe – an authoritarian honour roll.[55] Some countries, such as Russia and the Philippines, have cited Germany's Network Enforcement Act (often referred to as 'NetzDG'), which requires companies to take down 'illegal content' as defined by 22 statutes of the German criminal code, as inspiration for their own dictates.[56]

There is evidence that internet shutdowns may actually serve to increase violence. Roughly half of all internet shutdowns occur in India, often at the state level. The number is so high because the government uses shutdowns to control the frequent unrest in Kashmir. These shutdowns are often intended to disrupt peaceful protests by making it more difficult for opposition figures to organise. This may, however, encourage the opposition to turn to less organised tactics. As the author of one study put it, removing internet access 'can turn a predictable situation into one that is highly volatile, violent, and chaotic'.[57] Shutting down the internet can also have devastating economic consequences resulting from the loss of telecommunications networks, online-payment platforms and other business operations relying on internet connectivity. Although these consequences can vary depending on factors such as the level of internet use in the affected country, the economic effects can be considerable. After the 2019 terrorist attacks, shutting down Facebook and other platforms cost Sri Lanka more than $4m per day.[58] Sudan's 65-day-long internet and social-media shutdown cost the country $1.8 billion.[59]

In many countries, the information environment is limited or weak, and the government is one of the few sources of information during a crisis. In crisis situations today, many public services or other, less political outposts of government attempt to reach the public by posting information on social-media platforms.[60] In addition, social-media use by civil-society actors can be an important supplement to a diet of government-controlled television and print media. In Mexico, where state television often does not report on violence, activists use social media to highlight drug-related killings and to forge connections with like-minded activists and reporters both in Mexico and in the United States.[61] In such circumstances, over-policing is a danger. Removing too much content – for example, removing all references to violence involving a particular ethnic group – can prevent community associations, civil society and responsible journalists from reporting on the crisis and providing valuable warnings.

As noted, social media can play a vital role in a crisis by allowing family members to assess each other's safety. First responders may also rely on social media for information on how best to deploy their limited resources.

After the terrorist bombings in Brussels in 2016, first responders used social media to understand the scope and scale of the attacks, to communicate with the people affected and to locate the wounded, ultimately allowing for a better response.[62] Human Rights Watch criticised Myanmar for shutting down the internet in 2019 (a move the government claimed, ironically, was necessary because the rebel Arakan Army was spreading misinformation), warning that it prevented aid workers and human-rights monitors from carrying out their work.[63]

All this suggests that a poorly implemented shutdown or slowdown by a social-media company could cause more harm than good. Companies must be able to distinguish between violence perpetuated by states on social media and violence by states that is facilitated by an *absence* of social media. Even after making this distinction, temporarily shutting down operations to prevent state abuse, assuming this is possible from a business perspective, may still play into the hands of a repressive government.

The implications of content suppression for free speech and other democratic activities are also a concern. Most social-media companies are based in the United States, where objectionable content is legally allowed. Moreover, allowing some hateful speech that does not directly incite violence even from political leaders with large followings, such as Flynn's tweet, can serve the interests of free expression and a marketplace of ideas, though warning labels are usually in order in these cases. More importantly, it allows citizens to gain a sense of their leaders' motivations, statements and actions. In addition, it reduces the role of social-media companies as adjudicators of political debate, a role that they are often ill-equipped to play and that they do not embrace. Zuckerberg has said that he remains committed to his platform's original purpose of allowing anyone's voice to be heard, even if users say offensive or incorrect things.[64] Facebook thus seeks to err on the side of leaving content up rather than taking it down. Social-media companies also have a desire to be consistent. Since many of them operate around the world, designing policies on an ad hoc basis risks the excesses of over- or under-moderation. In addition, if a country objects to their policies, they are on firmer ground if they are able to point to a consistent standard used in other countries.

What can companies do?

So far, social-media companies appear at a loss for how to handle the problem of dangerous state behaviour on the internet. They have struggled to balance their commitments to free expression and a marketplace of ideas with the need to prevent harmful and hateful content. As noted, much of their effort has focused on terrorist or hate-group activity, a politically easier (though still messy) problem to deal with. Facebook has also endorsed some updates to existing 'digital literacy' programmes for Myanmar – which include modules such as 'Tips for Staying Safe on Facebook', 'Critical Thinking and Empathy' and 'Spotting False News' – and provides digital-literacy training through libraries and community centres across the country.[65] Facebook has also sought to build stronger relationships with civil society so as to develop its capacity to evaluate information.[66] Although these ideas sound good in theory, they are untested and difficult to implement on a mass scale or during a crisis, when new content spreads rapidly.

One approach would be for companies simply to permit all government content. This approach is easily implemented, allows for consistency and is usually in companies' financial interest. However, it also enables governments to manipulate online platforms in dangerous ways, potentially contributing to gross human-rights abuses. Conversely, companies could simply refuse to operate in dangerous areas. This approach, however, might be even riskier. It cedes the media environment to platforms such as radio and television, which governments are often well placed to dominate and manipulate. In addition, withdrawing services denies human-rights organisations and communities important resources for organising and drawing attention to their situation.

Companies should take a nuanced approach to state-backed hate. They could develop a set of emergency protocols to follow in dangerous situations to help them limit, but not stop, the flow of content. This would require determining the answers to three questions: what is an emergency, how do you know when an emergency is over and what should be done while the emergency is ongoing?

What is an emergency?

Defining an emergency could be likened to defining pornography: it can be hard to describe precisely, but one knows it when one sees it. It can be obvious from media reports that large-scale human-rights abuses are occurring, a situation that is clearly an emergency, but also one for which many preventive measures are too late.

Fortunately, a number of scholars and institutions have worked to develop a set of indicators that can suggest when a mass killing or another horrific crime is imminent. For example, scholars working on the US government-supported 'Political Instability Task Force' have identified hundreds of political, social and other measures that, taken together, can provide a 'fragility index' indicating when mass violence, such as civil war or genocide, might occur.[67] Indicators to pay attention to include a past history of violence, a failure by law enforcement to crack down on limited violence, or law enforcement's own use of excessive violence. Civil-society organisations such as Freedom House and the National Endowment for Democracy, as well as local organisations, can also be sources of relevant information. Such indicators can provide a general idea of how vulnerable a state or region might be to real-world violence. In 2018, Myanmar's fragility index was determined to be 18 out of 24, which flagged the country as in a state of war.

Assessments of this kind inevitably will be far from perfect, but a high fragility index, along with warnings from AI systems that sense an uptick in hate speech, reports from engaged governments and civil-society organisations, and other inputs should trigger close scrutiny. Even more robust internal-reporting systems could also help; lower-level Facebook employees warned of possible violence in India in August 2020 but were met with an inadequate response. Following preliminary warning signs, human analysts, as well as more senior staff at social-media companies, would then examine the situation to see if restrictions were in order and, if so, which ones. In addition, they would determine how any changes in conditions might lead to new restrictions and warn the governments in question to desist. They could also identify trusted news sources and other voices that could be elevated should an emergency occur, and enlist officials in other countries to try to counter the dangerous situation.

How do you end an emergency?

Almost as important as detecting an emergency is recognising when it is over. If an emergency drags on it can suppress important economic activity and hinder the return of normality. Unlike traditional wars, which often ended with the achievement of a clear territorial objective or an adversary's surrender, cases such as the violence in Myanmar and Sri Lanka can be more difficult to delineate, as persistent, underlying tensions give way to action. These emergencies are perhaps more comparable to the 'war on terror', which began with no clear vision of how the conflict would end and which continues to stumble on.[68] Drawing on this idea, companies may consider temporary victories, such as a certain number of days or hours without violence, as an indication that normal access to social media should be restored. In some cases, larger events, such as the announcement of elections, governmental reforms, negotiations between groups, or the return of refugees or displaced populations, could also indicate the end of a crisis. Reporting by other governments or non-governmental organisations could help to make this determination.

What is to be done during an emergency?

Companies have a number of tools at their disposal to inhibit the spread of dangerous content during emergency situations. These include warning labels, methods of limiting the visibility and virality of content, and steps that slow the overall working of the internet. The vigour of steps taken to prevent the spread of dangerous content should depend on the severity of the threat from government-initiated or -promoted content. The scale of the crisis may be determined by the presence of warning signs as discussed above, as well as by the extent to which hateful online content has spread. For instance, a single incendiary post in a time of high tension and instability, widespread borderline content in times of relative stability, and widespread hate speech in a highly tense and unstable situation may all provoke different responses.

Warning labels are a helpful tool that allows viewers to immediately question dubious claims and borderline content. In the case of emergencies such as the anti-racism protests that have gripped the United States, borderline content, especially content likely to go viral, can be hidden behind warning labels to allow it to stay up while encouraging users to question what they see. Twitter demonstrated this when it flagged President Trump's tweet in response to protests following the death of George Floyd. In this case, Twitter determined that the tweet violated its community guidelines, but allowed it to stay up due to its relevance for interpreting the United States' political and social environment. Still, the warning Twitter applied highlighted the inappropriate nature of the president's remark.[69]

Images and videos can be potent means of spreading misinformation and provoking violence, as they often evoke strong emotions while being more believable. In preparation for Myanmar's 2020 election, Facebook introduced an Image Context reshare product that warned users before they shared photos that were over one year old or were close to violating Facebook's policy on violent content.[70] Similar measures should be used elsewhere to prevent outbreaks of violence.

Limiting the visibility of dangerous content is something that many companies have taken steps to achieve, and is a strategy that should be aggressively used in crisis situations. Facebook has a strategy called 'remove, reduce, and inform', in which content that violates community standards is removed and the spread of borderline content reduced, while users are provided with additional information before they read, view or share content.[71] Facebook already 'downranks' posts identified as false, which moves them further down users' newsfeeds, and the company claims to distribute borderline content less than other types of post.[72] Facebook also has 'Recommendations Guidelines' that are more stringent than its community standards, and will not recommend questionable content even if it is allowed to stay online.[73] YouTube employs a similar strategy. Moving from a recommendation algorithm that promoted more extreme, misleading and generally attention-grabbing content, YouTube decided in 2019 to stop suggesting videos containing borderline content or misinformation, even if they did not directly violate its community guidelines. In particular, YouTube stopped recommending (and allowing the monetisation of) videos that promoted false medical cures for serious illnesses, flat-earth conspiracy videos and videos making 'blatantly false' claims about historic events such as 9/11.[74] Still, such videos were not taken down, and came up if searched for. Likewise, Twitter has removed trending topics if they are misleading or disruptive, such as two hashtags that spread in June 2020 falsely claiming that a blackout of communication devices had been imposed in Washington DC to silence protesters.[75] Such measures prevent exposure to content that may quickly spread between otherwise disconnected social networks and online communities. In times of crisis, these efforts should be significantly increased for content already identified by companies as problematic, such as clickbait and misinformation.[76] Furthermore, these measures should be applied to a wider range of borderline content.

Content visibility could also be reduced by putting problematic content in a sort of 'limited state'. YouTube has placed certain controversial videos involving conspiracy theories in such a state by disallowing advertising, comments and 'likes'. Similarly, Twitter, in addition to imposing a warning label on Trump's tweet, prevented it from being liked or retweeted if users did not first add a comment, limiting its visibility and rapid spread across the platform. In a crisis situation, social-media companies should ramp up such efforts, and could even apply a more general rule triggering this state for posts containing certain keywords, allowing AI-driven tools to work more effectively. In the past, keyword approaches have led to the over-removal of content. Therefore, this limitation could be implemented for a very short time while a company increased its understanding of the nuances of a situation, allowing at least some helpful information to reach users while avoiding the spread of inciteful content at the height of a crisis.

Social-media companies can also manipulate their recommendation algorithms to highlight positive and limit negative content. This would mean that, in a crisis, companies would not only block or demote certain content, but also increase the visibility of helpful information, allowing social-media users to gain rapid access to such information rather than being sidetracked by provocative or unhelpful content. Facebook appears to have the ability to elevate certain posts in its newsfeed and has changed its recommendation algorithm to increase 'meaningful' engagement by giving more weight to content that encourages substantial comments.[77] Thus, posts that encourage more genuine interaction are promoted, while more extreme posts that generate popularity through likes and shorter comments are less likely to appear at the top of newsfeeds. In a crisis, companies might make further changes to similarly elevate more trusted sources. Google could play an important role here given the ubiquity of its search engine.

Drawing on the relationships it has been cultivating with civil-society representatives to identify impending social crises, Facebook and similar companies should also determine, ideally in advance, which accounts it might elevate in cases where the immediate deployment of this tactic became necessary. Respected non-governmental and international organisations, such as the International Committee of the Red Cross, would be obvious candidates. Local civil-society organisations would also be likely contenders, though their ability to operate in an emergency may be limited. Elevating their accounts would make their information easier to find and share.

Companies might elevate trusted sources

One way of elevating such accounts is by whitelisting them. With whitelisting on social-media platforms such as YouTube Kids, users are able to explicitly approve the videos and channels that appear on their accounts to avoid harmful videos being put forward by the recommendation algorithm.[78] Whitelisting has also been applied at scale across the internet. When India first lifted the internet ban in Kashmir, it whitelisted 301 websites that could be accessed, including entertainment platforms and some international news outlets, while other sites remained blocked.[79] Social-media companies can combine these two approaches by whitelisting certain pre-approved accounts across their platforms while preventing access to others. Additionally, if certain information sources are whitelisted ahead of time, in a crisis, social-media companies can follow YouTube's model by creating an easily accessible tab at the top of the page called 'top news' or 'breaking news' that brings together the reputable sources it has already identified.[80]

Limitations on first-degree sharing can also prevent the spread of rumours. For example, in Sri Lanka and then Myanmar, Facebook limited message forwarding to five users.[81] This limit allows individuals to remain in contact with friends and family and to preserve their voice, but it prevents a small number of dangerous accounts from dominating the information space and rapidly disseminating false narratives. Facebook plans to roll out this limit on Messenger worldwide. This step would help mitigate crises and could be applied to other widely used messaging platforms such as WhatsApp when necessary.[82]

Slowing down the internet is another option for limiting the virality of internet content that could be used in the most extreme cases. In India, the government reinstated slower, 2G internet following a four-month shutdown in Jammu and Kashmir. Historically, militant organisations there had used social-media platforms, especially WhatsApp, to spread images, videos, memes and textual misinformation.[83] In a public statement and a legal affidavit opposing the restoration of 4G in Jammu and Kashmir, the government claimed that slower internet was necessary to prevent the spread of fake news, rumours, inflammatory material and large data files that could be used to plan attacks.[84] At the same time, the partial restoration of the internet theoretically allowed for access to essential services such as hospitals, banks, hotels, government offices and travel companies.[85] Allowing some internet activity might also help to prevent organised protest from transforming into disorganised violence, as happened with past internet shutdowns in Kashmir. Although the government's intentions in imposing 2G internet, as well as the consequences of this move, are still being hotly contested,[86] the idea of slowing down the internet to prevent certain content, especially images and videos, from going viral at the wrong moment is one that social-media companies should consider. By slowing down social-media platforms rather than the internet itself, companies could strike a balance between users having access to essential services and information while avoiding the uncontrolled spread of rumours.

In situations deemed emergencies, social-media companies should also consider deploying more resources and being more aggressive about identifying and suspending dangerous accounts, and disallowing borderline content. In Myanmar in 2019, for example, Facebook finally increased takedowns of borderline content and reduced content distribution by users with a history of violating community standards, including 600 inauthentic accounts and pages linked to the military.[87] There is, of course, a danger of over-policing. From a business and ideological perspective, these steps could undermine Facebook's commitment to showcasing diverse voices and individual content, thereby decreasing user trust in the platform. From a security perspective, there is a danger of suppressing helpful information along with misinformation. However, allowing borderline content, particularly in the form of violent graphics or videos, has been known to spark serious violence in the past, and the trade-offs involved in suppressing it are arguably justifiable to protect human life and safety in emergency situations.

Facebook's Crisis Response feature and similar tools can help to offset some of the risks posed by limiting social media in emergencies. Spanning Facebook and WhatsApp, Crisis Response's Safety Check feature asks users near an emergency if they are safe and then sends a notification to the user's network if they respond in the affirmative. Safety Check was widely used during the 2019 Sri Lanka attacks and was cited as a significant benefit of social media in the crisis.[88] Crisis Response contains other useful tools, such as functionalities to share requests or offers for help, and displacement and disaster maps to help guide first responders.[89]

*   *   *

Given their power and profitability, leading social-media companies such as Facebook and YouTube have a tremendous responsibility to ensure that their platforms do no harm. While social media has been abused to quickly spread hate, it also provides a new and unique opportunity to challenge destructive government narratives. None of the measures proposed here will solve the underlying causes of violence or otherwise end a given crisis. However, they can reduce the potentially dangerous role social-media companies play in emergencies and allow time for diplomacy, military action and other forms of intervention to bring an end to the killing.

Acknowledgements
The authors would like to thank John Bansemer, Miriam Estrin, Chris Meserole, Micah Musser and Jeremy Shapiro for their comments on previous versions of this article.

Notes

1   See Paul Mozur, 'A Genocide Incited on Facebook, with Posts from Myanmar's Military', *New York Times*, 15 October 2018, https://www.nytimes.com/2018/10/15/technology/myanmar-facebook-genocide.html; and Steve Stecklow, 'Why Facebook Is Losing the War on Hate Speech in Myanmar', Reuters, 15 August 2018, https://www.reuters.com/investigates/special-report/myanmar-facebook-hate/.

2   See 'Myanmar Rohingya: What You Need to Know About the Crisis', BBC News, 3 January 2020, https://www.bbc.com/news/world-asia-41566561. For the report of an extensive UN investigation, see Human Rights Council, 'Report of the Detailed Findings of the Independent International Fact-finding Mission on Myanmar', 10 September 2018, https://www.ohchr.org/Documents/HRBodies/HRCouncil/FFM-Myanmar/A_HRC_39_CRP.2.pdf.

3   Alexandra Stevenson, 'Facebook Admits It Was Used to Incite Violence in Myanmar', *New York Times*, 6 November 2018, https://www.nytimes.com/2018/11/06/technology/myanmar-facebook.html. See also Alex Warofka, 'An Independent Assessment of the Human Rights Impact of Facebook in Myanmar', Facebook, 5 November 2018, https://about.fb.com/news/2018/11/myanmar-hria/.

4   BSR, 'Human Rights Impact Assessment: Facebook in Myanmar', 2018, p. 3, https://about.fb.com/wp-content/uploads/2018/11/bsr-facebook-myanmar-hria_final.pdf.

5   Newley Purnell and Jeff Horwitz, 'Facebook's Hate-speech Rules Collide with Indian Politics', *Wall Street Journal*, 14 August 2020, https://www.wsj.com/articles/facebook-hate-speech-india-politics-muslim-hindu-modi-zuckerberg-11597423346.

6   *Ibid.*

7   Aditya Kalra and Nigam Prusty, 'India Parliamentary Panel to Question Facebook on Content Controversy – Source', Reuters, 21 August 2020, https://www.reuters.com/article/facebook-india-idUSL4N2FN19V.

8   Purnell and Horwitz, 'Facebook's Hate-speech Rules Collide with Indian Politics'.

9   See Andrew Liptak, 'Sri Lanka Restricts Access to Social Media Sites Following Terror Attack', *Verge*, 21 April 2019, https://www.theverge.com/2019/4/21/18510006/sri-lanka-restricts-access-social-media-sites-facebook-youtube-instagram-whatsapp-terror-attack; and Amanda Taub and Max Fisher, 'Where Countries Are Tinderboxes and Facebook Is a Match', *New York Times*, 21 April 2018, https://www.nytimes.com/2018/04/21/world/asia/facebook-sri-lanka-riots.html?module=inline.

10 Sarah Frier, 'Facebook's Crisis Management Algorithm Runs on Outrage', *Bloomberg Businessweek*, 14 March 2019, https://www.bloomberg.com/features/2019-facebook-never-ending-crisis/. See also Purnell and Horwitz, 'Facebook's Hate-speech Rules Collide with Indian Politics'.

11 See Sanjana Hattotuwa, 'Digital Blooms: Social Media and Violence

in Sri Lanka', Toda Peace Institute, no. 28, November 2018, p. 12; and Zaheena Rasheed and Amantha Perera, 'Did Sri Lanka's Facebook Ban Help Quell Anti-Muslim Violence?', Al-Jazeera, 14 March 2018, https://www.aljazeera.com/news/2018/03/sri-lanka-facebook-ban-quell-anti-muslim-violence-180314010521978.html.

12 See Meera Selva, 'Sri Lanka Attacks: Government's Social Media Ban May Hide the Truth About What Is Happening', Conversation, 22 April 2019, http://theconversation.com/sri-lanka-attacks-governments-social-media-ban-may-hide-the-truth-about-what-is-happening-115820; and James Griffiths, 'You Can Read This Article. An Internet Blackout Means No-one in Indian-controlled Kashmir Can', CNN, 9 August 2019, https://www.cnn.com/2019/08/08/tech/kashmir-internet-blackout-india-pakistan-intl-hnk/index.html.

13 See Yudhanjaya Wijeratne, 'The Social Media Block Isn't Helping Sri Lanka', *Slate*, 25 April 2019, https://slate.com/technology/2019/04/sri-lanka-social-media-block-disinformation.html.

14 *Ibid.*

15 See Freedom House, 'Freedom on the Net 2019: Sri Lanka', https://freedomhouse.org/country/sri-lanka/freedom-net/2019; and Louise Matsakis and Issie Lapowsky, 'Don't Praise the Sri Lankan Government for Blocking Facebook', *Wired*, 23 April 2019, https://www.wired.com/story/sri-lanka-bombings-social-media-shutdown/.

16 See Brian Fishman, 'Crossroads: Counter-terrorism and the Internet', *Texas National Security Review*, vol. 2, no. 1, February 2019, https://doi.org/10.26153/TSW/1942; and Samidh Chakrabarti and Rosa Birch, 'Understanding Social Media and Conflict', Facebook, 20 June 2019, https://about.fb.com/news/2019/06/social-media-and-conflict/.

17 See Dara Kerr and Shara Tibken, 'Amid George Floyd Protests, Weaponized Misinformation Floods Social Media', CNET, 16 June 2020, https://www.cnet.com/news/amid-george-floyd-protests-social-media-is-weaponizing-misinformation/.

18 See, for example, Laura W. Murphy and Megan Cacace, 'Facebook's Civil Rights Audit – Final Report', 8 July 2020, https://about.fb.com/wp-content/uploads/2020/07/Civil-Rights-Audit-Final-Report.pdf.

19 Michael Flynn (@GenFlynn), tweet, 26 February 2016, https://twitter.com/GenFlynn/status/703387702998278144.

20 Zachary Laub, 'Hate Speech on Social Media: Global Comparisons', Council on Foreign Relations, 7 June 2019, https://www.cfr.org/backgrounder/hate-speech-social-media-global-comparisons.

21 Tony Romm and Allyson Chiu, 'Twitter Flags Trump, White House for "Glorifying Violence" After Tweeting Minneapolis Looting Will Lead to "Shooting"', *Washington Post*, 29 May 2020, https://www.washingtonpost.com/nation/2020/05/29/trump-minneapolis-twitter-protest/.

22 Mike Isaac, Cecilia Kang and Sheera Frenkel, 'Zuckerberg Defends Hands-off Approach to Trump's Posts', *New York Times*, 2 June 2020, https://www.nytimes.com/2020/06/02/technology/zuckerberg-defends-facebook-trump-posts.html; and Murphy and Cacace,

'Facebook's Civil Rights Audit', p. 9.

23 See Genocide Archive of Rwanda, 'Radio Télévision Libre des Mille Collines', 2015, http://www.genocidearchiverwanda.org.rw/index.php/Radio_T%C3%A9l%C3%A9vision_Libre_des_Mille_Collines.

24 See Benjamin Wittes, 'Race Riot of '21', *Washington Post*, 1 February 2000, https://www.washingtonpost.com/archive/opinions/2000/02/01/race-riot-of-21/52c48b84-dafd-44fc-9b63-3c8e855dc6a9/.

25 Ian Bogost, 'When a Country Bans Social Media', *Atlantic*, 22 April 2019, https://www.theatlantic.com/technology/archive/2019/04/sri-lanka-social-media-ban-bigger-problem/587728/.

26 For a study of the effects of this phenomenon in the Philippines, see Henry Mihm, Ines Oulamine and Fiona Singer, 'The Philippines Deserves More from Facebook', Lawfare, 27 October 2019, https://www.lawfareblog.com/philippines-deserves-more-facebook.

27 Elise Thomas, 'Facebook Keeps Failing in Myanmar', *Foreign Policy*, 21 June 2019, https://foreignpolicy.com/2019/06/21/facebook-keeps-failing-in-myanmar-zuckerberg-arakan-army-rakhine/.

28 See Global Voices, 'Free Basics in Real Life', 27 July 2017, https://advox.globalvoices.org/wp-content/uploads/2017/08/FreeBasicsinRealLife_FINALJuly27.pdf.

29 See Mihm, Oulamine and Singer, 'The Philippines Deserves More from Facebook'.

30 See Kelly M. Greenhill and Ben Oppenheim, 'Rumor Has It: The Adoption of Unverified Information in Conflict Zones', *International Studies Quarterly*, vol. 61, no. 3, 1 September 2017, p. 661, https://doi.org/10.1093/isq/sqx015.

31 See Cynthia A. Andrews et al., 'Keeping Up with the Tweet-Dashians: The Impact of "Official" Accounts on Online Rumoring', in *Proceedings of the 19th ACM Conference on Computer-supported Cooperative Work & Social Computing – CSCW '16* (San Francisco, CA: ACM Press, 2016), pp. 451–64, https://doi.org/10.1145/2818048.2819986.

32 See *ibid.*; and Kate Starbird et al., 'Rumors, False Flags, and Digital Vigilantes: Misinformation on Twitter After the 2013 Boston Marathon Bombing', short paper, iConference 2014, https://faculty.washington.edu/kstarbi/Starbird_iConference2014-final.pdf.

33 See Davey Alba and Adam Satariano, 'At Least 70 Countries Have Had Disinformation Campaigns, Study Finds', *New York Times*, 26 September 2019, https://www.nytimes.com/2019/09/26/technology/government-disinformation-cyber-troops.html.

34 See Greenhill and Oppenheim, 'Rumor Has It', p. 663.

35 See Gary Alan Fine and Patricia A. Turner, *Whispers on the Color Line: Rumor and Race in America* (Berkeley, CA: University of California Press, 2001).

36 See Carly Nyst and Nick Monaco, 'State-sponsored Trolling: How Governments Are Deploying Disinformation as Part of Broader Digital Harassment Campaigns', Institute for the Future, 2018, https://

www.iftf.org/fileadmin/user_upload/
images/DigIntel/IFTF_State_
sponsored_trolling_report.pdf.

37   See Mark Zuckerberg, 'A Blueprint
for Content Governance and
Enforcement', Facebook, 15 November
2018, https://www.facebook.com/
notes/mark-zuckerberg/a-blueprint-
for-content-governance-and-enforcem
ent/10156443129621634/.

38   See Amy Pollard, 'Facebook Found
"Hate Speech" in the Declaration
of Independence', *Slate*, 5 July 2018,
https://slate.com/technology/2018/07/
facebook-found-hate-speech-in-the-
declaration-of-independence.html;
and David Hancock, 'N.Y. Columnist
Locked out of Facebook over N-word
Post', CBS News, 9 September 2016,
https://www.cbsnews.com/news/
shaun-king-n-y-columnist-locked-out-
of-facebook-over-n-word-post/.

39   See Elizabeth Dwoskin and Nitasha
Tiku, 'Facebook Sent Home
Thousands of Human Moderators
Due to the Coronavirus. Now
the Algorithms Are in Charge',
Washington Post, 24 March 2020,
https://www.washingtonpost.
com/technology/2020/03/23/
facebook-moderators-coronavirus/.

40   See Mark Scott and Laura Kayali,
'What Happened When Humans
Stopped Managing Social Media
Content', Politico, 21 October 2020,
https://www.politico.eu/article/face-
book-content-moderation-automation/.

41   See Rick Noack, 'The Coronavirus Is
Exacerbating a Crisis on Social Media.
Human Rights Activists Could Pay
the Price', *Washington Post*, 23 July
2020, https://www.washingtonpost.
com/world/2020/07/23/
coronavirus-is-exacerbating-crisis-
social-media-human-rights-activists-
could-pay-price/; and Scott and
Kayali, 'What Happened When
Humans Stopped Managing Social
Media Content'.

42   See Daisuke Wakabayashi, 'YouTube
Moves to Make Conspiracy Videos
Harder to Find', *New York Times*, 25
January 2019, https://www.nytimes.
com/2019/01/25/technology/youtube-
conspiracy-theory-videos.html.

43   See Zuckerberg, 'A Blueprint for
Content Governance and Enforcement'.

44   See Tom Simonite, 'Facebook's AI for
Hate Speech Improves. How Much Is
Unclear', *Wired*, 12 May 2020, https://
www.wired.com/story/facebook-ai-
hate-speech-improves-unclear/.

45   See Casey Newton, 'The Trauma
Floor', *Verge*, 25 February
2019, https://www.theverge.
com/2019/2/25/18229714/
cognizant-facebook-content-
moderator-interviews-trauma-
working-conditions-arizona.

46   See Stecklow, 'Why Facebook Is Losing
the War on Hate Speech in Myanmar'.

47   See *ibid*.

48   Elizabeth Dwoskin, 'Trump Lashes
Out at Social Media Companies
After Twitter Labels Tweets with Fact
Checks', *Washington Post*, 27 May
2020, https://www.washingtonpost.
com/technology/2020/05/27/
trump-twitter-label/.

49   See James Pearson, 'Exclusive:
Facebook Agreed to Censor Posts
After Vietnam Slowed Traffic',
Reuters, 21 April 2020, https://www.
reuters.com/article/us-vietnam-face-
book-exclusive-idUSKCN2232JX.

50   See Paresh Dave and Katie Paul,

'Facebook Defies China Headwinds with New Ad Sales Push', Reuters, 7 January 2020, https://www.reuters.com/article/us-facebook-china-focus-idUSKBN1Z616Q.

51 See Victor Cha, 'The NBA and China's Predatory Liberalism', Lawfare, 8 December 2019, https://www.lawfareblog.com/nba-and-chinas-predatory-liberalism.

52 Berhan Taye, 'The State of Internet Shutdowns Around the World: The 2018 #KeepItOn Report', https://www.accessnow.org/cms/assets/uploads/2019/07/KeepItOn-2018-Report.pdf.

53 Ibid., p. 14.

54 See Steven Feldstein, 'To End Mass Protests, Sudan Has Cut off Internet Access Nationwide. Here's Why', Washington Post, 13 June 2019, https://www.washingtonpost.com/politics/2019/06/13/end-mass-protests-sudan-has-cut-off-internet-access-nationwide-heres-why/.

55 See Tim Stelloh, 'Sri Lanka Attack: Internet Shutdowns Are More Common than You Think', NBC News, 22 April 2019, https://www.nbcnews.com/news/world/sri-lanka-attack-internet-shutdowns-are-more-common-you-think-n997301.

56 See Human Rights Watch, 'Germany: Flawed Social Media Law', 14 February 2018, https://www.hrw.org/news/2018/02/14/germany-flawed-social-media-law.

57 Jan Rydzak, 'Of Blackouts and Bandhs: The Strategy and Structure of Disconnected Protest in India', Social Science Research Network, 7 February 2019, p. 44, https://papers.ssrn.com/abstract=3330413.

58 Stelloh, 'Sri Lanka Attack'.

59 Yomi Kazeem, 'Internet and Social Media Shutdowns Cost African Economies over $2 Billion in 2019', Quartz Africa, 16 January 2020, https://qz.com/africa/1785609/internet-shutdowns-in-africa-cost-2-billion-in-2019/.

60 See US National Research Council and National Academies Press, Public Response to Alerts and Warnings on Mobile Devices: Summary of a Workshop on Current Knowledge and Research Gaps (Washington DC: National Academies Press, 2011); and CivicReady, 'The Importance of Social Media in Crisis Communications', https://www.civicplus.com/civicready/crisis-communications-guide.

61 See Celeste González de Bustamante and Jeannine E. Relly, 'Journalism in Times of Violence: Social Media Use by US and Mexican Journalists Working in Northern Mexico', Digital Journalism, vol. 2, no..4, 2 October 2014, pp. 507–23, https://doi.org/10.1080/21670811.2014.882067.

62 See Stelloh, 'Sri Lanka Attack'; and Hugo Marynissen and Mike Lauder, 'Stakeholder-focused Communication Strategy During Crisis: A Case Study Based on the Brussels Terror Attacks', International Journal of Business Communication, vol. 57, no. 2, April 2020, pp. 176–93, https://doi.org/10.1177/2329488419882736.

63 Human Rights Watch, 'Myanmar: Internet Shutdown Risks Lives', 28 June 2019, https://www.hrw.org/news/2019/06/28/myanmar-internet-shutdown-risks-lives.

64 Kara Swisher, 'Zuckerberg: The Recode Interview', Vox,

18 July 2018, https://www.
vox.com/2018/7/18/17575156/
mark-zuckerberg-interview-facebook-
recode-kara-swisher.

65 See Clair Deevy, 'Promoting Digital
    Literacy in Myanmar', Facebook, 4
    March 2019, https://about.fb.com/
    news/2019/03/digital-literacy-in-
    myanmar/; and Thomas, 'Facebook
    Keeps Failing in Myanmar'.

66 See Swisher, 'Zuckerberg'.

67 See Marcel Dickow and Daniel Jacob,
    'The Global Debate on the Future of
    Artificial Intelligence', SWP Comment,
    no. 23, May 2018, https://www.swp-
    berlin.org/fileadmin/contents/products/
    comments/2018C23_dkw_job.pdf; and
    Center for Systemic Peace, 'Integrated
    Network for Societal Conflict Research
    Data Page', http://www.systemicpeace.
    org/inscrdata.html.

68 See Ivo H. Daalder and James M.
    Lindsay, 'Nasty, Brutish and Long:
    America's War on Terrorism',
    Brookings Institution, 1 December
    2001, https://www.brookings.edu/
    articles/nasty-brutish-and-long-
    americas-war-on-terrorism/.

69 See Romm and Chiu, 'Twitter Flags
    Trump, White House for "Glorifying
    Violence" After Tweeting Minneapolis
    Looting Will Lead to '"Shooting"'.

70 Rafael Frankel, 'How Facebook
    Is Preparing for Myanmar's 2020
    Election', Facebook, 1 September 2020,
    https://about.fb.com/news/2020/08/
    preparing-for-myanmars-2020-election/.

71 Facebook Help Center, 'What Are
    Recommendations on Facebook?',
    25 September 2020, https://www.
    facebook.com/help/1257205004624246.

72 See Zuckerberg, 'A Blueprint
    for Content Governance and

Enforcement'; and Sheera Frenkel,
'Facebook to Remove Misinformation
that Leads to Violence', New York
Times, 18 July 2018, https://www.
nytimes.com/2018/07/18/technology/
facebook-to-remove-misinformation-
that-leads-to-violence.html.

73 Facebook Help Center, 'What Are
    Recommendations on Facebook?'.

74 See Wakabayashi, 'YouTube Moves
    to Make Conspiracy Videos Harder
    to Find'.

75 See Ben Collins, Brandy Zadrozny and
    Emmanuelle Saliba, 'White Nationalist
    Group Posing as Antifa Called for
    Violence on Twitter', NBC News, 1
    June 2020, https://www.nbcnews.com/
    tech/security/twitter-takes-down-
    washington-protest-disinformation-
    bot-behavior-n1221456.

76 See Zuckerberg, 'A Blueprint for
    Content Governance and Enforcement'.

77 See Fred Vogelstein, 'Facebook
    Tweaks Newsfeed to Favor Content
    from Friends, Family', Wired, 11
    January 2018, https://www.wired.com/
    story/facebook-tweaks-newsfeed-to-
    favor-content-from-friends-family/.

78 See Sarah Perez, 'YouTube Kids
    Adds a Whitelisting Parental Control
    Feature, Plus a New Experience for
    Tweens', TechCrunch, 13 September
    2018, https://social.techcrunch.
    com/2018/09/13/youtube-kids-adds-
    a-whitelisting-parent-control-feature-
    plus-a-new-experience-for-tweens/.

79 See Kai Schultz and Sameer Yasir,
    'India Restores Some Internet Access
    in Kashmir After Long Shutdown',
    New York Times, 26 January 2020,
    https://www.nytimes.com/2020/01/26/
    world/asia/kashmir-internet-
    shutdown-india.html.

80 See Elizabeth Dwoskin and Craig Timberg, 'Inside YouTube's Struggles to Shut down Video of the New Zealand Shooting – and the Humans Who Outsmarted Its Systems', *Washington Post*, 18 March 2019, https://www.washingtonpost.com/technology/2019/03/18/inside-youtubes-struggles-shut-down-video-new-zealand-shooting-humans-who-outsmarted-its-systems/.

81 See Colin Lecher, 'Facebook Says It's Taking New Steps to Stop Hate Speech in Sri Lanka and Myanmar', *Verge*, 21 June 2019, https://www.theverge.com/2019/6/21/18701073/facebook-myanmar-sri-lanka-messenger-hate-speech; and Frankel, 'How Facebook Is Preparing for Myanmar's 2020 Election'.

82 See Shannon Liao, 'WhatsApp Tests Limiting Message Forwarding After Violent Lynchings in India', *Verge*, 20 July 2018, https://www.theverge.com/2018/7/20/17595478/whatsapp-message-forwarding-end-violent-lynching-india.

83 See Kabir Taneja and Kriti M Shah, 'The Conflict in Jammu and Kashmir', Royal United Services Institute for Defence and Security Studies, Global Research Network on Terrorism and Technology, no. 11, 2019, p. 14.

84 Utkarsh Anand, 'No 4G Services in J&K, Faster Internet Will Be Used by Terrorists: UT Administration Tells SC', News18, 29 April 2020, https://www.news18.com/news/india/no-4g-internet-in-jk-will-be-used-by-terrorists-ut-administration-tells-sc-2598297.html.

85 See Safwat Zargar, 'The Internet Is Painfully Slow in Kashmir – But Users Have Found a Way to Access Restricted Websites', Scroll.In, 30 January 2020, https://scroll.in/article/951519/the-internet-is-painfully-slow-in-kashmir-but-users-have-found-a-way-to-access-restricted-websites.

86 A rationale for why 2G remains necessary can be found in Anand, 'No 4G Services in J&K, Faster Internet Will Be Used by Terrorists'. For discussion of the consequences and theories of why 2G continues, see Schultz and Yasir, 'India Restores Some Internet Access in Kashmir After Long Shutdown'; and Zargar, 'The Internet Is Painfully Slow in Kashmir'.

87 See Lecher, 'Facebook Says It's Taking New Steps to Stop Hate Speech in Sri Lanka and Myanmar'; and Facebook, 'Removing Myanmar Military Officials from Facebook', 28 August 2018, https://about.fb.com/news/2018/08/removing-myanmar-officials/.

88 See Matsakis and Lapowsky, 'Don't Praise the Sri Lankan Government for Blocking Facebook'.

89 See Sarah Perez, 'Facebook Updates Crisis Response Tools, Adds WhatsApp Integration', *TechCrunch*, 2 December 2019, https://social.techcrunch.com/2019/12/02/facebook-updates-crisis-response-tools-adds-whatsapp-integration/; and Sarah Perez, 'Facebook Centralizes Its Crisis Response Tools in a New Hub Called Crisis Response', *TechCrunch*, 14 September 2017, https://techcrunch.com/2017/09/14/facebook-centralizes-its-crisis-response-tools-in-a-new-hub-called-crisis-response/.

Digital Coloniser? China and Artificial Intelligence in Africa

Willem H. Gravett

China is aggressively pursuing artificial-intelligence (AI) capabilities, and spending billions on related research.[1] China uses these technologies domestically for surveillance and social control, spying on its citizens, learning about their private and public actions, and regulating their behaviour.[2] In Xinjiang, for example, authorities conduct mass collection of biometric data, including voice samples and DNA, and use AI-enabled facial-recognition technology to identify, classify and track Uighur Muslims.[3]

In 2015, Beijing launched its 'Made in China 2025' plan with an eye to dominating cutting-edge technology industries.[4] An integral part of China's strategy is to become the world's premier artificial-intelligence innovator by 2030, surpassing its rivals technologically, and to build a core domestic AI industry with gross output exceeding $150 billion.[5] The Chinese Communist Party envisions that AI will play a crucial role in maintaining social stability, not only in such areas as education, healthcare and environmental protection, but also in state security, where applications include internet censorship and analysing surveillance-camera footage to trace people's movements.[6] Kai-Fu Lee, one of China's best-known high-tech venture capitalists, has argued that China has an advantage in developing AI because its leaders are 'less fussed by "legal intricacies" and "moral consensus"'. According to him, the Chinese 'are not passive spectators in the story of A.I. – we are the authors of it' such that 'the values underpinning our vision of an A.I. future could become self-fulfilling prophecies'.[7]

Willem H. Gravett teaches law at the University of Pretoria.

Survival | vol. 62 no. 6 | December 2020–January 2021 | pp. 153–178   https://doi.org/10.1080/00396338.2020.1851098

Significantly for Africa, China hopes to become a world leader in AI in part by using developing countries as laboratories to improve its surveillance technologies. In March 2018, the Chinese AI start-up company CloudWalk Technology, based in Guangzhou, signed an agreement with the government of Zimbabwe to deploy facial-recognition technology there. Beijing touted the agreement as an example of 'win–win' diplomacy – Chinese AI companies would have the opportunity to train their algorithms on African faces to diversify their datasets and improve the accuracy of their products, and the Zimbabwean government would have access to cutting-edge technology to monitor its population.[8]

PricewaterhouseCoopers has estimated that AI technology could increase global GDP by $15.7 trillion – a full 14% – of which $1.2trn would be added for Africa.[9] AI could help solve some of Africa's most intractable development problems.[10] In particular, it could help farmers adapt to climate change, assist in predicting the outbreak of diseases and natural disasters, facilitate the protection of wildlife from poachers and help make congested urban centres more liveable. African nations have accordingly begun turning to AI for solutions.[11]

With this potential power, however, come possible abuses and unintended consequences.[12] In particular, the current use of Chinese technology exports to the continent, especially facial-recognition technology, raises grave human-rights concerns. Repressive governments in Africa could use centralised biometric databases to target political opponents and to reinforce discrimination against specific segments of the population.

Vectors of China's influence

Chinese technological penetration in Africa raises the spectre of digital neocolonialism – that is, China's application of economic and political pressures to control and strategically influence African governments. Although China's presence in Africa has been growing steadily for 20 years, it started escalating drastically in 2013 following Chinese President Xi Jinping's unveiling of the Belt and Road Initiative (BRI), a trillion-dollar international-development strategy to extend Beijing's influence in host countries through bilateral loans and infrastructure projects.[13] Most African countries have enthusiastically embraced the BRI.[14] China has emerged as the largest source of financing for infrastructure projects in Africa, and evidence of its influence is on wide display on the continent.[15]

China is also sponsoring training and education for the next generation of African leaders, bureaucrats, students and entrepreneurs, hosting tens of thousands of African university students annually, while the Chinese government offers thousands of scholarships to African students every year.[16] The Hanban (Chinese Language Council) has also founded 59 Confucius Institutes in Africa to spread Chinese language and culture.[17]

The BRI emphasises information technology.[18] And in Africa, China is unrivalled on the technological front.[19] Much of the continent has come to rely on Chinese companies for their telecommunications and digital services.[20] China Telecom plans to lay a 150,000-kilometre fibre-optic network covering 48 African nations.[21] Transsion Holdings, a Shenzhen-based company, has overtaken Samsung to become the leading smartphone provider in Africa.[22] Huawei, the Chinese telecommunications giant, has built 70% of the 4G networks and most of the 2G and 3G networks on the continent, vastly outpacing its European rivals.[23] The Kenyan government has appointed Huawei as principal adviser on its 'master plan' for information and communication technologies.[24] ZTE Corporation, the Chinese telecommunications conglomerate, provides the Ethiopian government with infrastructure to enable it to monitor communications by opposition activists and journalists.[25] Another Chinese company, H3C, won the contract to build a new telecommunications network for the Nigerian international airport in Abuja.[26] Hikvision has established an office in Johannesburg and, through a local video-surveillance provider, rolled out 15,000 cameras throughout the metropolitan area in 2019.[27]

Chinese companies play a clear role in Beijing's aspirations for global telecommunications dominance. Although some of these firms are ostensibly private enterprises motivated by market forces, all of them remain answerable to the government.[28] Hikvision, the world's leading manufacturer of surveillance-camera equipment, has strong ties to the Chinese government. The company disclosed in its 2018 annual report that the Chinese government was a controlling shareholder, and the company's chairman was appointed to the National People's Congress in 2018.[29] Similarly, a company owned by the Chinese government is the controlling shareholder in ZTE.[30] Huawei's founder is Ren Zhengfei, a former officer in the 'military technology division' of the People's Liberation Army.[31] Powerful ties between Huawei's management and the Chinese security and intelligence apparatus have continued.[32] The company reportedly receives billions of dollars in government subsidies.[33]

The Chinese Communist Party has systematically placed 'party cells' led by senior executives in technology companies to enhance its access to and control over these companies.[34] Moreover, a national-security law enacted in 2015 mandates that companies acquiesce to 'third-party' (read: government) access to their networks, source codes and encryption keys.[35] The significant inroads that especially Huawei has made in Africa – despite American warnings about corresponding cyber-security vulnerabilities – is evidence that for African governments and businesses, the imperative of greater internet access trumps all other considerations.[36]

Many African nations, further attracted by easy loans and investments, have become almost entirely dependent on China for their technology and services, and susceptible to pressure to subscribe to the Chinese notion of 'internet sovereignty'.[37] The danger is that this Chinese model of sprawling censorship and automated surveillance systems will lead to a dramatic reduction in digital freedom across the continent and imperil emerging democracy.[38] Ostensibly to help governments identify threats to 'public order', China appears to be promoting digital authoritarianism as a way for African governments to control their citizens through technology.[39] For example, the technology provided by ZTE over the past 20 years has been integral to the Ethiopian government's efforts to monitor private citizens and organisations, especially those who are critical of the government.[40] Huawei is the leading vendor of advanced surveillance systems worldwide by an enormous margin, and it is aggressively seeking new markets in sub-Saharan Africa. It is setting up advanced 'safe city' platforms, offering facial recognition and intelligent video-surveillance systems to repressive governments, and providing advanced analytic capabilities.[41] A recent *Wall Street Journal* investigative report found that Huawei technicians in both Uganda and Zambia had assisted government officials in spying on political opponents.[42]

Through seminars and official visits, the Chinese government is actively advising media elites and government officials in countries participating in the BRI to follow its lead on internet sovereignty. According to Freedom House, 'increased activity by Chinese companies and officials in Africa preceded the passage of restrictive cybercrime and media laws in Uganda and Tanzania' (whose largest trading partner is China), as well as in Nigeria, during 2018.[43] The governments of Cameroon, Chad and Togo have also ordered internet shutdowns and blocked websites and social-media platforms ahead of critical political moments, such as elections and protests.[44] The *Financial Times* reported that at least five governments in Africa – Chad, Democratic Republic of the Congo, Eritrea, Ethiopia and Mauritania – had shut down the internet in the first half of 2019, and that in June of that year the Sudanese government did so 'as soldiers from a government paramilitary force went on a killing spree in the capital Khartoum … preventing protesters from documenting the violence on social media'.[45] Benin, Tanzania, Uganda and Zambia have also started stifling freedom of expression through the imposition of social-media or 'blogger' taxes, 'leaving millions of Africans struggling to cover the costs of getting online'.[46]

The Chinese government's dominance over internet connectivity on the continent affords it significant leverage over African governments.[47] China could foster African nations' dependence on and financial obligation to China, echoing their relationships with their erstwhile colonisers. This could lead to China's inordinate political control over African governments and populations. The AI technology and data-mining techniques that China is providing constitute an especially acute temptation to such states, and could increase China's leverage.

Facial-recognition technology in China

China has become the fastest-growing user of facial-recognition technology.[48] This technology has proven to be a potent tool for maintaining control over Chinese society.[49]

Facial-recognition cameras are much more intrusive and discriminating than ordinary closed-circuit television (CCTV), which has been a mainstay of police forces for 25 years.[50] The technology, first developed and used in the West, is powered by AI algorithms. It analyses a person's distinctive facial features in minute detail, distinguishing them from thousands or even millions of potential matches. The algorithms can also assess in real time the number and density of people in a given frame, individuals' gender, their height, the characteristics of their clothing and even their gait. Facial-recognition cameras are often mobile and concealable. Thus, they can scan distinctive facial features in order to create detailed biometric maps or databases of individuals when they are walking down the street without their knowledge, let alone their consent. In effect, facial-recognition technology enables a government to remotely secure a GPS ankle monitor on any person.[51]

China's path to online censorship and digital surveillance started in the early 2000s with projects such as Golden Shield and continued thereafter with programmes like Skynet. In 2015, the Chinese Ministry of Public Security launched a project to establish the world's most powerful facial-recognition system, which will be able to identify any one of China's 1.393bn citizens within three seconds and with 90% accuracy. The system will be connected to surveillance-camera networks and will use cloud facilities to connect to data-storage and -processing centres across the country. Isvision, a security company based in Shanghai, is developing the system. It has set up similar systems for law-enforcement authorities in Xinjiang and Tibet.[52] In early 2018, Chinese police also deployed facial-recognition glasses. The Beijing-based company LLVision Technology sells basic versions of this technology to countries in Africa and Europe. Such glasses can be used to identify criminals, such as drug dealers and thieves, but also to hunt down human-rights activists and dissidents.[53]

China, of course, is not the only country experimenting with facial-recognition technology. The United States, which already had approximately 62 million CCTV security cameras installed as of 2016, has higher per capita penetration than China.[54] The FBI's Next Generation Identification System uses facial recognition to compare images from crime scenes with a national database of mug shots. But China's ambition sets it apart. Western law-enforcement agencies generally use facial recognition to identify criminal suspects – not to track social activists or dissidents, or to monitor entire ethnic groups. According to Maya Wang of Human Rights Watch, what distinguishes China is 'a complete lack of effective privacy protections, combined with a system that is explicitly designed to target individuals seen as "politically threatening"'.[55]

China's development of what Richard Fontaine and Kara Frederick call the 'autocrat's new tool kit' will have a profound impact on the rights and liberties of its citizens.[56] Indeed, the Uighurs have already felt that impact acutely.[57] The Chinese government has been waging a well-documented mass-surveillance and internment campaign against them in the fractious, far-western region of Xinjiang, where approximately one million people have been detained in 're-education' camps.[58] In Xinjiang, facial-recognition cameras have become ubiquitous at roadblocks, gas stations, airports, railways and bus stations, residential and university compounds,

The government uses data to track Uighurs

and entrances to Muslim neighbourhoods and mosques.[59] More than 2,500 cameras have also been installed in Ulan Bator, the capital of Mongolia.[60] The Chinese government is using biometric data, including facial recognition, iris scans and mass DNA collection, to track Uighurs and other minorities on an unprecedented scale.[61] Technology maps the target population's activities street by street and phone by phone. In the cities of Hotan and Kashgar there are poles bearing as many as ten video cameras at intervals of 100–200 metres along every street. As well as watching pedestrians, these cameras can read car number plates and correlate them with the faces of drivers. The cameras are equipped to work continuously, night and day.[62]

Thus, Xinjiang has become, in the words of Freedom House's Sarah Cook, 'a laboratory for testing big-data, facial recognition and smartphone-scanner technologies that can eventually be deployed across China and beyond'.[63] Several Chinese AI companies, including CloudWalk, Hikvision and SenseTime, have emerged on the cutting edge of this effort. Their work entails complicity in the oppression of Xinjiang's Uighur Muslim population and other groups.[64] Seen in a broader context, this is perhaps unsurprising. The Chinese state argues, and most of the Chinese population believes, that invasive surveillance practices have a specific and relatively narrow purpose – namely, to combat what Beijing calls the 'three evils' – terrorism, separatism and religious extremism – and that they are showing positive results. From this perspective, developing the world's leading AI algorithms is primarily a political and security endeavour rather than a commercial one. The Chinese companies' management, of course, sees their involvement in government monitoring and detention activities in Xinjiang as affording them a competitive edge in the international market, because access to large amounts of data is essential to developing and refining AI algorithms. Data on and images of ethnic Chinese and Turkic Uighurs could enable developers to correct common race-related errors – some stemming from biases inherent in Western training – in facial-recognition software and gain market share in other parts of the world.[65]

Authorities in Xinjiang have repeatedly stated that their goal is to achieve both 'ethnic unity' and 'social stability'.[66] The facial-recognition technology, which is integrated into China's rapidly expanding networks of surveillance cameras, looks exclusively for Uighurs based on their physical appearance, and maintains records of their movements for search and review. According to the *New York Times*, this is 'the first known example of a government intentionally using [AI] for racial profiling', and may usher in 'a new era of automated racism'.[67] It is facial recognition in aid of racial recognition.

In 2018, a respected US academic journal published a study entitled 'Facial Feature Discovery for Ethnicity Recognition', authored by one Australian and four Chinese scholars. The study determined that an effective way to automatically predict the ethnicities of minorities in China was for facial-recognition systems to focus on specific, T-shaped regions of their faces.[68] The researchers based this conclusion on more than 7,000 photographs that they took of Uighur, Tibetan and Korean students at Dalian Minzu University in northeastern China. The study sparked concern given that widespread use of pre-emptive racial profiling to guide detentions and arrests could violate the presumption of innocence and other human rights.[69]

A new generation of abundantly financed Chinese start-up companies are catering to Beijing's demand for emerging technologies, such as AI.

Most now sell analytic software that enables police to automatically distinguish Uighurs from others. Hikvision, in particular, has explicitly marketed its technology as a tool for racial and ethnic profiling.[70] Similar tools could incorporate biases based on the skin colour and other aspects of ethnicity of other groups elsewhere in the world. Clare Garvie of Georgetown University School of Law's Center on Privacy and Technology comments: 'If you make a technology that can classify people by ethnicity, someone will use it to repress that ethnicity.'[71]

In May 2019, David Kaye, the United Nations Special Rapporteur on freedom of expression and opinion, concluded that the problem of pervasive technological surveillance was serious enough to warrant not merely tighter regulation of surveillance exports and restrictions on their use, but also an immediate moratorium on the global sale and transfer of the tools of the private surveillance industry, until rigorous human-rights safeguards were put in place to regulate such practices.[72]

Some Chinese companies, such as YITU, CloudWalk and Hikvision, focus explicitly on exporting sophisticated surveillance technology to Africa. The Chinese authorities' ongoing persecution of Uighur Muslims suggests that these technologies, despite the limitations of sensors in rural areas, will allow African governments to track many of their citizens.[73] On a continent with a troubled history of genocide, ethnic violence and apartheid, this is an alarming prospect.

Chinese facial-recognition technology in Africa

China is projected to dominate the $7bn global market for facial-recognition devices, with a 44.59% market share by 2023 and CloudWalk leading all providers.[74] China also wants to use developing countries as laboratories for improving its own surveillance technologies.[75]

In April 2018, CloudWalk launched China's first AI project in Africa when it signed a strategic-cooperation agreement with the government of Zimbabwe to build a mass national facial-recognition database and monitoring system in Zimbabwe's cities and public-transport system, including smart financial systems (to integrate finance with technology), and airport, railway and bus-station security.[76] Under this arrangement, the Zimbabwean government will apparently provide biometric data on thousands of Zimbabweans to China, which will enable it to build a more comprehensive facial-recognition database reflecting greater ethnic diversity to train CloudWalk's AI programmes.[77]

Gaining access to a population with a racial mixture far different from that of China will give CloudWalk a crucial competitive edge. Well-documented difficulties in accurately recognising faces with darker skin tones have plagued commercial facial-recognition systems developed in the West and China. The Massachusetts Institute of Technology's (MIT) Media Lab tested the accuracy of the equipment of three major facial-recognition software providers – Microsoft and IBM, both American companies, and Megvii, a Chinese one. According to the MIT study, the error rate for identifying the gender of a person from photographs of lighter-skinned men was less than 1%, for darker-skinned women as high as 35%.[78] This is because the accuracy of AI depends on the data from which it learns, and facial-recognition AI has learned predominantly from Caucasian-male faces.[79] In this connection, it is worth noting that the Black Lives Matter protests that began in the United States prompted Amazon to impose a one-year moratorium on police use of its facial-recognition software, known as Rekognition, in part because it was inaccurate.[80]

The biometric records of Zimbabwean citizens are therefore crucial both for enhancing the Chinese government's own 'tech-infused policing capacity' and for making CloudWalk's products more effective and commercially attractive.[81] CloudWalk – and ultimately all Chinese AI technology – will benefit tremendously from this opportunity to rapidly improve its systems.[82] As with many of the agreements that China enters into in Africa, the facial-recognition technology was part of a comprehensive package under the wide-ranging BRI sweetened with soft loans, infrastructure development and technological assistance. That said, the Zimbabwean parties did not resist accepting the AI-related terms.[83] In essence, Zimbabwe is getting access to technology it would never be able to afford on the open market by using its own citizens' data as currency. Thus, this first foray of Chinese AI technology into Africa is occurring free of the ethical and legal questions that are raised in more developed markets.[84]

It is clear that CloudWalk intends to use Zimbabwe as a large research laboratory.[85] Amy Hawkins of *The Economist* has observed, other than possibly increased security and surveillance measures, the people of Zimbabwe will not see any return on the research that their personal data has facilitated. 'Acceleration is the whole point because the global AI race is ultimately a race to set standards', she writes.

> The Chinese government defines its ambitions as becoming the country that is 'setting the pace.' As racial upsets in facial recognition have shown, the standards in this field are still to play for. But with unprecedented access to a more diverse range of data, Chinese companies are edging ever closer to this goal – spreading their model of authoritarianism along the way.[86]

Hawkins may be exaggerating China's imperialism on this score. But the fact remains that legal loopholes have made it possible for Harare to share the data of thousands of Zimbabweans with CloudWalk, possibly compromising their personal privacy and safety.[87] Kuda Hove, a programme officer for the Media Institute of Southern Africa, which promotes freedom of expression in Zimbabwe, notes that

> people did not consent to the use of their biometric data in this way. Unfortunately, people do not have any way of holding the government accountable as there are no laws in place or any regulatory body tasked with the protection of people's privacy or data … Zimbabwe's 2002 Access to Information and Protection of Privacy Act doesn't cover biometric data or cross-border flows of data … The government has rarely ever acted in the people's interests.[88]

It goes almost without saying that the CloudWalk–Harare deal does not allow individual citizens to opt out of biometric-data collection. Thus, there appear to be no intra- and intergovernmental checks and balances establishing or regulating any relevant rights Zimbabweans may have to such data and who is responsible for protecting it.

China's mining of Zimbabweans' data also revives painful memories of the European powers' exploitation of Africa for its human and natural resources during the colonial era. Journalist and cognitive scientist Abeba Birhane writes:

> These firms take it for granted that such 'data' … automatically belongs to them. The discourse around 'data mining' and 'data rich continent' shows the extent to which the individual behind each data point is non-existent … [and] is symptomatic of how little attention is given to privacy concerns. The discourse of 'mining' people for data is reminiscent of the colonizer attitude that declares humans as raw material free for the taking.[89]

Especially given Africa's record of weak institutions, corruption and authoritarianism, government officials, civil-society leaders and technology entrepreneurs in Africa should be sensitive to the ways in which the collection, analysis and storage of Africans' biometric data might be dehumanising.[90] Of course, CloudWalk's AI technology does provide an attractive means for the Zimbabwe government – which has a bleak record on human rights – to manage its own surveillance programme, helping the government identify, track and monitor its people.[91] And the deal will enable Zimbabwe to replicate parts of the very surveillance infrastructure that has limited individual freedoms so severely in China. Indeed, live facial recognition has the potential to fundamentally change the relationship between people and the police, and even alter the very meaning of public space.[92] When Zimbabwean citizens walk past a facial-recognition camera, they will effectively be standing in a police line-up with other pedestrians alongside those suspected of crimes. Although the professed purpose of the technology is to combat crime in Zimbabwean cities, it could also be used to stifle opposition.[93] Zimbabwean journalist Garikai Dzoma believes that 'the benefits of using the database and technology to fight crime are far outweighed by the dangers the system poses to individual freedoms'.[94] For example, facial-recognition cameras could identify every individual who attends a protest.[95] They could automatically flag behaviour deemed suspicious, or people who look or act in a certain way.

This is not dystopian alarmism. It is precisely how the Chinese government is already using the technology. Freedom House ranks China at 14/100 and Zimbabwe at 30/100 in lack of internet freedom. It is unlikely that Zimbabwe will become freer – in the sense of more liberal – as a result of its collaboration with China on surveillance technology, even if the effort results in a reduction of crime. It's more probable that the Zimbabwean government intends to use this technology to attempt to monitor and control the population.

The Zimbabwean government has long curtailed freedom of expression by various means. In 2015, then-president Robert Mugabe accepted a gift of cyber-surveillance software from Iran, including international mobile subscriber identity (IMSI) catchers, which enable eavesdropping on telephone conversations.[96] Zimbabwe has also previously looked to China as a model for managing several aspects of society, including social media and communications. In 2016, Mugabe heralded China as an example of social-media regulation that he hoped Zimbabwe could emulate.[97] Zimbabwe's 2017 Cybercrime and Cybersecurity Bill criminalised communicating falsehoods online – the same legal pretext China has employed to stifle dissent.[98] The technology provided by the CloudWalk deal will leave government opponents in Zimbabwe with even fewer places to hide. Zimbabwe's post-Mugabe government seems even more determined to establish dominion over all aspects of its digital and public spaces.[99] In January 2019, after days of protests over a 100% increase in fuel prices, security forces launched a crackdown in which 12 people were killed and 600 were arrested. The government also ordered its first countrywide internet shutdown.[100]

Potential legal redress

Appropriately applied, the African Union Convention on Cyber Security and Personal Data Protection could minimise the type of exploitative data mining on the African continent threatened by the CloudWalk–Harare deal. Unfortunately, fewer than 20% of African nations have signed it, and Zimbabwe is not one of them.[101] But future abuses may produce national and international pressure on non-signatories to relent.

The convention mandates that the establishment of a regulatory framework on cyber security and personal data protection respect the rights of citizens, guaranteed under the fundamental texts of domestic law and protected by international human-rights conventions and treaties, particularly the African Charter on Human and Peoples' Rights. The convention also calls for the establishment of an appropriate normative framework consistent with the African legal, cultural, economic and social environment.

Under the convention, the processing of personal data is considered legitimate only when the subject has given his or her consent.[102] States are compelled to prohibit any data collection and processing revealing racial, ethnic or regional origin.[103] Significantly, an AU member state cannot transfer personal data to a non-member state, unless the latter state ensures the protection of the privacy, freedoms and fundamental rights of the person or persons whose data is transferred.[104] Additionally, individuals have the right to be informed before their personal data is disclosed for the first time to third parties, and to expressly object to such disclosure.[105]

In late 2019, the African Commission on Human and Peoples' Rights promulgated the revised Declaration of Principles on Freedom of Expression and Access to Information in Africa.[106] The declaration directly addresses the protection of personal information and communication surveillance in the context of the right to privacy. While the declaration is not a mandatory legal document, it is strongly precatory, and establishes the preferred legal framework for the protection of personal information that requires states to adopt laws regulating the processing of personal information.[107]

According to Principle 40, individuals have a right to privacy, including the right to protect personal information against access by third parties through digital technologies.[108] Principle 42 calls on states to ensure that individuals consent to the processing of their personal information; that the processing of personal information is 'in accordance with the purpose for which it was collected … and not excessive'; that the processing is transparent; and that the information is kept confidential and secure at all times.[109] In addition, every person has the right to control his or her own personal information.[110]

If Zimbabwe were to ratify the convention and respect the declaration, domestic Zimbabwean legislation would prohibit the government from gathering Zimbabweans' biometric data wholesale, allow individual citizens to opt out of the process and prohibit outright the transfer of citizens' biometric data to Chinese entities.

*   *   *

Many Africans worry that they will be left behind in the global AI race and the corresponding economic transformation. But the danger also looms that those in the developing world will become mere passive consumers – and potential victims – of AI systems developed elsewhere for different people, cultures and situations.[111] As China strives to become an AI powerhouse and the dominant force in AI technology on the African continent, the moral, ethical and cultural concerns raised by what Freedom House's Adrian Shahbaz has called China's 'techno-dystopian expansionism' deserve greater attention.[112] During a recent debate on AI ethics and norms, Chinese scholar Zhang Wei expressed China's chillingly doctrinaire approach to AI ethics: 'Chinese values means that China will value the security of the collective over the rights of the individual when it comes to AI.'[113] Facial-recognition technology has unprecedented potential for the large-scale invasion of privacy and erosion of individual rights. Sifting data to look for pickpockets, robbers and terrorists can easily morph into ferreting out and repressing political dissidents. Democratic governments should resist the temptation to undermine human rights in the name of safety and security, and refrain from sacrificing individual rights at the altar of innovation.[114]

African nations should take a step back and collectively consider to what extent they actually need or want widespread facial-recognition technology, what sensible measures of regulation or legislation might look like, and how to ensure that national law-enforcement and security agencies do not abuse the technology.[115] Africans themselves – in particular, entrepreneurs active in the AI field – should consider how AI can benefit local communities and not blindly import Chinese AI systems premised on authoritarian control, or, for that matter, Western AI systems spurred by excessive enthusiasm for technological advances or profit. They will have to distinguish between using new technologies legitimately for traditional law-enforcement, counter-terrorism and military purposes, and using them illegitimately to solidify single-party social control and curtail basic human rights.[116]

Lawmakers, civil-society leaders and technologists should press for appropriate safeguards to deal with the practical human-rights challenges arising from major AI-related programmes.[117] Unlike China, Zimbabwe and some other African countries have constitutions and laws that protect individual rights, including privacy and freedom of expression. Furthermore, Africans can call upon an international human-rights framework to address violations, and have access to a fairly robust regional human-rights system that could be mobilised to constrain potentially repressive Chinese technology.

Notes

1   See Arthur Gwagwa and Lisa Garbe, 'Exporting Repression? China's Artificial Intelligence Push into Africa', Council on Foreign Relations, 17 December 2018, https://www.cfr. org/blog/exporting-repression-chinas-artificial-intelligence-push-africa.

2   See Michael Cook, 'Exporting Enslavement: China's Illiberal Artificial Intelligence', Mercatornet, 15 August 2018, http://mercatornet. com/exporting-enslavement-chinas-illiberal-artificial-intelligence/23473/.

3   See Gwagwa and Garbe, 'Exporting Repression?'.

4   See Amy Hawkins, 'Beijing's Big Brother Tech Needs African Faces', Foreign Policy, 24 July 2018, https:// foreignpolicy.com/2018/07/24/beijings-big-brother-tech-needs-african-faces/.

5   See Jeffrey Ding, 'Deciphering China's AI Dream: The Context, Components, Capabilities, and Consequences of China's Strategy to Lead the World in AI', Future of Humanity Institute, University of Oxford, March 2018, p. 7,

https://www.fhi.ox.ac.uk/wp-content/ uploads/Deciphering_Chinas_ AI-Dream.pdf; Hawkins, 'Beijing's Big Brother Tech Needs African Faces'; Christina Larson, 'China's Massive Investment in Artificial Intelligence Has an Insidious Downside', Science, 8 February 2018, https://www. sciencemag.org/news/2018/02/ china-s-massive-investment-artificial-intelligence-has-insidious-downside; and Paul Mozur, 'Beijing Wants AI to Be Made in China by 2030', New York Times, 20 July 2017, https://www. nytimes.com/2017/07/20/business/ china-artificial-intelligence.html.

6   See Xiao Qiang, 'The Road to Digital Unfreedom: President Xi's Surveillance State', Journal of Democracy, vol. 30, no. 1, January 2019, pp. 25–39.

7   Quoted in 'For Artificial Intelligence to Thrive, It Must Explain Itself', The Economist, 15 February 2018, https://www.economist.com/ science-and-technology/2018/02/15/

for-artificial-intelligence-to-thrive-it-must-explain-itself.

8   See Gwagwa and Garbe, 'Exporting Repression?'.

9   Kwasi Gyamfi Asiedu, 'Google Is Throwing Its Weight Behind Artificial Intelligence for Africa', *Quartz Africa*, 14 June 2018, https://qz.com/africa/1305211/google-is-making-a-big-bet-on-artificial-intelligence-in-africa-with-its-first-research-center/. Of course, AI and other advanced technologies also have a downside for Africa. Many commentators, including Asiedu, have bemoaned a 'premature deindustrialization' to denote the industrial and factory employment that AI will put an end to – jobs that there were not enough of to begin with.

10 See Lindsey Andersen, 'Artificial Intelligence in International Development: Avoiding Ethical Pitfalls', *Journal of Public and International Affairs,* 20 May 2019, https://jpia.princeton.edu/news/artificial-intelligence-international-development-avoiding-ethical-pitfalls.

11 See Andersen, 'Artificial Intelligence in International Development'; Asiedu, 'Google Is Throwing Its Weight Behind Artificial Intelligence'; and Eshan Gul, 'Is Artificial Intelligence the Frontier Solution to Global South's Wicked Development Challenges?', *Towards Data Science*, 5 July 2019, https://towardsdatascience.com/is-artificial-intelligence-the-frontier-solution-to-global-souths-wicked-development-challenges-4206221a3c78.

12 See Andersen, 'Artificial Intelligence in International Development'. AI is not like a howitzer – most of the tech-nology is dual-use, meaning it can be used for both good and evil ends. See Cook, 'Exporting Enslavement'.

13 Antoaneta Roussi, 'China Charts a Path Into European Science', *Nature*, 8 May 2019, p. 326, https://www.nature.com/immersive/d41586-019-01126-5/index.html.

14 Thus far, 39 African countries and the African Union Commission have entered into BRI cooperation agree-ments, with others expected to follow suit. Antoaneta Roussi, 'China's Bridge to Africa', *Nature*, vol. 569, 16 May 2019, p. 325.

15 China funds one in five infrastruc-ture projects on the continent. See Bates Gill, Chin-hao Huang and J. Stephen Morrison, 'Assessing China's Growing Influence in Africa', *China Security*, vol. 3, no. 3, Summer 2007, p. 9; and Barry Sautman and Yang Hairong, 'Friends and Interests: China's Distinctive Links with Africa', *African Studies Review*, vol. 50, no. 3, December 2007, p. 80.

16 See Gill, Huang and Morrison, 'Assessing China's Growing Influence in Africa', p. 6. For example, China hosted almost 62,000 African univer-sity and post-graduate students in 2016, and the Chinese government offered 8,470 scholarships to African students in 2015. Roussi, 'China's Bridge to Africa', p. 326.

17 Joshua Eisenman and Joshua Kurlantzick, 'China's Africa Strategy', *Current History*, vol. 105, no. 691, May 2006, p. 221.

18 See Michael Abramowitz and Michael Chertoff, 'The Global Threat of China's Digital Authoritarianism', *Washington Post*, 1 November 2018,

https://www.washingtonpost.com/
opinions/the-global-threat-of-chinas-
digital-authoritarianism/2018/11/01/46
d6d99c-dd40-11e8-b3f0-62607289efee_
story.html; and Adrian Shahbaz,
'Freedom on the Net 2018: The Rise
of Digital Authoritarianism', Freedom
House, October 2018, https://freedom-
house.org/report/freedom-net/
freedom-net-2018.

19 See Roussi, 'China's Bridge to Africa',
p. 326.

20 See Hawkins, 'Beijing's Big Brother
Tech Needs African Faces'.

21 David Ignatius, 'China Has a Plan
to Rule the World', *Washington
Post*, 29 November 2017, https://
www.washingtonpost.com/
opinions/china-has-a-plan-to-rule-the-
world/2017/11/28/214299aa-d472-11e7-
a986-d0a9770d9a3e_story.html.

22 See Lynsea Chutel, 'China Is
Exporting Facial Recognition
Software to Africa, Expanding Its
Vast Database', *Quartz Africa*, 25 May
2018, https://qz.com/africa/1287675/
china-is-exporting-facial-recognition-
to-africa-ensuring-ai-dominance-
through-diversity/; and Hawkins,
'Beijing's Big Brother Tech Needs
African Faces'.

23 Amy MacKinnon, 'For Africa,
Chinese-built Internet Is Better
than No Internet at All', *Foreign
Policy*, 19 March 2019, https://
foreignpolicy.com/2019/03/19/
for-africa-chinese-built-internet-is-
better-than-no-internet-at-all/.

24 See Abramowitz and Chertoff 'The
Global Threat of China's Digital
Authoritarianism'.

25 Hawkins, 'Beijing's Big Brother Tech
Needs African Faces'.

26 Shahbaz, 'Freedom on the Net 2018'.

27 See Hawkins, 'Beijing's Big Brother
Tech Needs African Faces'; and
Heidi Swart, 'Video Surveillance
and Cybersecurity (Part Two):
Chinese Cyber Espionage Is a Real
Threat', *Daily Maverick*, 26 June 2019,
https://www.dailymaverick.co.za/
article/2019-06-26-video-surveillance-
and-cybersecurity-part-two-chinese-
cyber-espionage-is-a-real-threat/.

28 See Shahbaz, 'Freedom on the Net 2018'.

29 Charles Rollet, 'In China's Far West,
Companies Cash In on Surveillance
Program that Targets Muslims',
Foreign Policy, 13 June 2018, https://
foreignpolicy.com/2018/06/13/
in-chinas-far-west-companies-
cash-in-on-surveillance-program-
that-targets-muslims/. In a leaked
confidential investors prospectus, the
company candidly acknowledged
that '[our controlling shareholder]
… is subject to the control of the
People's Republic of China government … [and] will continue to be in a
position to exert significant influence
over our business'. Swart, 'Video
Surveillance and Cybersecurity'.

30 *Ibid*.

31 It has been reported that Zhengfei
may have been a 'high-ranking
Chinese spymaster and indeed may
still be'. Max Chafkin and Joshua
Brustein, 'Why America Is So Scared
of China's Largest Tech Company',
Bloomberg Businessweek, 23 March
2018, https://www.bloomberg.
com/news/features/2018-03-22/
why-america-is-so-scared-of-china-s-
biggest-tech-company.

32 'Sun Yafang, for example, chairwoman
of Huawei from 1999 to 2018, was

once employed in China's ministry of state security.' Steven Feldstein, 'The Global Expansion of AI Surveillance', Carnegie Endowment for International Peace, September 2019, p. 15, https://carnegieendowment.org/files/WP-Feldstein-AISurveillance_final1.pdf.

33   *Ibid.*, p. 15.

34   According to Zhang Lin, 'China's large privately-owned firms are becoming more like state-owned enterprises, as many in recent years have implanted in their businesses cells of the Communist Party, the Communist Youth League and even discipline inspection committees.' Zhang Lin, 'Chinese Communist Party Needs to Curtail Its Presence in Private Business', *South China Morning Post*, 25 November 2018, https://www.scmp.com/economy/china-economy/article/2174811/chinese-communist-party-needs-curtail-its-presence-private.

35   Feldstein, 'The Global Expansion of AI Surveillance', p. 15.

36   See MacKinnon, 'For Africa, Chinese-built Internet Is Better Than No Internet at All'.

37   See Scott N. Romaniuk and Tobias Burgers, 'How China's AI Technology Exports Are Seeding Surveillance Societies Globally', *Diplomat*, 18 October 2018, https://thediplomat.com/2018/10/how-chinas-ai-technology-exports-are-seeding-surveillance-societies-globally/.

38   See Samuel Woodhams, 'How China Exports Repression to Africa', *Diplomat*, 23 February 2019, https://thediplomat.com/2019/02/how-china-exports-repression-to-africa/.

39   See Abramowitz and Chertoff, 'The Global Threat of China's Digital Authoritarianism'.

40   See Romaniuk and Burgers, 'How China's AI Technology Exports Are Seeding Surveillance Societies Globally'.

41   Feldstein, 'The Global Expansion of AI Surveillance', p. 15.

42   Joe Parkinson, Nicholas Bariyo and Josh Chin, 'Huawei Technicians Helped African Governments Spy on Political Opponents', *Wall Street Journal*, 14 August 2019, https://www.wsj.com/articles/huawei-technicians-helped-african-governments-spy-on-political-opponents-11565793017.

43   Shahbaz, 'Freedom on the Net 2018'. See also Duniah Tegegn, 'African Union's Revised Declaration on Principles of Access to Information and Freedom of Expression', 13 December 2019, Amnesty International USA, https://medium.com/@amnestyusa/african-unions-revised-declaration-on-principles-of-access-to-information-and-freedom-of-2d7d636dddb2; and Woodhams, 'How China Exports Repression to Africa'.

44   'Report of the Special Rapporteur on the Rights to Freedom of Peaceful Assembly and of Association', UN General Assembly, Human Rights Council, 17 May 2019, p. 13, https://undocs.org/A/HRC/41/41.

45   David Pilling, 'The Fight to Control Africa's Digital Revolution', *Financial Times*, 20 June 2019, https://www.ft.com/content/24b8b7b2-9272-11e9-aea1-2b1d33ac3271.

46   Only in Benin did protests result in a quick abandonment of the tax plan. 'Taxing Social

Media in Africa', Internet Health Report 2019, April 2019, https://internethealthreport.org/2019/taxing-social-media-in-africa/.

47 Writes Amy MacKinnon: 'There is leverage that comes with being the low-cost solution provider to a country whose political leadership, might, in part, derive their popular support from being able to offer connectivity to their population.' MacKinnon, 'For Africa, Chinese-built Internet Is Better Than No Internet at All'.

48 Qiang, 'The Road to Digital Unfreedom', p. 56.

49 See Simon Denyer, 'The All-seeing "Sharp Eyes" of China's Security State', *Washington Post*, 8 January 2018, https://www.washingtonpost.com/news/world/wp/2018/01/07/feature/in-china-facial-recognition-is-sharp-end-of-a-drive-for-total-surveillance/.

50 See Feldstein, 'The Global Expansion of AI Surveillance', p. 18.

51 *Ibid.*, p. 10.

52 Stephen Chen, 'China to Build Giant Facial Recognition Database to Identify any Citizen Within Three Seconds', *South China Morning Post*, 12 October 2017, https://www.scmp.com/news/china/society/article/2115094/china-build-giant-facial-recognition-database-identify-any.

53 See Richard Fontaine and Kara Frederick, 'The Autocrat's New Tool Kit: The Next Generation of Repressive Technology Will Make Past Efforts to Spread Propaganda and Quash Dissent Look Primitive', *Wall Street Journal*, 15 March 2019, https://www.wsj.com/articles/the-autocrats-new-tool-kit-11552662637?.

54 Denyer, 'The All-seeing "Sharp Eyes" of China's Security State'.

55 Quoted in *ibid*.

56 Fontaine and Frederick, 'The Autocrat's New Tool Kit'.

57 See Alina Polyakova and Chris Meserole, 'Exporting Digital Authoritarianism: The Russian and Chinese Models', Brookings Institution, August 2019, https://www.brookings.edu/research/exporting-digital-authoritarianism/.

58 See Charles Rollet, 'Western Academia Helps Build China's Automated Racism', *Coda*, 6 August 2019, https://codastory.com/authoritarian-tech/western-academia-china-automated-racism/.

59 Denyer, 'The All-seeing "Sharp Eyes" of China's Security State'.

60 'Mongolia Installs 2,530 Surveillance Cameras in Capital', Xinhuanet, 18 June 2019, http://www.xinhuanet.com/english/2018-06/19/c_137264873.htm.

61 Rollet, 'Western Academia Helps Build China's Automated Racism'.

62 'China Has Turned Xinjiang Into a Police State Like No Other', *The Economist*, 31 May 2018, https://www.economist.com/briefing/2018/05/31/china-has-turned-xinjiang-into-a-police-state-like-no-other.

63 Sarah Cook, 'China's Cyber Superpower Strategy: Implementation, Internet Freedom Implications, and U.S. Responses', Freedom House, 28 September 2018, https://freedomhouse.org/article/chinas-cyber-superpower-strategy-implementation-internet-freedom-implications-and-us. Because the region is somewhat outside of the public eye, there can also be more experimentation in Xinjiang. See

Megha Rajagopalan, 'This Is What a 21st-century Police State Really Looks Like', BuzzFeed News, 17 October 2017, https://www.buzzfeednews.com/article/meghara/the-police-state-of-the-future-is-already-here.

64 In its marketing materials, CloudWalk touted its surveillance systems' ability to recognise 'sensitive groups of people'. Paul Mozur, 'One Month, 500,000 Face Scans: How China Is Using A.I. to Profile a Minority', *New York Times*, 14 April 2019, https://www.nytimes.com/2019/04/14/technology/china-surveillance-artificial-intelligence-racial-profiling.html.

65 See Cook, 'China's Cyber Superpower Strategy'.

66 Rajagopalan, 'This Is What a 21st-century Police State Really Looks Like'.

67 Mozur, 'One Month, 500,000 Face Scans'.

68 See Cunrui Wang et al., 'Facial Feature Discovery for Ethnicity Recognition', *Wiley Interdisciplinary Reviews: Data Mining and Knowledge Discovery*, vol. 9, no. 11, January–February 2019.

69 See Rollet, 'Western Academia Helps Build China's Automated Racism'. There is substantial and well-founded scepticism about these capabilities. Promoters of some particularly controversial apps claim they can gauge intelligence or sexual orientation, even emotion. This seems highly questionable. Not all ethnicities have clearly distinct markers; some are largely cultural constructs.

70 See Charles Rollet, 'In China's Far West, Companies Cash In on Surveillance Program that Targets Muslims', *Foreign Policy*, 13 June 2018, https://foreignpolicy.com/2018/06/13/ in-chinas-far-west-companies-cash-in-on-surveillance-program-that-targets-muslims/. The company has since removed the video making this claim. See Charles Rollet, 'Hikvision Markets Uyghur Ethnicity Analytics, Now Covers Up', IPVM, 11 November 2019, https://ipvm.com/reports/hikvision-uyghur.

71 Quoted in Mozur, 'One Month, 500,000 Face Scans'.

72 'Report of the Special Rapporteur on the Promotion and Protection of the Right to Freedom of Opinion and Expression', UN General Assembly, Human Rights Council, 28 May 2019, p. 3, https://undocs.org/A/HRC/41/35. Specifically with regard to facial-recognition technology, the Special Rapporteur tellingly concluded: 'Facial recognition technology seeks to capture and detect the facial characteristics of a person, potentially profiling individuals based on their ethnicity, race, national origin, gender and other characteristics, which are often the basis for unlawful discrimination … Perhaps no other environment demonstrates the comprehensive intrusiveness of these technologies better than China. Credible reporting suggests that the Government of China, using a combination of facial recognition technology and surveillance cameras throughout the country, looks exclusively for Uighurs based on their appearance and keeps records of their comings and goings for search and review. Much of the technology deployed by the Government appears to be produced domestically, by both State-owned and private enterprises' (p. 5).

73 See Abramowitz and Chertoff, 'The Global Threat of China's Digital Authoritarianism'.

74 This is a dramatic increase of the country's market share of 29.29% in 2017. See Chris Burt, 'Global Market for Facial Recognition Devices to Surpass $7 Billion by 2025, Led By CloudWalk', *Biometric Update*, 14 August 2018, https://www.biometricupdate.com/201808/global-market-for-facial-recognition-devices-to-surpass-7-billion-by-2025-led-by-cloudwalk. The 'Global Face Recognition Device Market Research Report 2018', referred to in Burt's article, can be accessed at https://genmarketinsights.com/report/global-face-recognition-device-market-research-report-2018/41637/.

75 See Hawkins, 'Beijing's Big Brother Tech Needs African Faces'.

76 See Garikai Dzoma, 'Zimbabwe Government Is Sending Our Faces to China so China's Artificial Intelligence System Can See Black Faces', *TechZim*, 8 November 2018, https://www.techzim.co.zw/2018/11/zimbabwe-government-is-sending-our-faces-to-china-so-chinas-artificial-intelligence-system-can-learn-to-see-black-faces/; Hawkins, 'Beijing's Big Brother Tech Needs African Faces'; Zhang Hongpei, 'Chinese Facial ID Tech to Land in Africa', *Global Times*, 17 May 2018, https://www.globaltimes.cn/content/1102797.shtml; Romaniuk and Burgers, 'How China's AI Technology Exports Are Seeding Surveillance Societies Globally'; Roussi, 'China Charts a Path Into European Science', p. 326; Adrian Shahbaz, 'Fake News, Data Collection, and the Challenge to Democracy: Freedom on the Net 2018 – The Rise of Digital Authoritarianism', Freedom House, October 2018, https://freedomhouse.org/report/freedom-net/freedom-net-2018; and Samuel Woodhams, 'How China Exports Repression to Africa', *Diplomat*, 23 February 2019, https://thediplomat.com/2019/02/how-china-exports-repression-to-africa/.

77 See especially Hongpei, 'Chinese Facial ID Tech to Land in Africa'. See also Chutel, 'China Is Exporting Facial Recognition Software to Africa, Expanding Its Vast Database'; Ryan Gallagher, 'Export Laws', Index on Censorship, 12 September 2019, https://journals.sagepub.com/doi/10.1177/0306422019876445; and Hanibal Goitom, 'Regulation of Artificial Intelligence: Sub-Saharan Africa', Library of Congress, January 2019, https://www.loc.gov/law/help/artificial-intelligence/africa.php.

78 See Joy Buolamwini and Timnit Gebru, 'Gender Shades: Intersectional Accuracy Disparities in Commercial Gender Classification', *Proceedings of Machine Learning Research Conference on Fairness, Accountability and Transparency*, vol. 81, 2018, pp. 6–12, http://proceedings.mlr.press/v81/buolamwini18a/buolamwini18a.pdf.

79 See Hawkins, 'Beijing's Big Brother Tech Needs African Faces'.

80 See Kari Paul, 'Amazon to Ban Police Use of Facial Recognition Software for a Year', *Guardian*, 11 June 2020, https://www.theguardian.com/technology/2020/jun/10/amazon-rekognition-software-police-black-lives-matter. See also Shita Ovide, 'A Case for Banning

Facial Recognition', *New York Times*, 9 June 2020, https://www.nytimes.com/2020/06/09/technology/facial-recognition-software.html.

81 See Shahbaz, 'Fake News, Data Collection, and the Challenge to Democracy'; and Woodhams, 'How China Exports Repression to Africa'.

82 See Hawkins, 'Beijing's Big Brother Tech Needs African Faces'. Commenting on the Zimbabwe agreement, Yao Zhiqiang, the chief executive officer of CloudWalk, stated: 'The difference between technologies tailored to an Asian face and those to a black one are relatively large, not only in terms of color, but also facial bones and features … The machine learning needed to expand the technology's capability would require sufficient data.' Quoted in Hongpei, 'Chinese Facial ID Tech to Land in Africa'.

83 The deal included dozens of cooperation agreements between Harare and Chinese technology and biotechnology firms. Yao Zhiqiang confirmed to China's *Global Times* that the 'Zimbabwean government did not come to Guanzhou purely for AI or facial ID technology, rather it had a comprehensive plan for such areas as infrastructure, technology and biology'. Quoted in Hongpei, 'Chinese Facial ID Tech to Land in Africa'. China has historically been a close partner of Zimbabwe, and remains the single biggest investor in the country's beleaguered economy, having sunk billions of dollars into diamond and platinum mines, new highways and electricity-generating dams. See Ray Mwareya, 'Zimbabwe Drifts Towards Online Darkness', *Coda*, 26 February 2019, https://www.codastory.com/authoritarian-tech/zimbabwe-drifts-towards-online-darkness/.

84 See Chutel, 'China Is Exporting Facial Recognition Software to Africa, Expanding Its Vast Database'.

85 See Chris White, 'Chinese Companies Using Zimbabweans as Guinea Pigs to Identify Black Faces', *National Interest*, 3 December 2019, https://nationalinterest.org/blog/buzz/chinese-companies-use-zimbabweans-guinea-pigs-identify-black-faces-report-101447.

86 Hawkins, 'Beijing's Big Brother Tech Needs African Faces'.

87 See Romaniuk and Burgers, 'How China's AI Technology Exports Are Seeding Surveillance Societies Globally'.

88 Quoted in Hawkins, 'Beijing's Big Brother Tech Needs African Faces'.

89 Abeba Birhane, 'The Algorithmic Colonization of Africa', *Real Life*, 18 July 2019, https://reallifemag.com/the-algorithmic-colonization-of-africa/.

90 See Gwagwa and Garbe, 'Exporting Repression?'.

91 Fontaine and Frederick comment: 'A political dissident in Harare may soon have as much to fear as a heroin smuggler in Zhengzhou.' Fontaine and Frederick, 'The Autocrat's New Tool Kit'. See also Ryan Khurana, 'The Rise of Illiberal Artificial Intelligence', *National Review*, 10 August 2018, https://www.nationalreview.com/2018/08/china-artificial-intelligence-race/; and Romaniuk and Burgers, 'How China's AI Technology Exports Are Seeding Surveillance Societies Globally'.

92 Frederike Kaltheuner, 'Facial

Recognition Cameras Will Put Us All in an Identity Parade', *Guardian*, 27 January 2020, https://www.theguardian.com/commentisfree/2020/jan/27/facial-recognition-cameras-technology-police.

93 See Woodhams, 'How China Exports Repression to Africa'.

94 Dzoma, 'Zimbabwe Government Is Sending Our Faces to China so China's Artificial Intelligence System Can See Black Faces'.

95 See Kaltheuner, 'Facial Recognition Cameras Will Put Us All in an Identity Parade'.

96 Hawkins, 'Beijing's Big Brother Tech Needs African Faces'.

97 Romaniuk and Burgers, 'How China's AI Technology Exports Are Seeding Surveillance Societies Globally'.

98 Hawkins, 'Beijing's Big Brother Tech Needs African Faces'.

99 See Mwareya, 'Zimbabwe Drifts Towards Online Darkness'.

100 Partial internet service was restored in February 2019, but social-media apps and communications services such as Facebook, WhatsApp and Twitter remained blocked for days longer.

101 Of the 55 member states of the African Union, the signatories to the convention are: Benin, Chad, Comoros, Congo, Ghana, Guinea-Bissau, Mauritania, Mozambique, Rwanda, São Tomé and Príncipe, Sierra Leone, Togo, Tunisia and Zambia. However, only Angola, Ghana, Guinea, Mauritius, Mozambique, Namibia, Rwanda and Senegal have ratified or acceded to the convention. See 'List of Countries Which Have Signed, Ratified/Acceded to the African Union Convention on Cybersecurity and Personal Data Protection', African Union, 18 June 2020, https://au.int/sites/default/files/treaties/29560-sl-AFRICAN%20UNION%20CONVENTION%20ON%20CYBER%20SECURITY%20AND%20PERSONAL%20DATA%20PROTECTION.pdf.

102 'African Union Convention on Cybersecurity and Personal Data Protection', Chapter II, Section 3, Article 13(1) of the Convention.

103 *Ibid.*, Chapter II, Section 3, Article 14(1).

104 *Ibid.*, Chapter II, Section 3, Article 14(6)(a). The prohibition is not applicable where, before any personal data is transferred to the third country, the data controller requests authorisation for such transfer from the national protection authority. Chapter II, Section 3, Article 14(6)(b).

105 *Ibid.*, Chapter II, Section 3, Article 18.

106 The declaration was adopted by the African Commission on Human and Peoples' Rights at its 65th ordinary session, held from 21 October to 10 November 2019 in Banjul, Gambia, and replaces its 2002 'Declaration of Principles on Freedom of Expression in Africa'. The declaration is a 'soft law' instrument that interprets Article 9 (right to receive information and free expression) of the African Charter on Human and Peoples' Rights. For the text, see African Commission on Human and Peoples' Rights, 'Declaration of Principles on Freedom of Expression and Access to Information in Africa', https://www.achpr.org/presspublic/publication?id=80.

107 See Principles 40–2 of the 'Declaration of Principles on Freedom of

Expression and Access to Information in Africa'.

108 *Ibid.*, Principle 40(1) and (2).

109 *Ibid.*, Principle 42(2).

110 *Ibid.*, Principle 42(4).

111 See Lindsey Andersen et al., 'Human Rights in the Age of Artificial Intelligence', Access Now, November 2018, p. 29, https://www.accessnow.org/cms/assets/uploads/2018/11/AI-and-Human-Rights.pdf.

112 See Shahbaz, 'Fake News, Data Collection, and the Challenge to Democracy'.

113 See 'Léifēng wǎng lùn dào AI ānquán yǔ lúnlǐ: Wǒmen néng dádào diànyǐng lǐ de zhìnéng ma? Zuì kěnéng shíxiàn de AI chǎngjǐng shì shénme? Rúhé kàndài AI zìzhǔ xìng?' [On AI safety and ethics: what is the most likely AI scenario? How to view AI autonomy?], Phoenix Network Technology, 3 June 2019, https://web.archive.org/web/20190628115141/http:/tech.ifeng.com/a/20190603/45601943_0.shtml.

114 See Andersen et al., 'Human Rights in the Age of Artificial Intelligence', p. 31; and Kaltheuner, 'Facial Recognition Cameras Will Put Us All in an Identity Parade'.

115 See Dylan Curran, 'Facial Recognition Will Soon Be Everywhere. Are We Prepared?', *Guardian*, 27 May 2019, https://www.theguardian.com/commentisfree/2019/may/21/facial-recognition-privacy-prepared-regulation.

116 See Birhane, 'The Algorithmic Colonization of Africa'.

117 See Gwagwa and Garbe, 'Exporting Repression?'.

Belarus and Russian Policy: Patterns of the Past, Dilemmas of the Present

Nigel Gould-Davies

On 9 August 2020, nationwide protests erupted in Belarus after a fraudulent presidential election. Their brutal suppression had the opposite effect to that intended: it outraged rather than intimidated, bringing more of the population onto the streets. Within days, the political landscape in Belarus had shifted dramatically. Peaceful citizens now confronted a violent state in a struggle to determine Belarus's future.

This historic moment for the country has also become an international event. Although the opposition's demands are focused on democratic transition, not foreign policy, the crisis has drawn in Russia and the West. From the start, the West has condemned human-rights violations. It has imposed sanctions, refused to recognise Alexander Lukashenko's inauguration as president and offered support to civil society.

Russia's response has been more complex. Initially, the Kremlin did not take a clear position. Without a steer from above, some media outlets expressed sympathy with beaten protesters, and criticised Lukashenko for his crackdown. Veteran nationalist politician Vladimir Zhirinovsky even predicted that the Belarusian president would have to give up power. But on 27 August, as the scale and resilience of the protests became clear, Russian President Vladimir Putin backed Lukashenko in a hastily prepared

Nigel Gould-Davies is Senior Fellow for Russia and Eurasia at the IISS. From 2000–10, he served in the UK Foreign and Commonwealth Office, including as ambassador to Belarus. He later held senior government-relations roles in the energy industry. He is author of *Tectonic Politics: Global Political Risk in an Age of Transformation* (Brookings Institution Press, 2019).

Survival | vol. 62 no. 6 | December 2020–January 2021 | pp. 179–198   https://doi.org/10.1080/00396338.2020.1851099

interview. He announced that he had created, at Lukashenko's request, a 'reserve group of law-enforcement personnel' to help restore order in Belarus if necessary.[1] He also endorsed Lukashenko's ban on Belarus's Coordination Council, which had been created by the leading opposition presidential candidate Svetlana Tikhanovskaya in August 2020 to facilitate a democratic transfer of power.

Russia then escalated its support for Lukashenko with several high-level visits. Prime Minister Mikhail Mishustin led a delegation to Minsk on 3 September. Defence Minister Sergei Shoigu and Foreign Intelligence chief Sergei Naryshkin also made visits. Lukashenko and Putin met in Sochi on 14 September. Russia's narrative also shifted decisively against the democratic movement. Senior figures and state media claimed that the West was directing the protests in Belarus in order to carry out a coup; that NATO was building up forces on Belarus's western border; and that specially trained Ukrainians had infiltrated Belarus to sow disruption.[2] Russian diplomats rejected repeated requests from the Belarusian opposition to meet.

Russia is Belarus's most powerful neighbour and closest partner. Its perceptions, interests and policies are therefore highly significant and will influence the course and outcome of the crisis. What are its goals, what means does it have to pursue them and what wider international circumstances will influence its actions?

Russia has a long history of responding to upheavals in the wider Central and Eastern European region of which Belarus is a part, and patterns of Russian policy in the region have been remarkably consistent over two centuries. But Russia's choices, and the methods it has used to enforce them, have varied with changes in the political geography of the region and in Russia's governing values. These themes and variations are relevant in interpreting Russia's approach to the Belarusian crisis today.

A history of opposing liberal change

Russia's interest in controlling domestic change in Central Europe dates from its emergence as an indisputably great power after its role in defeating Napoleon Bonaparte in 1815. It was a member of the Concert of Europe that sought to preserve great-power relations. But Russia's concept of international order went further. It proposed a Holy Alliance of all European states against revolutionary forces that threatened to undermine them from within. Other conservative powers, notably Austria-Hungary and Prussia, supported this, but it was Russia's idea, and Russia remained its keenest supporter.

Within a decade the Holy Alliance had faded away, but Russia, the most autocratic of the great powers, remained committed to resisting change, especially after the reactionary Nicholas I became tsar in 1825. His suppression of civil liberties in the Kingdom of Poland – a territory granted to Russia at the Congress of Vienna in 1815, but enjoying a high degree of autonomy under a liberal constitution – provoked an uprising in 1830. This revolt was also fuelled by Russian plans to use the Polish army to suppress two other revolutions, in France and Belgium, that had taken place earlier that year. Although thwarted by the Polish revolution, Russia's aspirations to intervene against liberal change had extended to Western as well as Central Europe.[3] In 1848, Europe's year of revolution, Russia intervened to help Austria crush a liberal-nationalist uprising in Hungary, earning Nicholas I the soubriquet of 'Gendarme of Europe'. A second revolution in Poland was suppressed in 1863. Thus, Russia was consistently a force of conservative reaction not only at home but also in its neighbours to the west.

Russia's role in Central Europe diminished from the 1870s as its geopolitical priorities turned south and east, and it became caught up in transformative domestic processes of modernisation, instability, war and collapse. The Bolshevik state that emerged from the 1917 revolution snuffed out the brief independence of Belarus and Ukraine, and expanded further in the wake of the 1939 Molotov–Ribbentrop Pact. But only at the end of the Second World War was the Soviet Union again strong enough to project power into the heart of Central Europe, as it had a century earlier.

The Soviet era and Eastern Europe

After 1945, the Soviet Union's military power, together with the region's exhaustion from years of war, occupation and genocide, gave Moscow greater dominance in Central Europe than ever before. The Soviet Union was not only more dominant than tsarist Russia had been, but also exercised its dominance differently, for two reasons. The first was ideology. The tsarist order had been a conservative autocracy that resisted change. The Soviet Union, by contrast, was defined by a universalistic, revolutionary creed that justified limitless expansion.

The second reason lay in the political geography of the region. Before 1914, Central and Eastern Europe comprised empires that divided up, or fought over, territory. After 1918, the collapse of these empires produced sovereign nation-states that were reconstituted after the Second World War. The Soviet Union occupied these, but did not absorb them. Instead, it devised a new system to control them suitable for an age of mass politics and total ideologies – and its own anti-imperialist claims. Each Central European state was turned into a miniature version of the Soviet Union, with a single, ruling communist party, a state-directed economy and a society in which no autonomous organisations were permitted.

This system centralised power in each country to an extraordinary degree. All major national institutions – party, military, security services and economic planning – were in turn subordinated to their Soviet counterparts, enabling Moscow to control each country without absorbing it. The states of the 'Eastern bloc' – a term coined during the Cold War to connote this distinctive pattern of control – were formally sovereign and internationally recognised. But in practice they were only semi-sovereign and thoroughly penetrated by mechanisms of Soviet control.

This was not a 'sphere of influence' in the traditional sense. Such spheres typically required small powers to align with a great power and respect its security interests, but granted them wide autonomy in domestic affairs. The Soviet Union sought not only to constrain external alignments but to transform internal structures too. This was an *ideological* empire in which Soviet power spread Marxism–Leninism to other states while imposing communist systems on them to help ensure their subordination to Soviet control.

The last country to succumb to this ideological and intrusive control was Czechoslovakia. The Soviet Union had allowed free elections to be held there in 1946. These produced a coalition government, with a large communist party that worked to maintain friendly relations with the Soviet Union while remaining democratic. But this experiment was snuffed out in the Prague coup of February 1948. Alarmed by the potential of Marshall Plan aid to revive Western Europe and attract Eastern Europe (the Czechoslovakian government had shown interest), Joseph Stalin abandoned his aspirations to extend looser Soviet influence across the continent and instead tightened control to secure what he could on the continent. This was the last time until 1989 that the Soviet Union tolerated democratic government in a territory under its control.

Eastern Europe's history over the next four decades was marked by a succession of national challenges to Soviet domination, and Soviet responses to them. These challenges and responses took different forms, but in each case the outcome – restoration of communist-party control and Soviet hegemony – was the same. Yet despite the Soviet Union's overwhelming strength, it repeatedly faced difficulties and dilemmas in exercising its control.

Moscow was concerned about contagion

The first major crisis erupted in East Germany in June 1953, when strikes against the adoption of harsher economic policies escalated into a full-scale uprising against communist rule. The Soviet Union crushed this quickly and ruthlessly, but required a massive commitment of troops to do so. Moscow was acutely concerned, as it would be in all subsequent crises, about the threat of contagion: the prospect that opposition to communist rule could spread not only to other Eastern European countries, but to the Soviet Union itself.[4]

In October 1956, mass unrest swelled in Poland. The strength of Polish nationalism, and the country's history of difficult relations with Russia, made the Soviet Union especially reluctant to intervene militarily. It found in Władysław Gomułka a communist leader who was both loyal enough to assuage Moscow's concerns and legitimate enough in Polish eyes to restore domestic stability. By squaring the circle of communism and nationalism, Gomułka resolved the crisis without Soviet military force.

The following month, Soviet forces sent to suppress a revolt in Hungary met with such fierce local resistance that they withdrew from Budapest. The Soviet Union even sought to reach a compromise with the government of prime minister Imre Nagy to remove its forces from the country entirely.[5] One of the biggest revelations to emerge from the Soviet-bloc archives is how seriously, if briefly, the Soviet leadership considered abandoning Hungary.[6] In the end, it chose to crush the uprising in what was to be the bloodiest of its interventions in Eastern Europe.

The origins of the next crisis, in Czechoslovakia in 1968, lay in reforms introduced by new communist leader Alexander Dubček intended to create 'socialism with a human face'. He did not seek to dismantle communism or revise the country's relationship with the Soviet Union, having understood from the Hungarian experience that any challenge to Moscow would be unacceptable. But his limited initial reform awakened demands in civil society for greater pluralism and further freedoms. When the Soviet leadership under Leonid Brezhnev concluded that this posed a threat to key institutions of state socialism – above all, the leading role of the communist party – it authorised a Warsaw Pact invasion to restore control. But despite occupying the country with overwhelming force, the Soviet Union did not find it easy to pacify the country. The Czechoslovakian opposition conducted an ingenious and versatile civil-resistance campaign for almost a year before 'normalisation' entrenched a post-Dubček regime and subdued the population.

The Prague Spring sought domestic liberalisation and was not anti-Soviet in character. But its fate showed clearly that the Soviet Union would not tolerate the granting of any significant domestic freedom in the Eastern bloc, even if this did not challenge Soviet primacy. The Brezhnev Doctrine, formulated to justify the invasion, explicitly limited the sovereignty of Eastern-bloc countries by making the Soviet Union the arbiter of domestic change.

Interventions fuelled resentment of the Soviet Union. This, and the stagnation of the state-owned economies imposed on the region, forced Moscow to subsidise Eastern Europe at growing cost to itself – creating a unique 'reverse empire' in which the dominant state financed, rather than extracted from, subordinate states. But this 'welfare authoritarianism' was not enough to prevent further protests in Poland, culminating in 1980 in major strikes that forced the government to accept the legalisation of the Solidarity trade-union movement and other major concessions. The Soviet Union could not tolerate this challenge, but understood the risks of intervening even as it drew up contingency plans to do so.[7] The solution was to pressure Poland into declaring martial law in December 1981. In effect, the country invaded itself.

Although in relative decline, the Soviet Union remained strong enough to keep Eastern Europe subordinate and under tight control. This changed only when Mikhail Gorbachev fundamentally revised Soviet foreign policy. Drawing on 'new thinking' about cooperative security with the West, and a misplaced confidence in the potential of socialism to renew itself, he refused to intervene to prevent popular demands for change that had themselves been encouraged by Gorbachev's reforms in the Soviet Union. Indeed, he even used mechanisms of bloc control to prevent hardliners, notably in East Germany, from attempting the 'Chinese solution' of a violent crackdown to secure the regime's survival.

There were many paths from socialism in the 'miracle year' of 1989: negotiated transitions in Poland and Hungary, regime collapse in East Germany and Czechoslovakia, and the toppling of long-standing leaders in Bulgaria and Romania. Free from Soviet control, what had been the Eastern bloc was restored as a Central

Freedom emboldened some Soviet republics

Europe of sovereign states. Such change proved contagious. Newly won freedom emboldened some Soviet republics, notably the Baltic states, to press for independence. In this way, the disintegration of the outer empire of Eastern Europe corroded the inner empire of the Soviet Union itself, culminating in its break-up two years later.[8]

By 2001, following the wars in Yugoslavia (where Soviet writ had never run) and the ouster of Serbian leader Slobodan Milosevic, the whole of Europe – including two Soviet successor states, Ukraine and Moldova – was sovereign, and at least partially democratic, for the first time. The sole exception was Belarus. As in many Soviet republics, a reform movement had mobilised there in the late 1980s. A physicist turned democratic politician, Stanislav Shushkevich, led the country to independence and hosted the meeting that dissolved the Soviet Union in December 1991.

But the election of former collective-farm chairman Alexander Lukashenko as president in 1994 led to the return of harsh authoritarian rule. Though Minsk lay further west than the capital of any other former Soviet republic (apart from the Baltic states), the country now suffered the most repressive regime outside Central Asia. As the rest of Central Europe continued its transition towards the West, both domestically and in foreign policy, Belarus moved in the opposite direction. It grew steadily more anti-democratic and anti-Western, and closer to Russia – even as Russia itself rebuilt an authoritarian system and increasingly defined itself in opposition to the West.

Continuities of Russia's Central Europe policies

The history of Russia's relations with Central Europe offers four lessons that are relevant today. The first concerns Russian goals. Ever since Russia became strong enough to intervene in the region, it has sought to control its domestic affairs – specifically, to suppress liberalising change. This impulse has remained constant across two centuries, two very dissimilar regimes and several leaders. In the tsarist era, suppression of change mostly took the form of periodic military interventions. In the Soviet era, control was systemic and continuous, with resort to military interventions when uprisings nonetheless erupted.

Russia's concern with controlling both the domestic systems and foreign alignments of Central Europe meant that it treated the region not only as a geographical space defined by territory, but also as an ideological one defined by values. As a state, Russia controlled territory offensively, as a springboard for potential invasion, and defensively, as a security buffer. As a regime, it controlled its neighbours' domestic systems offensively, as part of its commitment to spread socialism, and defensively, to prevent contagion of a hostile ideology.

The singular exception to this pattern came in 1989. Only when the Soviet Union abandoned its ideology did it give up its concern with that of other states. Gorbachev's willingness to allow Eastern European states to choose their own future – founded partly on optimistic delusions about the choices they would make – was a striking departure from long-standing Russian and Soviet practice. It is also a rare example of a major power voluntarily giving up control of territory that it had previously considered a vital interest. The exceptional nature of Gorbachev's 'new political thinking' is unlikely to be a precedent or guide for Russian policy in the foreseeable future.

The second lesson concerns Russia's instruments of control. Maintaining control was costly, especially in its intrusive and systemic Soviet form. Propping up state-planned satellites imposed a financial burden that only grew larger with time. Although the Soviet Union enjoyed overwhelming military superiority, intervention carried risks and was always a last resort after negotiations failed. Where possible it was avoided, as in Poland in 1956 and 1981. Where it was carried out, as in Hungary and Czechoslovakia, it proved more difficult than expected.

The third lesson concerns Russia's international environment. Western policies towards Soviet domination of Eastern Europe were ambiguous. On the one hand, the West opposed this domination and sought to undermine it. By supporting human rights, especially after the 1975 Helsinki Final Act formally committed Eastern European states to respect these, Western governments sought to delegitimise the ideological basis of Eastern-bloc regimes. West Germany's Ostpolitik also weakened the security case for Eastern Europe's acceptance of the Soviet Union as a guarantor against German revanchism.

On the other hand, some Western policies facilitated Soviet domination. While the West condemned interventions, it never directly challenged them. Despite early rhetoric of 'rollback', the United States was in practice preoccupied with averting escalation, and sought to reassure more than restrain the Soviet Union during crises in the Eastern bloc.[9] Furthermore, by extending major loans to Eastern European governments in the 1970s and 1980s, Western banks helped prolong their survival. Stagnating economies borrowed heavily from the capitalist world even as they were increasingly subsidised by the Soviet Union.

The fourth lesson concerns local leadership. Soviet domination of the region enabled it to appoint and remove leaders. Yet the crises that threatened Soviet control usually took place during, or soon after, leadership change. This was true in Hungary, where Nagy became prime minister after two unpopular leaders, Mátyás Rákosi and Ernő Gerő, were removed under Soviet pressure in the space of three months in 1956; in Poland, where Gomułka succeeded Edward Ochab and Bolesław Bierut that same year; and in Czechoslovakia, where the Soviet Union approved the replacement of Antonín Novotný by Dubček in 1968.[10]

Russia and the Belarus crisis

Under Lukashenko, Belarus has been a close and reliable partner for Russia. In domestic policy, the Belarusian president has suppressed civil society and Western values. His personalistic rule is even more control-ling than was communist-party rule in the Eastern bloc, where senior party officials and their factions struggled for influence within the collec-tive leadership – including in all the crises discussed earlier. In Belarus, Lukashenko rules alone.

In foreign policy, Lukashenko has kept Belarus close to Russia and has repeatedly declared the 'brotherhood' of the two countries. His vaunted 'balancing' between Russia and the West is much overstated. He has shown no interest in building a significant relationship with Western states, and the openings and concessions he has made to them have been limited, grudg-ing and reversible. The political and psychological centre of gravity of the Soviet-minded Lukashenko lies firmly in the east, and in the past.

As a bulwark against domestic liberalisation and Western alignment, Lukashenko has served Russia's interests extremely well. Russia has not incurred the costs or opprobrium of Cold War-style control to achieve this. Nor is Russia resented as an occupying force in Belarus, as the Soviet Union was in Eastern Europe. The only real cost to Russia has been the provision of cheap energy and loans to Belarus's largely unreformed economy – much as the Soviet Union subsidised the reverse empire of Eastern Europe. But these costs are modest and easily manageable. Seen in the context of two centuries of Russian attempts to control the domestic and foreign affairs of its neighbours, the Belarusian model seems the ideal solution.

Yet even this has not been enough for Russia. For over a decade, Putin has tried to use Belarus's economic dependence to pressure it into accepting de facto integration with Russia by turning the 'Union State', established by the two countries in 1999 but so far existing mainly on paper, into a reality. Lukashenko has largely succeeded in resisting this, but the two countries have become locked in a toxic embrace characterised by fractious disputes interspersed with declarations of Slavic unity. By seeking to impose a degree of dominance that no sovereign state could accept, Russia has managed to contrive a poor relationship with a country that should be an ideal partner.

By late 2019, this relationship had deteriorated so much, and Lukashenko had become so concerned about Russian pressure, that he hosted, for the first time, visits by US national security advisor John Bolton and Secretary of State Mike Pompeo. Lukashenko even agreed to the appointment of the first US ambassador to Minsk since he forced the previous one out in 2008. Shortly before the presidential election in August 2020, Belarusian authorities arrested 33 members of the Wagner Group – which bills itself as a 'private military company' but is closely tied to the Russian state – in Minsk, and accused them of planning to destabilise the country. Of course, this has not prevented Lukashenko from seeking, and receiving, Putin's support against opposition protests.

Russia's long history of involvement in the wider Central European region helps explain its behaviour in this crisis. Russia sees Belarus as it once saw Central Europe, in both territorial and ideological terms. Just as tsarist Russia and the Soviet Union each sought to control Central Europe according to the political geographies they faced (empires, nation-states) and the values they espoused (monarchical conservatism, state socialism), so too do political geography and values shape Russia's policies towards Belarus today.

Russia does not occupy Belarus in any of the various ways that tsarist Russia and the Soviet Union controlled Eastern Europe. In particular, it does not stand to lose a subordinate national army, military bases or logistical and communications links within a much larger, integrated bloc as it might have done in the event of regime change in Eastern Europe during the Cold War.[11] Hungary's withdrawal from the Warsaw Pact and adoption of neutrality, for example, would have been an enormous setback for the Soviet Union. Nagy's push for this, more than anything else, triggered Soviet intervention. By contrast, contemporary Belarus is not Russia's to lose in military terms. A change in the country's regime would not diminish Russia's hard power.

But with Russian–Western relations once again marked by deep mutual distrust, the Kremlin may fear that, however well disposed towards Russia Belarus's population may be, and despite the absence of a foreign-policy agenda among the democracy movement there, a free Belarus might in due course seek a more Western orientation – as the rest of Central Europe did when it began its democratic transition. Since the country borders not only Russia but three EU and NATO member states, as well as Ukraine (with which Russia has been de facto at war since 2014), a closer Belarusian relationship with the West would be inherently threatening to a Russia that once again sees relations with the West in zero-sum terms.

Nonetheless, if Putin's main reason for supporting Lukashenko and opposing democratic change were a concern about Belarus's future alignment, this would be a potentially resolvable problem. Solutions are available that might satisfy both Russia's need for security and Belarus's desire for freedom, such as a constitutional commitment to non-alignment or neutrality. Ukraine's June 2010 law ruling out NATO membership (overturned after Russia annexed Crimea in 2014) could serve as a precedent. Such solutions might be controversial, but they could at least be discussed. Some Belarusians might reasonably see a case for accepting international neutrality as the price of domestic freedom if this would assuage Russian security concerns.

> *Putin is hostile to liberal democracy*

But Russia has always conceived of European space in ideological as well as territorial terms. It no longer seeks to spread a grand doctrinal system as it did in Soviet times, but Russia's conservative nationalism under Putin is hostile to liberal democracy and seeks to disrupt it in Europe and beyond. It is also determined to prevent the inflow into Russia of liberal and democratic ideas that would threaten the stability of its own regime.

Indeed, the Kremlin may now be more vulnerable to such contagion than it has been for most of its history. Despite growing domestic repression, Russia remains freer than in the Soviet era, and is much more internationally open and connected. Furthermore, contagion-by-example from Belarus would be especially potent. This eastern Slavic neighbour, culturally similar and with close ties to Russia, has been ruled by a highly authoritarian leader for 26 years. Lukashenko's overthrow by peaceful protesters after a rigged election would set an uncomfortable precedent for Putin, who will have been in power for 24 years when Russia's next presidential election is held in 2024. For these reasons, the Kremlin's ideological concern about democratic change in Belarus may be even more significant than its preoccupation with territory. Lukashenko has played on this sensitivity, warning Putin that 'the threat now is not to Belarus alone … The defence of Belarus today is nothing less than the defence of our entire space – the Union State and its example to others. If Belarusians can't hold the line, this wave will roll [to Russia] too.'[12]

If Russia considers a democratic Belarus to be intrinsically threatening, it will see no case for genuine dialogue or compromise that might bring the Belarusian opposition to power. It will always prefer the authoritarian Lukashenko – however non-compliant and difficult to deal with – precisely because he is authoritarian.

Some analysts speculate that Moscow could replace Lukashenko with another leader acceptable to both Russia and Belarus – a Belarusian Gomułka, who would square the circle of external loyalty and domestic legitimacy. There are three reasons to doubt this is feasible. Firstly, it is far from clear that Russia could achieve this; it does not dominate Belarus in the way that allowed the Soviet Union to remove leaders at will in the Eastern bloc. Secondly, as noted earlier, the record of Soviet-enforced leadership changes shows that such changes are as likely to exacerbate as resolve crises. Thirdly, Belarusian society is now so mobilised around the demand for democracy that any successor to Lukashenko would be obliged to submit to a free and fair election to be considered legitimate. No authoritarian alternative would be acceptable.[13]

If Russia's overriding goal is to prevent a democratic Belarus, what instruments are available to it? It might try to prop up the current regime by reinforcing the three pillars of any political order: legitimacy, funding and force. To help with legitimacy, Russia has sent journalists (replacing local ones on strike) and political advisers to Minsk to reinforce domestic propaganda. A month after the election, a group of senior editors, including RT head Margarita Simonyan, interviewed Lukashenko to try to burnish his image. There is little evidence that any of this has been effective in shoring up support. If anything, the reported use of Russian, rather than Belarusian, spellings – including for the word 'Belarusian' itself – undermined the credibility of such efforts.

Russia has also provided money, agreeing a $1.5 billion loan at the Putin–Lukashenko meeting in Sochi. This will help avert a financial crisis in the short term, but on its own it is no solution to declining reserves, let alone the country's longer-term economic stagnation. Some argue that Belarus's current economic dependence (a consequence of Lukashenko's failure to reform the state-dominated economy, rather than an existential fact) puts Russia in a strong position to dictate its future. But it is unclear how Russia could use this. Moscow can hardly hope to achieve its goal of preventing democratic change by withdrawing economic support from the current regime. The same dilemma faced the Soviet Union during the turmoil in Poland in 1980–81. While it considered reducing aid in order to press the Polish leadership to resolve the crisis, it concluded that this only risked deepening the crisis that was fuelling popular support for Solidarity, and ended up increasing aid instead.[14]

This leaves the use of force. Putin's announcement of a law-enforcement reserve to help Lukashenko signalled his readiness to avail himself of this option. His ambiguous formula covers a wide spectrum, from sending regular police, to deploying 'little green men' of the kind used to annex Crimea, to launching an overt military intervention. Short of this last, most extreme variant, it is not clear how effective Russian force would be. Subduing a whole country is a very different matter from annexing a peninsula.

Nonetheless, there is no doubt that Russia has the capacity to occupy Belarus with a full-scale intervention. For this reason, many in the West assume that Russia's military power will make it the arbiter of the crisis. But intervention is likely to be a last resort for Russia, as it was during the Eastern-bloc crises of the Cold War. Recent experience in Ukraine reinforces this lesson. Enjoying the advantage of surprise, and the presence of a major military base, Russia annexed Crimea quickly. But it failed to achieve its wider goals. Ambitions to create a Russian-controlled 'Novorossiya' across a large part of Ukraine were scaled back and then abandoned in the face of Ukrainian resistance. No less significant, this catalysed a stronger Ukrainian identity and support for closer relations with the West – exactly the opposite of what Putin intended or wished.

Even if military intervention were to face little resistance, the political costs would be high. It would turn a population that is well disposed towards Russia into one that sees it as an oppressor. And while intervention would prevent a democratic transition, it is less clear what outcome it would produce. It is unlikely to lead to a Czechoslovakian-style 'normalisation': the Belarusian regime has been reduced to an occupation regime – more domestically isolated than even the Eastern European governments had become by the 1980s. Russian forces would face the prospect of remaining stationed in Belarus, among a newly embittered population, to keep the regime in power.

Russia is also likely to find the wider international environment more difficult. Western investments in Belarus, unlike those in Eastern Europe during the Cold War, are small: as of March 2020, less than 10% of Belarus's bilateral and multilateral loans came from Western sources.[15] These loans neither keep Belarus afloat nor moderate Western policy.[16] Meanwhile, because a full Russian occupation of Belarus would make it easier to isolate the Baltic states from the rest of NATO by cutting the Suwalki Gap that connects them with Poland, any Russian intervention in Belarus would alarm NATO more acutely than Soviet interventions during the Cold War did.

But the most significant difference in the international environment compared to the Cold War is Russia's closer economic and financial relationship with the West. Just as Russia is today more vulnerable to ideological contagion that could undermine its regime, so too is it more vulnerable to sanctions that could punish the regime. Western sanctions imposed since 2014 have had an unwelcome and cumulative impact. There is evidence, too, that the threat of more severe measures may have deterred specific military operations in Ukraine.[17] Russia's use of force in Belarus would likely incur major new sanctions targeting elite figures and institutions. There is already appetite, and draft sanctions bills, in the US Congress to punish Russia more harshly, especially since the poisoning of Russian opposition leader Alexei Navalny with Novichok in August 2020. Even more than during the Cold War, Russian intervention would carry major costs and risks.

*   *   *

For two centuries, Russian policies towards Central and Eastern Europe have been driven by a distinctive impulse. Treating the region as an ideological as well as a territorial space, Moscow has sought to control not only its external alignments but also the domestic values and structures that govern it. The Gorbachev era was the only period in which it was capable of enforcing this will but chose not to do so.

These impulses were expressed in different ways in the tsarist and Soviet periods as a consequence of changes in Europe's political geography and the values of the Russian regime. But the patterns of Russian conduct have nevertheless exhibited striking continuity. In the Belarusian crisis, these same impulses are refracted through a new set of circumstances. Understanding the current situation in these terms yields three conclusions.

Firstly, until the political earthquake triggered by the rigged August 2020 election, Lukashenko was the best partner for Russia. Under his long rule, Belarus has been reliably authoritarian and aligned with Russia, allowing Moscow to secure its priorities without incurring the costs of subordinating another country. But Russia demanded subordination too, pressuring Lukashenko with impossible demands and predictably souring a relationship that should have been strong. Had Russia, in the months and years leading up to the election, supported rather than coerced Belarus, especially economically, the country's politics might not have taken such an adverse turn. In retrospect, Russia's pressure has been remarkably counterproductive.

Secondly, Russia's major concern is not only – and perhaps not primarily – with securing territory, but with protecting itself from ideas and examples that might undermine its regime. Repressive measures taken over the past year confirm the authorities' growing sensitivity to the perceived threat of opposition political activity.[18] This concern with contagion from without is more salient than in the past, and has only been enhanced by the similarities between Belarus and Russia.

Thirdly, Russia's presumed dominance of Belarus is overstated, and there is less to Moscow's instruments of influence than meets the eye. The bluntest of these, military intervention, would be politically more costly than in the past. Russia might appear to have a strong hand, but it faces difficult choices.

All this explains the essential features of Russia's response to the unfolding Belarusian crisis. The limits of Russian power (as well as uncertainty about the strength of the popular challenge to Lukashenko) explain its initial reluctance to take a clear official position, and failure to act decisively since. The Kremlin's overriding concern to prevent the spread of democracy explains Putin's decision to back Lukashenko, despite their toxic relationship. It also explains Moscow's refusal to engage with opposition leader Tikhanovskaya and the Coordination Council, and the escalating efforts of senior officials and the state media to malign them as witting or unwitting agents of the West.

Two implications follow. Firstly, Russia is unlikely to agree to a democratic transition in Belarus. It will only accept this as an outcome if it is unable to prevent it, or judges the risks and costs of preventing it to be too high. This zero-sum approach is consistent with its long-standing attitude to so-called 'colour revolutions' in the former Soviet Union.

The second implication points to the larger significance of Russia's Belarus policy before the crisis. As noted earlier, Lukashenko was an ideal partner for Putin's Russia. Yet despite the natural affinity of the two regimes, and their broadly similar interests and priorities, Russia repeatedly made unacceptable demands that poisoned the relationship. In this light, the prospects for the West achieving a stable and tolerable accommodation with Russia, at least under its present leadership, look bleak.

Notes

[1] President of Russia, 'Interview with Rossiya TV Channel', 27 August 2020, http://en.kremlin.ru/events/president/news/63951.

[2] See, for example, 'About 200 Extremists Trained in Ukraine Currently in Belarus – Lavrov', Tass, 2 September 2020, https://tass.com/politics/1196457; and 'Shoigu zayavil o popytke smeny vlasti v Belarusi pri politicheskoi i finansovoi podderzhke Zapada', tut.by, 27 October 2020, https://news.tut.by/world/705566.html#ua:main_news~.

[3] I am grateful to Max Fras for a helpful exchange on this point. See also Tom Junes, 'A Century of Traditions: The Polish Student Movement, 1815–1918', Central and Eastern European Review, vol. 2, 2008.

[4] See Mark Kramer, 'The Early Post-Stalin Succession Struggle and Upheavals in East–Central Europe: Internal–External Linkages in Soviet

Policy Making (Part 3)', *Journal of Cold War Studies*, vol. 1, no. 3, Fall 1999, pp. 36–41.

5   See Csaba Békés, 'The 1956 Hungarian Revolution and World Politics', Cold War International History Project, Working Paper No. 16, Washington DC, September 1996, pp. 9–12.

6   See Mark Kramer, 'The Soviet Union and the 1956 Crises in Hungary and Poland: Reassessments and New Findings', *Journal of Contemporary History*, vol. 33, no. 2, April 1998, especially pp. 187–90.

7   Contingency planning to provide military support began as early as August 1980, before the signing of the Szczecin and Gdańsk agreements that legalised Solidarity. See 'Special Dossier on the Polish Crisis of 1980', 28 August 1980, Dmitry Antonovich Volkogonov papers, 1887–1995, mm97083838, reel 18, container 27, History and Public Policy Program Digital Archive, Library of Congress, Manuscript Division, https:// digitalarchive.wilsoncenter.org/ document/111230. Translated by Malcolm Byrne.

8   For a comprehensive overview of these events, see Jacques Lévesque, *The Enigma of 1989: The USSR and the Liberation of Eastern Europe* (Berkeley, CA: University of California Press, 1997).

9   See John Lewis Gaddis, *We Now Know: Rethinking Cold War History* (Oxford: Oxford University Press, 1998), p. 235. Note, though, that in 1980 US national security advisor Zbigniew Brzezinski warned the Soviet Union that 'the U.S. would not interfere if the Soviets did not invade Poland, but that the U.S. would not be passive if the Soviets did'. 'Stanislaw Kania, 92, Polish Leader During Solidarity's Rise, Dies', *New York Times*, 3 March 2020, https:// www.nytimes.com/2020/03/03/world/ europe/stanislaw-kania-dead.html.

10   In Poland in 1980, the pattern was reversed: leadership change followed liberalisation and preceded crackdown. Edward Gierek was removed just a week after signing the Szczecin and Gdańsk agreements that legalised Solidarity. His successor, Stanisław Kania, was in turn replaced by Wojciech Jaruzelski two months before the imposition of martial law in December 1981.

11   Russia has two small military facilities in Belarus: a naval-communications relay station at Vileika and an early-warning radar at Hantsavichy. As of November 2020, Lukashenko had not agreed to a renewal of the lease for the latter, which was due to expire. Since 2014, Russia has pressed Minsk to agree to an air base, without success.

12   'Lukashenko: ne nado ubayikivat' mirnymi aktsiyami, my bidim, chto v glubine proskhodit', *Belta*, 15 August 2020, https://www.belta.by/ president/view/lukashenko-ne-nado-ubajukivat-mirnymi-aktsijami-my-vidim-chto-v-glubine-proishodit-402937-2020/?utm_source=belta&utm_ medium=news&utm_ campaign=accent.

13   Speculation has centred on Viktor Babariko, the popular presidential candidate arrested in June 2020 who has long-standing ties to Russia through his chairmanship

of the Belarusian–Russian bank Belgazprombank. Unconfirmed reports suggested that Putin and Lukashenko discussed Babariko at their Sochi meeting. In October 2020, Lukashenko visited Babariko and other political prisoners for an unprecedented four-hour meeting in the KGB prison in Minsk where they were being held. But even if Russia could force out Lukashenko, the record of Eastern-bloc leadership change suggests this could aggravate the crisis rather than resolve it in Russia's favour.

14 See Mark Kramer, 'Soviet Deliberations During the Polish Crisis, 1980–81', Cold War International History Project, Working Paper No. 1, Woodrow Wilson International Center for Scholars, Washington DC, April 1999, especially pp. 17–22, https://www.wilsoncenter.org/sites/default/files/media/documents/publication/ACF56F.PDF.

15 Ben Aris, 'Belarus's Economy in Danger of a Crisis in the Face of Sustained Popular Protests, Says IIF', bne IntelliNews, 2 September 2020, https://intellinews.com/belarus-s-economy-in-danger-of-a-crisis-in-the-face-of-sustained-popular-protests-says-iif-190979/?source=Belarus.

16 Contrast this with some Western businesses during the Cold War, which not only called for greater official engagement with Eastern-bloc countries but even criticised Solidarity for disrupting the Polish economy. See, for example, 'Money Is Often Bottom Line in East–West Ties', Washington Post, 11 May 1982, https://www.washingtonpost.com/archive/politics/1982/05/11/money-is-often-bottom-line-in-east-west-ties/f521c391-9d49-4a72-af3c-a4ad7ae3dd74/.

17 See Nigel Gould-Davies, 'Russia, the West and Sanctions', Survival, vol. 62, no. 1, February–March 2020, pp. 7–28.

18 Examples include the exclusion of independent and opposition candidates from local elections; arrests and prison sentences for those protesting against this; raids on Alexei Navalny's Anti-Corruption Foundation and on the vote-monitoring organisation Golos; the poisoning of Navalny; and the arrest of Khabarovsk governor Sergei Furgal for alleged murders carried out more than 15 years earlier.

The Sino-Russian Relationship and the West

Marcin Kaczmarski

Western policymakers have been growing uneasy about China and Russia's strategic convergence. From right-wing US President Donald Trump to centre-left European leaders such as French President Emmanuel Macron, they have concluded that the West needs to act decisively to prevent Russia from falling into Beijing's arms.[1] Underpinning this assessment and related policy prescriptions are two assumptions, both of which are questionable.

The first is that the West's recent geopolitical losses have resulted from Sino-Russian cooperation. In 2019, the congressional US–China Economic and Security Review Commission for the first time devoted one of its annual report's sections to Sino-Russian relations.[2] It concluded that Russia and China jointly opposed the US and its allies in a number of areas and were working together to undermine the current international order. The report's authors accused both states of interfering in democratic states' domestic politics, championing the idea of a 'sovereign internet' and coordinating their anti-US activities in United Nations forums. An editorial in the *New York Times* argued that Sino-Russian cooperation poses 'a strategic challenge to the United States'.[3] Other commentators shared these sentiments, emphasising that 'the depth of relations between Beijing and Moscow has exceeded what observers would have expected just a few years ago'.[4]

Marcin Kaczmarski is a lecturer in security studies at the University of Glasgow, and author of *Russia–China Relations in the Post-crisis International Order* (Routledge, 2015).

Survival | vol. 62 no. 6 | December 2020–January 2021 | pp. 199–212   https://doi.org/10.1080/00396338.2020.1851101

The second assumption is that reversing Russia's foreign-policy course and making it 'European' again is a viable response. On this view, Russia's rapprochement with China is a temporary aberration, a result of Western, and primarily American, policies. It was a tacit premise of the Obama administration's attempt to 'reset' relations with Russia. Macron, speaking about the growing imbalance in the Sino-Russian relationship, asserted that Vladimir Putin 'can see things are changing, and I'm not sure he likes it'.[5] The self-interest of the Kremlin would help the West in its efforts to pull Russia away from China. Both the congressional report, speaking about 'an uneasy entente', and the 2020 Munich Security Conference paper reflected this hope.[6] The belief that the Russian ruling elite is repressing fears of subordination to China is widespread among scholars. Some argue that Russia is 'terrified' of China but 'does not want to acknowledge this reality'.[7] Others point to the absence of China on the Kremlin's strategic horizon: 'Russian leaders tend to focus solely on some challenges, such as NATO, and under-appreciate other risks, such as China's military buildup.'[8] The upshot is that the West – as the major force behind the Sino-Russian rapprochement – is capable of reversing it. To an extent, Russian scholars who blame Western policies for pushing Moscow towards Beijing share this view.[9]

These two assumptions need to be qualified. Western observers exaggerate the negative implications of Sino-Russian cooperation for Europe and the US, as well as the West's ability to weaken this relationship or to reverse its course. Undoubtedly, closer ties between Moscow and Beijing limit the West's room for manoeuvre in international politics. However, the West does not face a true alliance, as Moscow and Beijing diverge on a number of relevant issues and do not actively support each other's most aggressive political moves. Furthermore, substantial aspects of Sino-Russian cooperation, including in the energy realm, do not have a direct impact on the West. Instead, parallel and often uncoordinated actions by Russia and China, for instance in the Middle East or the Balkans, pose the most serious challenge. Finally, Sino-Russian collaboration is not based solely on geopolitical considerations involving the US and Europe. Other drivers, such as regime survival, have figured into the relationship between Russia and China.

Kindred spirits

Without doubt, authoritarian trust has arisen between Moscow and Beijing over the past decade. Each regime is now confident that the other will not stab it in the back by joining the West in criticising it or supporting more punitive measures, such as sanctions, against it. This factor sets clear limitations on policies the West can successfully implement towards Russia and China. Western states cannot count on isolating either Russia or China in the international arena, be it in the UN Security Council or in groupings such as the G20. This became evident in the aftermath of Russia's wars against Georgia in 2008 and Ukraine in 2014. While Russian actions – the recognition of the independence of South Ossetia and Abkhazia, and the annexation of Crimea, respectively – marked a clear departure from the Sino-Russian declaratory stance against separatism and non-interference, Beijing refrained from open criticism and sought ways to exonerate Moscow. Russia has responded in kind – for instance, by supporting China's rejection of the Permanent Court of Arbitration's ruling on the territorial disputes in the South China Sea.[10]

Collaboration with Russia in the security and defence arena has allowed China to embark on the path towards military modernisation despite the Western embargo imposed after the 1989 Tiananmen Square crackdown. China's most recent acquisitions – Su-35 fighter jets and S-400 missile-defence systems – have substantially improved Beijing's power-projection and anti-access/area-denial capabilities in its near seas, the South China Sea and the Taiwan Strait in particular. Russia's assistance in constructing an early-warning missile-attack system may reinforce China's nuclear posture.[11] Joint military exercises are useful as signals to the West, especially when conducted in regions witnessing tensions with Western actors, such as the Baltic Sea or the South China Sea.

The economic dimension is more complex. China could provide Russia with a lifeline should Russian–Western conflict intensify. But, as post-2014 developments illustrated, Beijing has chosen to walk a fine line in responding to Western economic sanctions on Russia. On the one hand, China did not extend enough help for Russia to offset pressure from Europe or the United States. Chinese companies have generally been unwilling to forgo profit for the sake of geopolitical gestures or to risk sanctions by Western financial authorities, and the Chinese leadership appears to support that restraint. The low level of Chinese investment in the Russian economy after 2014 confirmed this risk-averse attitude.[12] On the other hand, Beijing has offered targeted support to Putin's regime and his cronies. Chinese banks provided multi-billion-dollar loans to Novatek, a liquefied-natural-gas (LNG) producer with reputed links to the Kremlin, which enabled the company to weather Western sanctions and to start its flagship enterprise, the Yamal LNG project, ahead of schedule.[13] Beijing also refused to cancel arms contracts with Rosoboronexport, the Russian state defence export/import agency, despite US sanctions against Chinese companies.[14]

Reciprocated assistance, however, is not feasible. Even assuming maximum political goodwill, Russia could not offset Chinese losses from the trade war with the US nor offer substantial help if the US or the European Union adopted tougher economic measures against Chinese companies such as Huawei.[15] The Russian economy does not offer access to leading-edge technologies, rich consumer markets or established brands, nor opportunities to invest in them. This asymmetry affords Western states leverage vis-à-vis both Russia and China.

To the casual observer, Moscow and Beijing may seem to be meticulously coordinating their activities on the international stage and challenging the West at every possible opportunity to reinforce their rigid conception of sovereignty. Using their status as permanent members of the UN Security Council and becoming more involved in the daily work of UN organisations, both states have prevented the emergence of a new consensus on the Responsibility to Protect.[16] They have promoted a 'sovereigntist' agenda on internet and cyberspace governance.[17] Joint summits display Sino-Russian unity. In annual communications, the two states express shared positions on issues at the top of the international agenda.[18] Every couple of years, Russia and China publish a special communication that outlines their broader views on the international order.[19]

Practical coordination remains much narrower. The rhetoric at Sino-Russian summits broadly condemns Western hegemony but is usually scarce on detail.[20] Moscow and Beijing rarely propose any viable alternatives.

A typical example is the language on the conflict in Afghanistan in a June 2019 communiqué: Russia and China merely pledged 'close coordination of efforts in bilateral and multilateral formats to promote Afghan national reconciliation' and to 'stabilize the situation'.[21] Sino-Russian coordination is, of course, conspicuous in the UN Security Council, where Moscow and Beijing can achieve it with relative ease, but it is essentially negative: no concrete joint actions have to follow vetoes on whatever the West is proposing. Consider the civil war in Syria. Sino-Russian opposition to the West in the political–diplomatic realm did not translate into joint action on the ground. Each state pursued its own policy. Russia intervened militarily and took over the role of key diplomatic broker, setting up the Astana process with Iran and Turkey. China chose to stay on the sidelines and hold back on economic assistance, limiting its engagement to political support.[22] There has been a similar lack of ground-level cooperation with respect to Iran. Russia and China both chastised the Trump administration for withdrawing from the Joint Comprehensive Plan of Action, and offered political support to Tehran.[23] Both states also conducted joint naval exercises with the Iranian navy towards the end of 2019.[24] But Moscow and Beijing have not rushed to challenge US sanctions crippling the Iranian economy. China withdrew from a gas-exploration project, unwilling to risk a clash with Washington.[25] Russia has taken its time in deliberating on Iran's request for a $5 billion loan for infrastructure investments.[26]

Each state pursued its own policy

While cooperation between Moscow and Beijing in the security and defence realm has reinforced each side's military capabilities, it has not transformed the relationship into a fully fledged alliance of two revisionist powers, whereby each side offers security guarantees to the other. Their joint bomber patrol, conducted near Japan and South Korea, shows strategic solidarity and a capacity for tactical coordination but hardly amounts to a concerted provocation.[27] Moreover, Moscow and Beijing are not ready to legitimise each other's most aggressive policies.[28] China did not recognise Abkhazia's or South Ossetia's independence; nor did it accept Crimea as part of the Russian Federation. Beijing has continued to develop economic and, more cautiously, political ties with Ukraine.[29] Russia, in turn, has endeavoured to stay neutral in China's territorial disputes with other East Asian nations over islands in the South and East China seas, and refrained from supporting Chinese territorial claims. Moscow maintains close ties with Vietnam – a target of China's territorial depredations – including through joint oil exploration in contested waters and the steady supply of weapons.[30]

Each side's restraint is attributable to several factors. These include pragmatic unwillingness to overstrain relations with the West, normative opposition to separatism and reluctance to strengthen an already powerful partner. If Russia or China decides to challenge the West on fundamental issues of the international order, it will have to do so individually. In turn, the prospect of its partner offering merely 'friendly neutrality' rather than unconditional support may moderate anti-Western sentiments in Moscow and Beijing.

It's not always about the West

Much of Sino-Russian cooperation has little bearing on the EU and the US, even if Russian policymakers and commentators might portray it as focused on the West.[31] A case in point is energy. In the oil sector, flourishing cooperation between Russia and China does not target or harm Western interests. China, having emerged as Russia's biggest customer for Russian crude oil, can hardly be considered Europe's competitor. The global oil market gives the buyer an opportunity to choose among producers, and historically low prices have made it all the more favourable to buyers. Europe and China alike may see Russia as a stable alternative to the turbulent Middle East, but it is Russia that needs customers.

In the case of natural gas, the hype surrounding the $400bn 2014 Sino-Russian contract was unjustified.[32] Gazprom, Russia's state-controlled energy company, began to export gas to China using the newly completed Power of Siberia pipeline in late 2019. However, the opening of the Chinese market to Gazprom in no way diminishes the importance of the European market for Russia. Once the Power of Siberia reaches its maximum capacity in five years, it will provide only 38bn cubic metres (bcm) of gas to China. The capacity of the Nord Stream pipeline to Germany is 55 bcm (to be doubled by Nord Stream II, although EU regulations may not allow Gazprom to use it to the full extent), Yamal 33 bcm, Blue Stream 16 bcm and TurkStream 31 bcm. Overall, gas exports to Europe exceed those to China by several times. Claims that 'Russia can ship its output to the east' and 'the west may need to pay more to ensure supplies' play into the ominous Russian narrative but belie the reality on the ground.[33]

Furthermore, gas exported to China comes from newly explored fields in eastern Siberia that are not connected to the European market; western Siberian fields that supply the European market are physically separate. Moscow spent more than a decade fruitlessly trying to sell Beijing on its idea of the Altai gas pipeline that would link western Siberian fields with north-western China. The construction of such a pipeline would have been a game changer, allowing Moscow to 'switch' between consumers in the east and west. China patiently took part in negotiations and signed numerous memoranda of understanding, later presented as 'final' documents by the Russian side. But Beijing has since shied away from the project, considering its value dubious given the existing Central Asia–China gas-pipeline system.

Russia's and China's parallel activities

Close Sino-Russian cooperation has had a limited impact on the West. What most diminishes the West's position, reduces the effectiveness of its policies and narrows its room for manoeuvre are parallel and often uncoordinated activities of Russia and China that they implement with the best tools at hand – security and military assets in the case of Russia, economic and financial ones in the case of China. Their efforts have been notable in the Middle East, the Balkans and, more recently, sub-Saharan Africa, weakening American and European influence.

For Moscow, Syria has served as a showcase for Russian military prowess and geopolitical heft, elevating its status as a great power and increasing its leverage vis-à-vis the US. There, Moscow has become a risk-taker, sending military advisers, supplying the Assad regime with weapons, and directly using military force to capitalise on domestic and international crises. China has increased its economic presence in the Middle East, emerging as a major trading partner, lender and infrastructure developer (including telecommunications, 5G technology and submarine cables) in the region and its largest foreign direct investor. At the same time, it has avoided military involvement and limited its political engagement.[34]

Russia's and China's activities in the Balkans reflect a similar pattern. Russia put its political weight behind Serbia in campaigning against international recognition of Kosovo and offering military and technical assistance, including joint exercises in 2019.[35] Moscow has also attempted to prevent a pro-Western tilt in North Macedonia. Meanwhile, China focused on investments in infrastructure in the region, provided loans to the Balkan states and set up the '17+1' economic-cooperation framework for former communist countries in Central and Eastern Europe.[36]

Overall, Russia is eager to provide local actors with political support, arms, security advisers and, in special cases, direct military support. China furnishes credits, infrastructure investment and local business investment, as well as political support. The EU is not inclined to match Russia's military strength and China's largesse. The US, while rhetorically stressing the growing challenge from Russia and China, has appeared disinclined to engage in long-term and costly influence-building, defaulting to a form of retrenchment.

An appropriate Western response

The 2019 US congressional report identified a number of weaknesses and limitations of the Sino-Russian relationship, complacently concluding that each country sees the other as 'the long-term geopolitical threat' that impedes 'the positive development of the relationship'.[37] Other American analysts acknowledge that the Moscow–Beijing axis could become more formidable and argue that it is up to the United States to stop this from happening.[38]

Were the Sino-Russian relationship exclusively about the West, reversing its course could be feasible by way of a compromise with Russia. Moscow, however, has embraced the rising China not just because of its desire to stem the expansion of the West but also to firm up regime security, serve the parochial interests of the Russian elite and encourage China's self-restraint towards Russia. These additional factors have led Russia to enter a much closer and less symmetrical relationship than the Kremlin might have initially intended.

Domestic politics have also facilitated Russia's cooperation with China in spite of the growing power imbalance between the two states. From the Kremlin's point of view, power asymmetry does not threaten Russia's domestic stability or Putin's regime survival because China – unlike the US – does not seek to interfere in Russian domestic politics. Dominant members of Putin's clique also benefit economically from growing ties with China. As a result, there is no domestic anti-Chinese lobby in the Russian corridors of power. In addition, China has adopted a policy of restraint towards Russia, manifested especially in self-imposed limitations on the pursuit of power in the post-Soviet space, especially Central Asia, convincing Russian elites of its benign intentions.[39] China deferred to Russia's great-power image, for instance when accepting the Kremlin's notional vision of 'Greater Eurasia', and showed patience even when Moscow's actions embarrassed Beijing.[40]

This is not to say that the Sino-Russian relationship is set in stone, as some Russian and Chinese commentators tend to portray it.[41] Both are dissatisfied with the post-Cold War order, but their expectations regarding its future shape differ. Being highly dependent on the external world, Beijing wants to strengthen economic globalisation, even if it would prefer to strip it of Western liberal underpinnings. Chinese elites may sympathise with the sovereigntist language of populists, but they are also leery of the populist tendency – demonstrated by Trump in the US and President Jair Bolsonaro in Brazil – to bash China.[42] Moscow, much less dependent on the external world, thrives on regional instability and does not perceive protectionism as a major problem. Russian elites see the wave of right-wing populism as proof of Western decline and a source of new opportunities. Russia's military adventurism may harm China's pursuit of economic interests as it has in the past. The annexation of Crimea, for instance, excluded one of the railway routes for the Belt and Road Initiative via Ukraine, and foreclosed the prospect for a China-built deep-sea port in Crimea. Beijing feels compelled to weigh the political benefits of close cooperation with Moscow against the economic losses stemming from Russia's sometimes rogue conduct.

Domestic politics can also imperil cooperation. For example, CEFC China Energy – a very large, private Chinese conglomerate – was on the verge of striking a landmark deal by purchasing 14% of shares of Russia's state-owned oil behemoth Rosneft for about $9bn from a Glencore–Qatari consortium. Chinese domestic politics intervened.[43] The CEFC chairman was arrested for suspected 'economic crimes' and the company effectively nationalised before the deal could be completed.

Conversely, Russian domestic politics may also inhibit Sino-Russian cooperation. In states with close economic ties to China – for instance, Sri Lanka or Malaysia – cooperation with Beijing has raised fears of inordinate Chinese leverage and become a salient domestic political liability for those in power.[44] Perceptions of Russia as a weaker partner in the bilateral relationship, worries about economic co-optation or coercion on Beijing's part, suspicions of Beijing-fuelled corruption, and anxiety about Russia's technological dependency on China and its exploitation by Chinese intelligence could provide the Russian opposition with potent political ammunition. Any Chinese shift away from the policy of restraint would also weaken Russian incentives for closer cooperation.

*   *   *

The idea that China and Russia are strategically aligned against the West often obscures relevant details and exaggerates negative implications of Sino-Russian ties for the West. At the same time, self-assuring observations about the lack of trust between Moscow and Beijing or an imminent clash of interests in the post-Soviet space constitute an insufficient basis for Western policy. A more nuanced understanding of the Sino-Russian relationship, with greater focus on the drivers of Sino-Russian cooperation, would help Washington and European capitals to formulate and implement more effective responses to the challenges it poses. In particular, it is worth pondering why the Russian elite has gradually accepted Russia's role as China's junior partner and its loss of influence to China, even as it has vigorously sought to counter a similar dynamic in its relations with the West.

Notes

1   See 'Emmanuel Macron In His Own Words (English)', *The Economist*, 7 November 2019, https://www. economist.com/europe/2019/11/07/ emmanuel-macron-in-his-own-words-english; and Simon Tisdall, 'Donald Trump Attempting to Play Nixon's "China Card" in Reverse', *Guardian*, 12 December 2016, https:// www.theguardian.com/us-news/2016/ dec/12/donald-trump-us-china-relations-taiwan-nixon.

2   US–China Economic and Security Review Commission, *2019 Report to Congress*, 116th Congress, First Session (Washington DC: US Government Publishing Office, 2019), https://www. uscc.gov/sites/default/files/2019-11/2019%20Annual%20Report%20 to%20Congress.pdf.

3   Editorial Board, 'What's America's Winning Hand if Russia Plays the China Card?', *New York Times*, 21 July 2019, https://www.nytimes. com/2019/07/21/opinion/russia-china-trump.html.

4   Andrea Kendall-Taylor and David Shullman, 'A Russian–Chinese Partnership Is a Threat to U.S. Interests', *Foreign Affairs*, 14 May 2019, https://www.foreignaffairs.com/ articles/china/2019-05-14/russian-chinese-partnership-threat-us-interests.

5   'Emmanuel Macron in His Own Words (English)'.

6   US–China Economic and Security Review Commission, *2019 Report to Congress*; and Munich Security Conference, 'Munich Security Report 2020: Westlessness', https:// securityconference.org/assets/user_

upload/MunichSecurityReport2020.pdf.

7   Stephen K. Wegren, 'Introduction: Prospects During Putin's Fourth Term', in Stephen K. Wegren (ed.), *Putin's Russia: Past Imperfect, Future Uncertain* (Lanham, MD: Rowman & Littlefield, 2019), p. 19.

8   Céline Marangé, 'Russia', in Thierry Balzacq, Peter Dombrowski and Simon Reich (eds), *Comparative Grand Strategy: A Framework and Cases* (Oxford: Oxford University Press, 2019), pp. 51–2.

9   See Alexander Lukin and Anatoly Torkunov, 'Trump's Policies and the Sino-Russian Entente', *Survival*, vol. 62, no. 2, April–May 2020, pp. 29–30.

10 See Alexander Korolev, 'Russia in the South China Sea: Balancing and Hedging', *Foreign Policy Analysis*, vol. 15, no. 2, April 2019, pp. 263–82.

11 See Mathieu Duchatel, 'How China Is Relying on Russia to Achieve "Strategic Stability" with the US', *South China Morning Post*, 13 October 2019, https://www.scmp.com/news/ china/diplomacy/article/3032436/ how-china-relying-russia-achieve-strategic-stability-us.

12 See Nicholas Trickett, 'Russia's FDI Outlook Grim, with No Chinese Rescue in Sight', Russia Matters, 11 July 2019, https://www.russiamatters. org/analysis/russias-fdi-outlook-grim-no-chinese-rescue-sight.

13 See Stephen Bierman and Elena Mazneva, 'Russia LNG Plant Gets $12 Billion from China amid Sanctions', Bloomberg, 29 April 2016, https://www.bloomberg. com/news/articles/2016-04-29/

russian-lng-project-gets-12-billion-china-loans-amid-sanctions.

14   See Lesley Wroughton and Patricia Zengerle, 'U.S. Sanctions China for Buying Russian Fighter Jets, Missiles', Reuters, 20 September 2018, https://www.reuters.com/article/us-usa-russia-sanctions/u-s-sanctions-china-for-buying-russian-fighter-jets-missiles-idUSKCN1M02TP.

15   See Zak Doffman, 'Huawei Soars in Russia as Putin Engages in New "Technological War"', *Forbes*, 3 November 2019, https://www.forbes.com/sites/zakdoffman/2019/11/03/huawei-soars-in-russia-as-putin-engages-in-new-technological-war/.

16   See Zheng Chen and Hang Yin, 'China and Russia in R2P Debates at the UN Security Council', *International Affairs*, vol. 96, no. 3, May 2020, pp. 787–805.

17   See Joe Uchill, 'Russia and China Get a Big Win on Internet "Sovereignty"', Axios, 21 November 2019, https://www.axios.com/russia-china-united-nations-internet-sovereignty-3b4c14d0-a875-43a2-85cf-21497723c2ab.html.

18   See, for instance, President of Russia, 'Joint Statement of the Russian Federation and the People's Republic of China', 8 June 2018, section III, http://kremlin.ru/supplement/5312.

19   See, for instance, President of Russia, 'Joint Statement of the Russian Federation and the People's Republic of China on Strengthening Global Strategic Stability in the Modern Era', 5 June 2019, http://kremlin.ru/supplement/5412; and President of Russia, 'Joint Statement of the Russian Federation and the People's Republic of China on the Current Situation in the World and Important International Problems', 4 July 2017, http://kremlin.ru/supplement/5219.

20   For instance, in 2019 both sides vowed to 'continue to make joint efforts to counter the politicization of the international human rights agenda, the application of a "double standards" policy and the use of human rights as a pretext for interfering in the internal affairs of sovereign states'. President of Russia, 'Joint Statement by the Russian Federation and the People's Republic of China on the Development of Comprehensive Partnership and Strategic Interaction Entering a New Era', 5 June 2019, http://kremlin.ru/supplement/5413.

21   *Ibid.*

22   See John Calabrese, 'China and Syria: In War and Reconstruction', Middle East Institute, 9 July 2019, https://www.mei.edu/publications/china-and-syria-war-and-reconstruction.

23   See Mark Landler, 'Trump Abandons Iran Nuclear Deal He Long Scorned', *New York Times*, 8 May 2018, https://www.nytimes.com/2018/05/08/world/middleeast/trump-iran-nuclear-deal.html.

24   See 'China, Russia and Iran Begin Joint Naval Drills', Al-Jazeera, 27 December 2019, https://www.aljazeera.com/news/2019/12/china-russia-iran-joint-naval-drills-191227183505159.html.

25   See Benoit Faucon, 'China Pulls Out of Giant Iranian Gas Project', *Wall Street Journal*, 6 October 2019, https://www.wsj.com/articles/china-pulls-out-of-giant-iranian-gas-project-11570372087.

26   See Olga Solovyeva, 'Rossiya investiruyet v okhvachennyi besporiyadkami Iran' [Russia invests

in unrest-ridden Iran], *Nezavisimaya Gazeta*, 21 November 2019, http://www.ng.ru/economics/2019-11-21/1_7733_iran.html.

[27] See Franz-Stefan Gady, 'The Significance of the First Ever China–Russia Strategic Bomber Patrol', *Diplomat*, 25 July 2019, https://thediplomat.com/2019/07/the-significance-of-the-first-ever-china-russia-strategic-bomber-patrol/.

[28] See Korolev, 'Russia in the South China Sea'.

[29] See Valbona Zeneli and Nataliia Haluhan, 'Why China Is Setting Its Sights on Ukraine', *Diplomat*, 4 October 2019, https://thediplomat.com/2019/10/why-china-is-setting-its-sights-on-ukraine/.

[30] See Bennett Murray, 'Russia's Awkward Dance with Vietnam', Foreign Policy Research Institute, 14 October 2019, https://www.fpri.org/article/2019/10/russias-awkward-dance-with-vietnam/.

[31] See Frank Sieren, 'Sieren's China: Rapprochement with Russia – EU Must Act', Deutsche Welle, 9 December 2019, https://www.dw.com/en/sierens-china-rapprochement-with-russia-eu-must-act/a-51581496.

[32] See, for example, Jane Perlez, 'China and Russia Reach 30-year Gas Deal', *New York Times*, 21 May 2014, https://www.nytimes.com/2014/05/22/world/asia/china-russia-gas-deal.html.

[33] Olga Tanas, Anna Shiryaevskaya and Dan Murtaugh, 'How Russia–China Gas Pipeline Changes Energy Calculus', Bloomberg, 25 November 2019, https://www.bloomberg.com/news/articles/2019-11-25/how-russia-china-gas-pipeline-changes-energy-calculus-quicktake. See also Pierre Noël, 'Nord Stream II and Europe's Strategic Autonomy', *Survival*, vol. 61, no. 6, December 2019–January 2020, pp. 89–95.

[34] See Henrik Stålhane Hiim and Stig Stenslie, 'China's Realism and the Middle East', *Survival*, vol. 61, no. 6, December 2019–January 2020, pp. 153–66.

[35] See Vuk Vuksanovic, 'Why Serbia Won't Stop Playing the Russian Card Anytime Soon', Carnegie Moscow Center, 28 October 2019, https://carnegie.ru/commentary/80188; and Maksim Samorukov, 'Novyy brat luchshe. Pochemu pomoshch' Rossii Balkanam ne dayet bylogo effekta' [The new brother is better. Why Russia's aid to the Balkans does not give its former effect], Carnegie Moscow Center, 28 April 2020, https://carnegie.ru/commentary/81657.

[36] See Jacob Mardell, 'China's Economic Footprint in the Western Balkans', Asia Policy Brief, Bertelsmann Stiftung, 2020, https://www.bertelsmann-stiftung.de/en/our-projects/germany-and-asia/news/asia-policy-brief-chinas-economic-footprint-in-the-western-balkans; and Heather A. Conley et al., 'China's "Hub-and-Spoke" Strategy in the Balkans', CSIS, April 2020, https://www.csis.org/analysis/chinas-hub-and-spoke-strategy-balkans.

[37] US–China Economic and Security Review Commission, *2019 Report to Congress*.

[38] See, for example, Michael O'Hanlon and Adam Twardowski, 'An Alliance Between Russia and China Is the Next Military Threat', *Hill*, 13 December

2019, https://thehill.com/opinion/
national-security/474424-an-alliance-
between-russia-and-china-is-the-next-
military-threat.

39   See Nadège Rolland, 'A China–Russia
Condominium over Eurasia', *Survival*,
vol. 61, no. 1, February–March 2019,
pp. 7–22.

40   For instance, when Moscow's use of
force against Georgia in 2008 over-
shadowed the opening of the 2008
Beijing Olympic Games.

41   See, for instance, Zhou Bo, 'As
China and Russia Draw Closer,
It Would Be a Fool's Errand for
Trump to Try to Separate Them',
South China Morning Post, 23 August
2019, https://www.scmp.com/
comment/opinion/article/3024049/
china-and-russia-draw-closer-it-

would-be-fools-errand-trump-try.

42   See Antonio C. Hsiang, 'Why Latin
American Populism Is Bad News for
China', *Diplomat*, 13 August 2019,
https://thediplomat.com/2019/08/
why-latin-american-populism-is-bad-
news-for-china/.

43   See Dmitry Zhdannikov, 'China's
CEFC Investigation Hits $9 Billion
Russian Oil Deal', Reuters, 22
August 2019, https://uk.reuters.com/
article/uk-rosneft-cefc/chinas-cefc-
investigation-hits-9-billion-russian-oil-
deal-idUKKBN1GY2XX.

44   See Tim Fernholz, 'China's
"Debt Trap" Is Even Worse than
We Thought', *Quartz*, 28 June
2018, https://qz.com/1317234/
chinas-debt-trap-in-sri-lanka-is-even-
worse-than-we-thought/.

Robert Stone's Fight for His Flag

Jonathan Stevenson

Child of Light: A Biography of Robert Stone
Madison Smartt Bell. New York: Doubleday, 2020. $35.00. 615 pp.

The novelist Robert Stone, who died in 2015 at age 77, never knew his father. His mother was a schizophrenic who was sometimes institutionalised. At age 17 and semi-orphaned, having been kicked out of his Catholic high school and become disenchanted with the prospect of death by switchblade as a member of an Irish-American street gang, he enlisted in the US Navy in search of a more abundant life. Thus he vaulted from the streets of New York to the world stage, and embraced geopolitics. From the attack transport ship USS *Chilton*, in Port Said, he saw French *Mirage*s mowing down helpless Egyptians during the Suez crisis of 1956. That inaugural fusion of individual quest and national identity helped mould his soul as a man and a writer. Fifteen years later, in South Vietnam to research *Dog Soldiers* (1974), his searing novel of that war's evisceration of America and winner of the National Book Award, he witnessed *Operation Dewey Canyon* II, in which US forces re-established an American base in Khe Sanh and supported South Vietnamese units infiltrating Laos to disrupt the North Vietnamese army's logistical operations on the Ho Chi Minh Trail. He did not directly experience much more of war, but he was compelled, perhaps uniquely, to inhale its fumes wherever they arose – as they did far from the actual field

Jonathan Stevenson is Managing Editor of *Survival* and IISS Senior Fellow for US Defence.

Survival | vol. 62 no. 6 | December 2020–January 2021 | pp. 213–222   https://doi.org/10.1080/00396338.2020.1851102

of battle – reporting, for instance, on navy deserters in Stockholm, where the novel actually took root. This expansive empathy made him one of the most astute chroniclers of Cold War America's veiled iniquity, and therefore of the American conscience writ large.[1]

He was discharged from the navy in 1958, got married in New York, started writing for newspapers and enrolled in New York University. Ever the romantic itinerant, he and his wife Janice took flight to New Orleans. Though he never finished college, his autodidacticism and narrative talents blossomed and, on the basis of chapters from what would eventually become *A Hall of Mirrors*, his prescient first novel about right-wing America, he received a fellowship at Stanford. In San Francisco he

met Ken Kesey, author of the iconic *One Flew Over the Cuckoo's Nest* and conductor of the 'acid tests', who introduced him to LSD. Now a father, Stone saw the Merry Pranksters off from California in Kesey's 'magic bus' *Furthur*, and greeted them months later in New York, having moved back to the Upper West Side. He got to know Neal Cassady and, less amiably, Jack Kerouac. The title of Stone's sardonic memoir *Prime Green: Remembering the Sixties* (2007) refers to a particularly vivid pre-dawn colour of the California light, ideally appreciated high. Drugs and excess permeated his fiction, and he recognised that his generation sometimes 'confused self-destructiveness with virtue and talent, obliteration with ecstasy, heedlessness with courage'.[2]

As Madison Smartt Bell shows in his effusive and unabashedly votive biography *Child of Light* – he and Stone were good friends, Bell enjoyed Janice's close cooperation, and he appears as a character in the book – Stone was a person of considerable warmth, candour and indeed weakness, but one who never let sentimentality get in the way of his hard-nosed assessments of humanity's innate vice. Though adulatory, Bell mounts no concerted argument for Stone's pre-eminence as a novelist. He seems content largely to proclaim extravagantly that Stone was a great writer and a great guy, crossing the boundary of acceptable indulgence with a saccharine and ill-advised 'Coda'. This is not the stuff of transcendent literary or political biography. The book, however, frequently reflects Bell's own acumen as a novelist and scholar. It is densely and agreeably picaresque, relaying telling anecdotes, deftly summarising and analysing plots, and duly arraying reviews good and bad. And *Child of Light* satisfyingly affirms Stone as a weathered observer of the American Century who, forged in the sixties, absorbed America's pain, saw through its grandiosity and called out its hypocrisy and delusion.

Quarrels with America

Of *A Hall of Mirrors*, Stone said, 'I had taken America as my subject, and all my quarrels with America went into it' (p. 108). His best-remembered books are big, political novels of ideas featuring people who want to put them into action and get it wrong. He believed that was how history got made. His characters screwed up because they were human. What passed for civilisation in the twentieth century was all about mistakes, and there wasn't much to be done about that except to situate the transgressions and the culprits in clarifying stories and control the damage. 'The purpose of fiction', he said in a famous 1985 interview in the *Paris Review*, 'is to help us answer the question we must constantly be asking ourselves: Who do we think we are and what do we think we're doing?'[3] His fiction did not embody reactive philippics; rather, it secreted sharp and considered judgements in rich narrative, 'fusing topical issues to eternal questions' (p. 231). His subjects remained, resolutely, 'America and Americans'.[4]

In *Dog Soldiers*, Ray Hicks, a viciously disaffected ex-marine looking to sell heroin smuggled from Vietnam to California, intentionally overdoses a counter-culture poseur named Gerald, drawing the panicked wrath of the middleman who has put the two together. As Gerald foams at the mouth, Hicks leaves it to the other guy to bring him back – if he's not already gone. Marge, the estranged wife of the squirrelly war correspondent who scored the heroin in Vietnam, is shocked and asks Hicks why he did it. 'I'm a Christian American who fought for my flag', says Hicks. 'I don't take shit from Martians.'[5] This has to be one of the most flatteningly mordant – and mordantly humanistic – lines in American literature.

Gerald's patronising, downwardly mobile pretence to the junkie valour that Hicks believed he had earned cost Gerald, and Stone rates Hicks's unforgiving unity of thought and action as admirable on a purely existential level as well as a reflection of America's self-abasement.

Like many of Stone's characters, Hicks is a victim of history, and in particular war. Yet *Dog Soldiers* involves no combat, and the story merely starts in Vietnam, moving quickly to California. The book's brilliance lies in its fierce demonstration that the Vietnam War contaminated the American homeland as well as destroying distant lands. Bell makes the point nicely:

> Stone had always intended to set this story in the United States, but it took him years of struggle to understand that its lodestone was in Vietnam – not so much in the combat zones, or even among the increasingly obscure issues and ideologies supposed to be at stake, but in the corrupt penumbra surrounding the American involvement. As in *A Hall of Mirrors*, he would find himself tracing the edges of a fissure in American society, in this case treating the Vietnam War as a wound. (p. 160)

A diligent researcher, Bell unearths in Stone's National Book Award acceptance speech his understanding of the diabolical circuit of American hubris, overreach and loss that he traced in his novel. The Vietnam era, said Stone, was one 'dominated by the good intentions of the American middle class; abroad it was a time of chaos and war because of those good intentions; while they are a generally progressive force domestically, they do not travel well' (p. 173).

Stone was not content merely to expose the toll of American peremptoriness. He also took pains to highlight the way in which it had been cynically internalised as practically unavoidable. In *A Flag for Sunrise* (1981), alongside *Dog Soldiers* probably Stone's finest book, burnt-out anthropologist Frank Holliwell, who had been in Vietnam with the CIA, is importuned by an old friend from the agency, worried about a dangerously left-leaning Catholic mission that is defying requests to leave a brutal Central American client state called Tecan, to discreetly assess the situation. There Holliwell links up with Tom Zecca, a jaunty CIA case officer, also scarred by his time in Vietnam but convinced of the sufficiency of his ethics. During a drunken car ride from neighbouring Compostela to Tecan, the two men, joined by a shaky reporter and his fretful wife, engage in an agonising exchange of moral relativism and acquired callousness. Zecca boasts that he never killed civilians, butchered corpses, torched hamlets or tortured Vietcong suspects. 'I don't claim virtue', he says. 'I don't claim to be a kindly man. I claim to be capable of honor.'[6] Stone accepts Zecca's resignation and questions Holliwell's quest for vindication. In the Cold War world, pragmatic results fell chronically short of ideals and good intentions, so being merely capable of honour and able to conjure it upon occasion was frequently the best a good man could do. In a related passage towards the end of the book, the fatalistic Father Egan notes that 'the truth was a fine thing, but it had to be its own reward'.[7] Bell suggests, credibly, that the line 'could stand as a late twentieth-century novelist's credo' (p. 224).

In *Outerbridge Reach* (1992), Stone uses Vietnam to address generational self-respect more explicitly. As the book begins, Owen Browne – a former naval officer and Vietnam veteran, now a weary yacht broker – has aborted a boat delivery due to a faulty bilge pump and wistfully reunited with a couple of Naval Academy classmates in Annapolis. Returning home to Connecticut via New York, he sits under the 'piss-yellow light of Penn Station', trying to remember how he felt in 1964 when he boarded a train for Annapolis to start his four years at the academy:

> The image would have been a romantic one, but romantic in the postwar modernist style. Its heroic quality would have been salted in stoicism and ennobled by alienation. As an uncritical reader of Hemingway, he would have imagined his future self suitably disillusioned and world-weary. On the morning in question, he would not have had the remotest conception of what such attitudes entailed. He would have awaited world-weariness and disillusionment impatiently, as spurs to higher-class and more serious fun. Of course, not even Hemingway enjoyed them much in the end.[8]

Neither did Browne, whose inability to forgive himself and his world for their failures spells his demise. He lets himself drown, lost at sea in an around-the-world, single-handed ocean race – cuckolded, ashamed and 'thinking it would be wonderful to have back the man he once had been'.[9] The tragedy of Vietnam, along with his country's ingrained and amnesiac venality, has robbed him of his faith in his own rectitude, and beyond that his capacity for contentment.

While Stone's quarrels with America never ended – how could they? – they receded a little in his later years, as he explored more intensely personal quandaries in two collections of short stories and, in his final novel, *Death of the Black-haired Girl* (2013), examined abortion and other domestic issues in the haze of 9/11. But he could not completely resist geopolitical subtext, however localised the context. In the overtly satirical story 'The Wine-dark Sea', from his second collection, Stone imagines a US secretary of defense blending the arrogance of Donald Rumsfeld and the mental decline of James Forrestal (the first occupant of the office, a suicide) who is holding a conference on a quaint Connecticut island.[10] Eric Floss, a bad-boy journalist who enjoys baiting provincials with conspiracy theories about 9/11, has heard about the secretary's 'spectacular mood-swings'.[11] Floss triggers a series of events that culminates in the secretary's public tantrum. Having drunkenly made a play for his ex-girlfriend's married sister, who has graciously provided him lodging, Floss blows off the story he's been commissioned to write. But a bystander's video goes viral and the secretary resigns, ending up in an institution, writing doggerel and attempting to end his life. A Stone novel wouldn't wind up so neatly, but he did summon a piquant symbol of what had then become – and is now again, in spades – a nasty, clueless US government.

Enlightened realist

The finiteness of US power is an implicit premise of the complicated, overly expository and undeniably ambitious *Damascus Gate* (1998), which concerns the Arab–Israeli conflict during the intifada. Even in the late 1990s, with the parties moving towards a two-state agreement brokered by the Clinton administration, the conflict seemed barely susceptible to US mediation. Here Stone confronts the matter of faith, as opposed to politics or state, more directly than he had before, casting Jerusalem and Gaza as vortices of outside as well as local religious agendas. Christopher Lucas, a guileless

American journalist, half-Jewish and raised Catholic, is looking for truth in Israel that he can't seem to find elsewhere. He uncovers a plot to blow up the Temple Mount hatched not by militant Palestinians or fanatical Israelis but by two unhinged American Jews who have formed an eclectic cult combining apocalyptic elements of Judaism, Christianity and Islam. Stone thus reveals his knowing sense of humour and the considerable weight he assigns to religion – also evident in *A Flag for Sunrise*, in which Holliwell falls in love with Sister Justin Feeney, a defiantly naive nun who is martyred. Putatively a non-believer, Lucas is nonetheless attracted to religion. Yet, faithful to Stone's realistic default, he novel's breathless climax turns not on any triumph of faith but on preventing its violent excesses – a far more basic imposition of minimal decency, and, again, often all that broken people under duress can manage.

Stone was a long way from a moral purist or a human perfectionist. Even so, given his richly counter-cultural and presumptively iconoclastic pedigree, it's a little jarring that his and Janice's marital dynamics verged on literary cliché: he played the wayward prodigy, she the near-saintly enabler. Bell faithfully reports the facts – his alcoholism, serial infidelity and eventual drug addiction, Janice's forbearance, succour and loyalty – and enshrines Janice's testimony that they stood 'two against the world' even if 'the ground sometimes seemed less than solid' (p. 189). He is also forthcoming about her acquiescence to the role, recounting that she 'would wryly describe herself as a "handmaid to genius"' and noting that 'the phrase was ironic on the surface but in fact she took this vocation with complete seriousness and had devoted most of her life to it' (p. 384). They did seem to exemplify a genuine form of *Zweisamkeit*. But this biographer also strains to sanctify even the most bourgeois thoughts of Robert and Janice as universally worthy – for example, fatuously endorsing their observation that the Third World poor handled their privation with dignity as identifying 'a transitive property of peasant cultures the world over' (p. 195). And Bell makes too much of Stone's being a political agent – 'a player of some significance on the world stage' (p. 242). Although some fiction writers do have zeitgeist moments, and Stone had at least a brief one when nuns were murdered in Central America as Sister Justin was in fictional Tecan, they tend to be fleeting.

Certain insights shine through the gauze of flattery and special pleading. In particular, Bell identifies Stone's conviction that ambition – the instinct for betterment – while motivationally useful, traffics in perilous delusion. 'Élan vital', the biographer writes, 'is what carried the pioneers over the next hill; it also engenders chronic dissatisfaction. In a Robert Stone novel, the quest for life more abundant always turns out to be folly. In this way, American dream becomes nightmare' (p. 448). With mankind's trajectory thus crushed, Stone felt obliged to pay serious attention to the generally low quality of human life. Bell quotes from an unpublished paper that Stone wrote: 'We want human suffering to mean something … We think it must. We insist on it' (p. 242). This imperative gives Stone's work its purpose, and redeems it. Reviewing *Children of Light* (1986) – his fourth novel, about shattered pilgrims of the film trade – for the *New York Times Book Review*, writer and critic Jean Strouse observed that Stone, somewhat like Graham Greene before him, was 'the apostle of strung out' (p. 278).[12] But he never succumbed to abject despair.

For Bell, Stone was a poignantly stoic figure. He staggered into old age, racked with emphysema yet still determined to live as he had, winding down his searching time on earth almost incidentally, with Janice by his side on the bathroom floor in his home in Key West. It was a fitting Mecca for an inheritor of the realist tradition of Ernest Hemingway, whose dramatic way out Stone fortunately abjured, even if he identified more with Joseph Conrad as an outsider haunted by the spectre of 'a flabby, pretending weak-eyed devil of a rapacious and pitiless folly' (pp. 164, 285).[13] For all his pessimism, Stone's idea of America had a basic if submerged integrity. In *Prime Green*, as Bell notes (p. 476), Stone wrote: 'My generation left the country better in some ways, not least in destroying the letter of the laws of racism and sexual discrimination. We were one of the generations to which the word "Romantic" might be applied – the offspring of a period inclined by history to highly value the Dionysian and the spontaneous, to exalt freedom over order, to demand more of the world than it may reasonably provide. We saw – may we not be the last to see – this country as blessed in its most generous hopes.'[14]

Stone himself fought for his flag, and made no apologies for doing it his way. 'Measuring ourselves against the masters of the present', he reflected at the end of his memoir, 'we regret nothing except our failure to prevail'.[15] He penned those words during the George W. Bush administration, as the Iraq and Afghanistan wars raged, and he died during Barack Obama's second term. He judged his country harshly but with qualified hope. Witnessing an America wilfully burning its virtues, Robert Stone's laments would be so much graver now.

Notes

[1] Parts of this essay draw on an article I wrote on Stone's work, published shortly after his death. See Jonathan Stevenson, 'Battered Souls: The Fiction of Robert Stone', *Commonweal*, 7 October 2015, https://www.commonwealmagazine.org/battered-souls.

[2] Robert Stone, *Prime Green: Remembering the Sixties* (New York: Ecco, 2007), p. 229.

[3] William C. Woods, 'Interview: Robert Stone, the Art of Fiction No. 90', *Paris Review*, no. 98, Winter 1985, https://www.theparisreview.org/interviews/2845/the-art-of-fiction-no-90-robert-stone.

[4] *Ibid.*

[5] Robert Stone, *Dog Soldiers* (Boston, MA: Houghton Mifflin, 1974), p. 202.

[6] Robert Stone, *A Flag for Sunrise* (New York: Alfred A. Knopf, 1981), p. 170.

[7] *Ibid.*, p. 437.

[8] Robert Stone, *Outerbridge Reach* (New York: Ticknor & Fields, 1992), pp. 11, 12.

[9] *Ibid.*, p. 383.

[10] Robert Stone, 'The Wine-dark Sea', in Robert Stone, *Fun with Problems: Stories* (Boston, MA: Mariner Books, 2010), pp. 56–100. Bell reports that an incident involving Robert McNamara was the initial inspiration (p. 479).

[11] *Ibid.*, p. 63.

[12] Jean Strouse, 'Heebiejeebieville Express', *New York Times Book Review*, 16 March 1986, https://archive.nytimes.com/www.nytimes.com/books/98/04/26/specials/stone-children.html.

[13] The epigraph of *Dog Soldiers* is a quote from Marlow out of Conrad's *Heart of Darkness*. In full, it reads: 'I've seen the devil of violence and the devil of greed and the devil of hot desire; but, by all the stars! these were strong, lusty, red-eyed devils that swayed and drove men – men, I tell you. But as I stood on that hillside, I foresaw that in the blinding sunshine of that land, I would become acquainted with a flabby, pretending weak-eyed devil of a rapacious and pitiless folly.' Joseph Conrad, *Heart of Darkness* (New York: Dover, 1990), p. 13.

[14] Stone, *Prime Green*, p. 228.

[15] *Ibid.*, p. 229.

Review Essay

Uncle Sam's Hidden Empire

Russell Crandall and Frederick Richardson

How to Hide an Empire: A History of the Greater United States
Daniel Immerwahr. New York: Farrar, Straus & Giroux, 2019.
$30.00. 528 pp.

The 1899 Greater America Exposition was intended to familiarise mainland Americans with their country's diverse colonial holdings. Taking place in the prairie metropolis of Omaha, Nebraska, the fair's primary draw was a series of staged villages housing Cubans, Filipinos, Hawaiians and Puerto Ricans, which were to allow fairgoers to admire the 'natives' that Uncle Sam had recently taken charge of through territorial acquisitions. With help from the army and president William McKinley, the organisers of the fair managed to get 35 Filipinos onto the USS *Indiana*, which then set sail for San Francisco, California. However, the ambiguous status of the United States' territories meant that, although the Filipinos believed themselves to be US citizens, the port authorities would not let them enter the country due to anti-immigration laws. Eventually, the Filipinos were allowed to make their way to Omaha, but the men who arrived were nothing like the 'half-wild, monkey-like dwarfs' that the organisers had envisioned. Instead, they were 'stylish dressers' who seemed to share few cultural differences with the white fairgoers (pp. 82–3).

Russell Crandall is a professor of American foreign policy and international politics at Davidson College in North Carolina, and a contributing editor to *Survival*. His latest book is *Drugs and Thugs: The History and Future of America's War on Drugs* (Yale University Press, 2020). **Frederick Richardson** graduated from Bowdoin College in 2019 and is a master's student at Johns Hopkins University's School of Advanced International Studies (SAIS).

Survival | vol. 62 no. 6 | December 2020–January 2021 | pp. 223–230   https://doi.org/10.1080/00396338.2020.1851103

This episode speaks to several core themes from American historian Daniel Immerwahr's *How to Hide an Empire*. The Greater America Exposition sought to educate an American public that had little understanding of what constituted the United States and, as Immerwahr demonstrates, this blindness to the extent of US empire has remained constant in every era, from the eighteenth century through to today. Moreover, while the Filipinos rightly considered themselves to be US citizens, their interaction with the immigration authorities demonstrated that definitions of citizenship were malleable, and that, just because a territory was technically part of the United States, this did not necessarily mean that the US was willing to treat its people as citizens. While an advertisement for the exposition included a tropical Uncle Sam with a banner reading 'The White Man's Burden' –

referencing the supposed responsibility of the United States to 'civilise' non-white populations – the horrific abuses that occurred in many of America's overseas holdings proved that Washington rarely felt burdened by legal or moral constraints. From using Panamanian jungles to test chemical weapons during the Second World War, to contaminating Bikini Atoll with nuclear tests during the Cold War, to the modern-day torture of prisoners in Cuba's Guantanamo Bay detention facility, the 'Greater United States' has often played host to nefarious activities that would have carried severe consequences on the mainland. With this in mind, Immerwahr aims to expand our view of the US to include these often-forgotten lands while conveying the steep costs of their neglect.

The western frontier and beyond

Immerwahr's story of the American empire begins even before independence from Great Britain, with the westward expansion led by frontiersmen such as Daniel Boone. Boone's establishment in 1769 of a settlement in Kentucky led the charge of white settlement past the Appalachians and the subsequent displacement of Native Americans from their land into a western area that president Andrew Jackson designated 'Indian Country'.

But white 'pioneers', as they fancied themselves, soon hungered for these lands, and the US government gave its approval, eventually forcing Native American tribes from all corners of the country into modern-day Oklahoma. Indeed, nearly all the territory represented on the present-day US 'logo map' (the most reproduced depiction of the country that includes only the lower-48 states) was, at one point, part of the Greater United States. Over time and through settlement, the US integrated these territories to such an extent that they form the present core of the American empire. But Immerwahr reminds us that 'the tendency of today's borders to stick in place can make the shapes of countries seem inevitable', which often reduces the story of American expansion to the construction of a 'jigsaw puzzle' in which each state falls nicely into place after a purchase or conquest (p. 46). In reality, American expansion was a lurching, messy process that was anything but inevitable.

After the continental United States had been consolidated, the desire to expand remained embedded in the American psyche. This, coupled with industrialisation, led to a bizarre, virtually unknown and undeniably fascinating chapter of American history in which the US annexed nearly 100 guano islands. As industrialisation progressed in the latter half of the nineteenth century, agriculture had to keep up with rising populations – and bird guano was the solution. In order to ensure a reliable supply of the potent (and acrid) fertiliser, president Franklin Pierce helped push through the Guano Islands Act of 1856, which allowed for any island containing guano deposits to be incorporated into the United States, provided that the island was previously unpopulated and unclaimed. By 1902, the United States had claimed 94 guano islands that were feeding the industrialised agriculture of the mainland. However, guano extraction was labour-intensive, and working conditions on these barren rocks were wretched. As Immerwahr quips: 'It offered all the backbreaking labor and lung damage of coal mining, but to do the job, you had to be marooned on a hot, dry, pestilential, and foul-smelling island for months' (p. 53). In one instance, black labourers who had been tricked into working on such an island revolted, killing five white overseers. Their defence, which reached the US Supreme Court, argued that the United States could not convict the men because the island did not fall under US jurisdiction. They lost and a dangerous precedent was set: Washington could claim dominion overseas no matter how flimsy its governance was on the ground.

Immerwahr's telling of the guano saga highlights one of the reasons that *How to Hide an Empire* is so compelling. The book draws examples from obscure corners of American history that keep the reader engaged while the author probes the consequences of overseas expansion. Even for the most informed of history buffs, *How to Hide an Empire* is sure to surprise as the author hammers home the bizarre and tragic nature of US imperialism.

One of the greatest boosters of US imperialism was New York governor – and later US president – Theodore Roosevelt, who believed that the frontier was integral in shaping American values, and who lamented its exhaustion in the American West. But, if the American frontier was gone, in his eyes there remained frontiers in foreign lands where 'wild' peoples, danger and adventure beckoned. When the USS *Maine* blew up in Havana Harbor in early 1898, Roosevelt's eye for adventurism compelled him to push the United States into a 'splendid little war' and lead the vaunted (especially in the infamous pro-war 'yellow press' dailies) Rough Riders' capture of San Juan Hill – cementing his legend and vaulting him to the vice presidency. Following a treaty with Madrid, Washington coolly assumed control of Cuba, the Philippines and Puerto Rico. In the aftermath, the US logo map no longer sufficed; many maps produced around the turn of the century added the new possessions of Hawaii, the Philippines, Puerto Rico, Samoa and Wake Island to the iconic outline of the lower 48. However, printing new territories on maps said nothing of the messy dynamics of incorporating new peoples into the American empire. Now that these new territories were officially part of the United States, the process of implementing American authority on the ground began.

To demonstrate the unreality of the American overseas project, Immerwahr traces how attitudes on the American mainland translated into US policy in its territories. For instance, in one particularly illuminating chapter, he details how the architecture and scale of the 'White City', a group of buildings erected for the 1893 World's Columbian Exposition in Chicago, Illinois, were brought to Manila more than a decade later. The architect of the White City, Daniel Burnham, was enlisted by authorities in the Philippines to bring order to what they perceived as an 'ancient pest-hole' (p. 125). Mainland attitudes – in this case the planning and structure of the so-called 'Progressive Era' – could be taken to extremes in the territories, which served as 'spaces for bold experimentation where ideas could be tried with practically no resistance, oversight, or consequences' (p. 124). In Chicago, Burnham had been forced to cut through endless amounts of red tape, but in the Philippines, he could simply dictate that a building go up and it would be executed without opposition.

Out of sight, out of mind

The use of overseas possessions for experimentation was not confined to architecture. Dr Cornelius P. Rhoads came to Puerto Rico to eradicate the hookworm parasite, but employed vastly different methods there than on the mainland. He selected certain patients to leave untreated in order to have a control group, and admitted in a letter to 'killing off 8 [Puerto Ricans] and transplanting cancer into several more' (p. 144). When the letter was made public it ignited a media firestorm that helped catalyse the rise of Puerto Rican nationalism. Rhoads claimed he was joking, and the affair did little to hinder his career. Indeed, during the Second World War Rhoads was commissioned as a colonel, put in charge of the Chemical Warfare Service's (CWS) medical service and oversaw gas testing on US soldiers – many of whom were Puerto Rican. For jungle tests, the CWS used an island off the coast of Panama, and although many of the soldiers suffered horrible after-effects, the dark legacy of the programme remained largely obscured until the 1990s – such was the advantage of taking non-white test subjects to a location away from the continental United States.

As Burnham's and Rhoads's stories demonstrate, US territories, which were often out of sight and out of mind for the American public, were not subject to the same regulatory or legal constraints as the continental United States. US authorities could get away with far more in the territories, and they often equated a lack of oversight with impunity. That being said, with the outbreak of the Second World War, once-distant locales such as Alaska, Guam, Hawaii and the Philippines suddenly came to the fore of America's preoccupations as they played host to the Japanese advance. As Immerwahr observes, 'across the empire, backwaters became battle stations' as troops and money flowed across America's far-flung holdings (p. 172). But while the US war machine was spread out across the empire, it was primarily concerned with defending the logo map. Consequently, staggering civilian casualties in the territories were largely swept under the rug.

Along with killing on an unprecedented scale, the Second World War also brought great leaps of innovation. At the beginning of the war, Japan had conquered territories that had formerly supplied the United States with rubber, putting the rubber-dependent US war machine at risk. Fortunately, American chemists, backed by substantial government funding, made breakthroughs that allowed Washington to use artificial rubber – negating its reliance on rubber plantations halfway across the world. But rubber was hardly the only raw material that the US was able to substitute through laboratory breakthroughs. As Immerwahr points out, 'silk, hemp, jute, camphor, cotton, wool, pyrethrum, gutta-percha, tin, copper, tung oil – for one after another, the United States found synthetic substitutes. Throughout its economy, it replaced colonies with chemistry' (pp. 270–1). These wartime innovations dramatically altered the post-war world. Colonies that had once provided vital resources were no longer all-important, as the homes of Americans became filled with plastics, nylon and polyester, and count-less other synthetic innovations. Immerwahr makes the argument that these synthetics in part allowed the United States to divest itself of its massive post-war territorial holdings. In late 1945, 51% of the population of the Greater United States (including occupied territories) lived outside the logo map. After the US granted the Philippines its independence the following year, ended the occupations of Japan and Germany in 1951 and 1955 respec-tively, and accepted Hawaiian and Alaskan statehood in 1959, only 2% of the population remained outside the 50 states. Obviously, the independence movements within the formerly held US territories played a role in winning autonomy for their nations, but the synthetics boom was a factor in allowing Washington to give up the vast majority of its overseas territory.

While the war reduced the United States' dependence on foreign com-modities, it also reinforced the need to maintain the 'pointillist empire'

(p. 390). The US military's strategy of 'island hopping' across the Pacific as a way to defeat Imperial Japan demonstrated that, with advancements in logistics and aviation, power could be exercised from strategic points around the globe without the need to hold significant swathes of territory. Therefore, the United States gradually traded its large colonies for tiny points on a map – points which could harbour planes, communications and, later, nuclear weapons. Over the years, the US has amassed some 800 of these overseas bases, which allow it to maintain a global military presence. However, in keeping with the tradition of past overseas territories, the legal ambiguity of these bases allows Washington to act in ways that it could not on the mainland.

It is no coincidence that, when the nuclear tests in Utah became untenable due to the fallout, the United States made Bikini Atoll its primary testing site. US citizens had recourse to fight the testing; the Bikinians did not. Similarly, when looking for a place to detain suspected terrorists indefinitely after 9/11, the CIA chose Guantanamo Bay – 'the least worst place', as secretary of

> *The US has engaged in cultural imperialism*

defense Donald Rumsfeld so chillingly put it – due to its purported lack of US sovereignty. Of course, this was later challenged in the courts, but the lesson remains: the pointillist empire is at once everywhere and nowhere. It is global in reach, but its absence from the public conscience has allowed for repeated abuse by Washington. Immerwahr's call for greater awareness of what goes on outside the logo map is well made: only by recognising the extent of US power can we curtail its abuses.

How to Hide an Empire also makes the case that American imperialism cannot be fully described in terms of territory. Since the Second World War, the United States has engaged in cultural imperialism in which its standards, language and products have spread globally, much like a virus. As Immerwahr describes it, in today's world 'powerful countries project their influence through globalization rather than colonization'. Most of the rest of the world has adopted American standards, creating 'stupefying privilege' for the US (pp. 264, 313). English has become the de facto global language, while everything from music to aviation has been standardised according to an American model. This has given the United States a home-court advantage in terms of production and globalisation, and has disadvantaged other countries as they struggle to adapt. The examples in *How to Hide an Empire* with respect to the cultural component of imperialism are compelling (stop signs, ASCII characters) and add a unique, if unexpected, angle to Immerwahr's argument. While the adoption of standards comes from the bottom up and is therefore less dramatic than the taking of territory, it nonetheless reflects the ever-advancing conquest of other cultures and peoples.

*   *   *

Overall, *How to Hide an Empire* is an expansive, meticulously crafted book with a strong argument. Immerwahr could have easily gotten lost in the details of his examples or stumbled over the sheer chronological diversity of the subject, but he maintains an even hand throughout, steadily guiding the reader through the development of the American empire. He has a talent for picking stories that both advance his case and draw readers in, and his research was predictably thorough for a trained academic. Immerwahr is no fan of America's hidden empire, but he never lets his distaste overwhelm his objectivity. His carefully curated primary sources are a particular highlight, and he analyses them with a wittiness that is sure to win him acclaim among casual readers. *How to Hide an Empire* proves the importance of including the Greater United States in any US history, and Immerwahr's talented storytelling makes the book a joy to read.

Book Reviews

United States
David C. Unger

We're Still Here: Pain and Politics in the Heart of America
Jennifer M. Silva. Oxford and New York: Oxford University
Press, 2019. £16.99/$24.95. 206 pp.

Ever since Donald Trump's upset 2016 victories in former blue-collar Democratic bastions such as Michigan, Pennsylvania and Wisconsin, a growing number of political scientists, sociologists, historians and journalists have sought to explain to themselves and their readers why working-class people made the electoral choices they did that year – including the choice, in many cases, of not voting at all.

Jennifer Silva's *We're Still Here* is one of the best such books I have read. Chief among its merits are the diverse range of people Silva interviews – young, middle-aged, single, coupled, divorced, white, African American and Latinx – and her skill at letting them tell their own stories in their own distinctive and revealing ways. Silva freely shares her scholarly interpretations of their stories, but she does not allow her comments to drown them out.

Silva's sociological analyses will likely be familiar to readers of *Survival*, but the autobiographical stories her subjects tell, and their explanations of how and why they vote (or don't), read like tales from a completely different world, one scarcely known to people ensconced in comfortable middle-class or professional lives. Taking in these searing accounts of chronic struggle and suffering, and reading about the very different ways the author's interviewees have found to retain some dignity and carry on from one day to the next, immerses the reader in a culture where presidential candidates and party platforms seem almost irrelevant.

Survival | vol. 62 no. 6 | December 2020–January 2021 | pp. 231–238   https://doi.org/10.1080/00396338.2020.1851104

Silva, who teaches sociology at Indiana University, conducted her research in a region she calls 'Coal Brook', in the anthracite-coal counties of northeastern Pennsylvania, an area that was already beginning to undergo economic decline when the family of presidential candidate Joe Biden moved from Scranton to Delaware in the early 1950s. Since then, most of the coal seams have been abandoned and the region's economic decline has grown exponentially worse. Coal Brook today is a place where intact families are rare, opioid addiction is widespread and the granddaughters of white coal miners live alongside people of colour fleeing the gun violence of inner-city Philadelphia. Steady jobs are hard to find and hold in Coal Brook, but housing there is cheaper than anywhere else nearby, making it difficult for many to consider moving away.

Silva tells us she is interested in deciphering 'the puzzle of working-class politics' – broadly, why working-class people seem to vote against their own supposed economic interest. Her definition of 'working class' is robust and nuanced, built around the material circumstances, family patterns and life-styles of her subjects, and how they define themselves. She does not rely on dry statistical categories such as 'non-college-educated white males', or on regression analyses drawn from batteries of carefully phrased polling questions. Her subjects are people who think of themselves as working-class individuals from working-class families in working-class towns. Yet, to return to Silva's 'puzzle', their attitudes towards politics have little to do with unions or any traditional notions of labour solidarity at the workplace or the ballot box.

Silva expresses hope that the people she spoke with will find their way to new kinds of social solidarity by drawing on their shared pain and experience of addiction, but there is little evidence that her interview subjects are prepared for a reorientation from individual coping strategies to group action. These are people who believe they have learned the hard way not to trust anyone but themselves.

Coal Brook is a very particular slice of America that may not be broadly representative of places outside Appalachian coal country. But the community and its inhabitants are real, and still there.

Manufacturing Decline: How Racism and the Conservative Movement Crush the American Rust Belt
Jason Hackworth. New York: Columbia University Press, 2019.
£25.00/$30.00. 316 pp.

In this well-researched, data-driven book, Jason Hackworth makes a persuasive case that the devastating demographic and fiscal declines that have turned once-thriving rust-belt cities into quasi-wastelands were not simply the result of impersonal market forces or the supposedly spendthrift policies of left-wing mayors, but were the predictable, if not always intended, result of neoliberal nostrums such as 'right-sizing', the systematic demolition of residential properties, and regulatory and tax constraints imposed by state governments. Not so coincidentally, he continues, struggling cities such as Detroit, Flint and Saginaw, Michigan; Youngstown, Ohio; and Rochester, New York, have large African-American and other minority-group populations, while their state legislatures are generally more politically responsive to largely white suburban and rural electorates. Hackworth also shows how African-American neighbourhoods within these cities have been specially targeted for downsizing and right-sizing projects, while their mythologised racial 'otherness' has been weaponised to mobilise white suburban and rural voters to elect legislators who compel cities to adopt these neoliberal policies.

Manufacturing Decline has a clear point of view but is not a polemical tract. Hackworth, who teaches geography and planning at the University of Toronto, critically examines governmental and non-governmental planning documents for each city he discusses. He makes good use of comparative property-value tables, which he cross-correlates with census data on demographic patterns and voting data to illustrate his arguments, and to counter some of the more airy and wishful data-free formulations of conservative and libertarian think tanks.

Hackworth concedes that, done properly, right-sizing could produce benefits. Demolishing vacant hulks and replacing them with green space, for example, could improve living conditions and raise property values for remaining residents. Pruning infrastructure systems built to service the larger populations of past decades could free up scarce fiscal resources for more immediately valuable uses. He notes the pledges of today's right-sizing planners to avoid repeating the acknowledged mistakes of the urban-renewal schemes of the 1960s that uprooted neighbourhoods and came to be disparagingly relabelled 'negro removal'.

But how, asks Hackworth, can the projected savings from consolidating infrastructure systems be reconciled with contemporary planners' explicit claims that no existing residents will be displaced? As he pointedly notes, plans for demolition are elaborately spelled out and budgeted for, but plans for rehousing displaced residents are left vague and aspirational.

Hackworth understands that the decline of rust-belt cities has deeper causes, such as the offshoring of the American manufacturing economy, that reach well beyond the political and racial calculations of state legislators or the ideological agendas of think tanks. What he seeks to demonstrate in this book is that the way these global economic trends actually play out in the lives of rust-belt city residents – how the burdens of urban decline are distributed and how much

scope elected municipal governments have to protect the interests of their constituents – are essentially political decisions.

**The Politics of Losing: Trump, the Klan, and the
Mainstreaming of Resentment**
Rory McVeigh and Kevin Estep. New York: Columbia University
Press, 2019. £28.00/$34.00. 310 pp.

Donald Trump's appeals to the resentful, to people on the losing end of globalisation, to white supremacists: these are themes that have been explored again
and again since Trump's surprise victory in the 2016 presidential election. This
volume, which co-authors Rory McVeigh and Kevin Estep tell us they started
writing weeks before that election, offers something different, more ambitious
and more valuable. *The Politics of Losing* is a comparative historical study explor-
ing the nature of the ideological and sociological appeals that brought the Ku
Klux Klan to its three periods of peak membership – during Reconstruction,
in the 1920s and in reaction to the 1960s civil-rights movement – and comparing those appeals with the messaging and voter targeting of the 2016 Trump
campaign. Originally intended to trace historic continuities on the margins of
mainstream politics – neither author thought Trump had any chance of winning
– it turned into a case study of what happens when a once marginal movement
takes over a mainstream political party.

McVeigh, who teaches sociology at the University of Notre Dame, and Estep,
who teaches cultural and social studies at Creighton University, found that the
main theme linking 2016 Trump voters with past iterations of the Klan was
not white racism or white nationalism per se, but a belief that self-styled 'real
Americans' were losing economic ground, social status and political dominance to newly enfranchised or newly arrived populations – be they African
Americans, immigrants, Roman Catholics, Jews or whomever. The authors
point out that the 2016 Trump campaign, like the Klan before it, appealed to
the need these voters felt to defend their relative status and their views of what
America ought to be before it was too late.

The crucial difference separating these historical episodes is that the Trump
movement succeeded in taking over one of the major political parties, something the Klan repeatedly tried, and failed, to do. That difference could prove
decisive. In each of the earlier episodes, one or the other of the mainstream
parties managed to co-opt enough of the Klan's support base to send it into steep
organisational decline while holding on to its own, more centrist, political identity. But that history may not be a reliable guide to what will happen this time.
Trump did not so much lead his base into mainstream Republicanism as lead

the mainstream Republican Party into his own particular brand of resentment politics – hence the subtitle of this book. Republicans have been tapping into the politics of resentment for half a century, since the days of Richard Nixon's 'silent majority', if not earlier. But before Trump, this strategy was intended mainly to attract votes for a much broader Republican agenda, including trickle-down tax cuts, free-trade agreements, business deregulation and a muscular, militarised foreign policy. Some elements of that older Republican agenda remained visible in Trump's 2020 re-election campaign, while others, such as free trade and military muscle-flexing abroad, were unceremoniously discarded.

As sociologists in good standing, McVeigh and Estep construct a model featuring a supply-and-demand market for social status, in which, for example, the influx of women voters after the adoption of the 19th Amendment to the US Constitution threatened the status of male voters, just as the prospect of increased black voting in the Reconstruction era, and then again in the civil-rights era, threatened the status of white voters. But if sociological models are not your thing, the historical narratives amply suffice to make the authors' point. White nationalism, they conclude, will remain a potent political force until such time as America achieves full social integration. Despite the heartening surge of white support for the Black Lives Matter movement, that day now appears far off.

The Cult of the Constitution
Mary Anne Franks. Stanford, CA: Stanford University Press, 2019. £20.99/$26.00. 256 pp.

Mary Anne Franks believes that American gun enthusiasts, and especially the National Rifle Association (NRA), have built a cult around the Second Amendment, wrenching it from its constitutional context and wielding it in ways that especially constrain the rights of women, African Americans and other less-privileged people to public expression, personal privacy and physical security. Franks, a law professor at the University of Miami School of Law, cites ample evidence to prove her case. She points out that the NRA's Second Amendment fundamentalism in its present extreme form is a relatively recent development, driven by the evolution of American fundraising and lobbying techniques over the past few decades, which have created organisational incentives to adopt ever more extreme positions.

In line with mainstream Second Amendment scholarship, Franks situates the amendment's intent and meaning in its militia clause, which guarantees to states a mechanism for resisting potential federal tyranny. As such, it is not about the individual's right to bear arms, be it for the purposes of hunting, home defence, standing one's ground and so on. That mainstream interpretation was, however, set aside by the Supreme Court's *Heller* decision in 2008, and an individual right to bear arms is now the law of the land.

Franks is far from alone in arguing that the NRA promotes a constitutionally distorted and socially damaging interpretation of the Second Amendment. But her argument stands out from the mainstream view for its strong rooting in feminist and identity-politics theory. For Franks, the Second Amendment, even in its non-distorted form, is shadowed by the original sin of having been drafted by an assembly of white, propertied men, doubly suspect for being part and parcel of a centuries-old constitutional order based on white supremacy and patriarchy, and condemned anew in the present for its adverse effects on women and minorities.

Franks is in more controversial territory when it comes to what she calls 'First Amendment fundamentalism'. She aims her fire at civil-liberties groups in general and, in particular, the American Civil Liberties Union (ACLU) and Electronic Frontier Foundation (EFF), for erecting what she sees as a cult surrounding the First Amendment's guarantee of free speech. In the case of the ACLU, she sees the same kind of fundraising and lobbying dynamics at work as those that pushed the NRA to adopt more and more extreme positions. Particularly where internet speech is concerned, she condemns both the ACLU and the EFF for weaponising the First Amendment to enable and incentivise social networks, tech giants and other assorted bad actors to intimidate, silence and inflict harm on women and other targets. She is particularly, and rightly, concerned with the way social-media companies have misused Section 230 of the Communications Decency Act of 1996 to shield themselves from accountability.

First Amendment fundamentalism – which tends to dismiss other constitutionally protected rights, such as privacy, in the name of free speech, and to stretch the Constitution's guarantee against government censorship to apply to private-sector actors as well – is a genuine and widely acknowledged problem. The ACLU itself wrestled with some of these dilemmas after drawing internal criticism for litigating on behalf of organisers of the deadly 2017 'Unite the Right' rally in Charlottesville, Virginia.

But Franks's broad-brush approach undermines the power of her argument. She is sometimes overhasty in imputing motives based on what is at best circumstantial evidence, such as the identities of funders for research projects, causes, parties or candidates, or implying guilt by association, for example in condemning the ACLU based on the politics of its clients.

In her efforts to cite written sources who agree with her, Franks sometimes puts advocacy journalism on the same level as legal and academic scholarship.

It's fine to cite and footnote both kinds of sources. But I wish she had taken more care to indicate in the text which was which. These techniques may work in the courtroom, but they are a weakness here.

Franks's approach is at times avowedly illiberal. She sees traditional liberal values as reflecting their origins in a white, male, privileged world and upholds as a counter-value the rights of oppressed groups. She concludes with a paean to the equal-protection clause of the 14th Amendment. But there is tension she can never overcome between upholding constitutional equality for all and implementing special protections for some based on their less-privileged place in society.

Breaking the Two-party Doom Loop: The Case for Multiparty Democracy in America
Lee Drutman. Oxford and New York: Oxford University Press, 2020. £18.99/$27.95. 272 pp.

Lee Drutman offers an immodest proposal to purge toxic partisanship from the American electoral system and thereby save American democracy. If we fail to act now, he warns, America's democratic system will succumb to a death spiral that has, in fact, already begun.

Drutman offers a menu of democracy-saving solutions. One is ending first-past-the-post voting for most federal offices and replacing it with the kind of ranked-choice voting and proportional representation used by other democracies to create incentives for multiparty coalitions. Another is ending congressional primaries to encourage the selection of more moderate party nominees. Yet another is to expand the House of Representatives to bring its members closer to their constituents. These are sweeping changes, as Drutman acknowledges, but all could be achieved without amending the Constitution if enough support could be enlisted from the political beneficiaries of the present system. Under the right circumstances, Drutman argues, it should be possible to do so.

A political scientist who teaches at the Johns Hopkins University Center for Advanced Governmental Studies, Drutman is not big on understatement or subtlety. Even with its scholarly apparatus, *Breaking the Two-party Doom Loop* sometimes brings to mind the 'for Dummies' manuals that became popular in the 1990s. Frequent subheadings and guideposts to the argument can be helpful, giving the reader an opportunity to absorb and reflect. But in this book, the sub-headings are so frequent and melodramatic that they leave the reader with the feeling of being hustled and hyped along towards the author's preconceived menu of electoral reforms.

These stylistic annoyances are all the more regrettable since Drutman has serious arguments to make and serious remedies to propose. He starts from the premise that, 40 years ago, America had what was only nominally a two-party system. In reality, he explains, it was more like a four-party system, populated by liberal Republicans, conservative Republicans, liberal Democrats and conservative Democrats. The internal diversity of the two major parties made possible a politics of compromise and shifting coalitions, ideally suited, as Drutman points out, to America's constitutional structure of checks and balances and separation of powers.

Over the past four decades, however, the Democrats and Republicans have developed into ideologically sorted, hierarchically dominated parties in do-or-die competition with each other. As a result, each party now battles to delegitimate, destroy and marginalise the other, a process, Drutman believes, that is already well on the way to destroying American democracy.

Drutman sees the destructive political developments of recent decades as largely the result of inappropriate party structures. Checks and balances depend on the avoidance of national parties with national agendas – which Founding Father James Madison warned against as 'factions' – and on achieving compromise solutions. The de facto four-party system, in Drutman's account, favoured such practices, but the current two-party system makes them impossible. Since Drutman sees no way of returning to the four-party past, he proposes leaping forward into a formal multiparty future. Federal representatives would be elected from multi-member districts, which would permit replacing first-past-the-post voting with systems of ranked choice or proportional representation. Although presidential and senatorial races must produce sole winning candidates by constitutional design and dictate, ranked-choice voting and proportional representation could still be used to encourage coalition government.

But what if the United States' growing political polarisation is less a function of how Americans vote than of the wrenching economic and social changes of globalisation? Similar political trends have appeared in other industrialised countries, as outsourcing and austerity have alienated centre-left and centre-right parties from their old working- and middle-class bases of electoral support, with more polarising parties rising to fill the void. In that case, even the most radical of electoral reforms might yield only marginal political effects. Germany's Weimar constitution of 1919 was based on proportional representation and multiparty competition. But it was an artificial graft, not deeply rooted in Germany's political culture, and Adolf Hitler proved able to game it to notoriously immoderate and uncompromising ends.

Europe
Hanns W. Maull

The Last President of Europe: Emmanuel Macron's Race to Revive France and Save the World
William Drozdiak. New York: PublicAffairs, 2020. £20.00/$16.99.
256 pp.

This concise, elegant and very readable portrait of Emmanuel Macron builds on several interviews that author William Drozdiak was able to conduct with the French president. We therefore get a strong flavour of how Macron sees the world around him, his tasks and his role as a political leader. The book is organised into three parts, which cover France, Europe and the world at large. This closely follows the logic of Macron's political project, the first step of which was to launch reforms to rebuild the socio-economic foundations of France. This persuaded Germany to join France in providing political leadership for Europe's internal reconstruction and its transformation into a global player. The goal was 'strategic autonomy' – a Europe that could hold its own in a world of geopolitical competition and power politics.

After detailing a blizzard of domestic reforms implemented during Macron's first two years in office, Drozdiak then turns to the challenge of the Yellow Vests movement that starkly exposed the divide separating rich and poor, metropolitan and rural France – a divide that for too long has been neglected by French elites. Macron astutely responded to this challenge by reinventing his presidency (and himself as president) through a series of town-hall meetings across France, lasting a total of 39 hours. During these meetings Macron met with some 2,300 mayors and other elected representatives, along with 1,000 young people, 400 environmental activists and 150 community planners. In-person meetings were backed up by a massive online effort to record grievances and collect suggestions and ideas. The government's response was to be presented in a speech, carefully prepared for weeks, that was to be televised on Monday, 15 April 2019 at 8pm on major radio and TV channels. According to Drozdiak, the speech was a powerful one. Yet it was never broadcast, because at seven o'clock that evening word reached Macron that Notre Dame, the 850-year-old cathedral that is perhaps the most powerful symbol of France as a nation, stood in flames. This was a tragedy that shook the whole country; Macron almost immediately decided to cancel his speech.

In retrospect, this tragedy was but the forerunner of another devastating blow: the COVID-19 pandemic, which hit France after Drozdiak completed his book. Yet the pandemic was to produce an outcome that Macron had sought

Survival | vol. 62 no. 6 | December 2020–January 2021 | pp. 239–245   https://doi.org/10.1080/00396338.2020.1851105

from the first day of his presidency: a close rapport with German Chancellor Angela Merkel around an ambitious agenda for the European Union. Merkel had hesitated for years, diluting or stalling Macron's rapid-fire European initiatives; it was only the devastations of the pandemic in France, Italy and Spain that finally persuaded her of the need for bold advances. The result was the €500 billion Franco-German European Recovery Fund launched in May 2020, which cleared the way for a massive European effort to overcome the damage of the pandemic and modernise the European economy.

The third part of *The Last President of Europe* deals with Macron's efforts to position France as, in his own words, a 'key mediating power' in pursuit of an international order that will make 'globalization a little more human and humanist' (p. 168). In pursuit of this mission, Macron has tried to cultivate ties with Donald Trump and Vladimir Putin, hoping to make France an effective interlocutor for both the United States and Russia. Overall, this is perhaps the most interesting and revealing part of the book, not least in its description of Trump's appalling performance as an ally. The chapters on France in the world vividly demonstrate the limitations of a country that, without Europe, will not be able to hold its own. Macron is well aware of this predicament, and has tried hard to mitigate and overcome it. Yet, as Drozdiak concludes:

> Whether Macron can restore momentum to the cause of a more integrated Europe … remains uncertain. If he succeeds, he could infuse a new life into Europe's ambition to serve as a shining beacon of democracy, freedom, and prosperity … But if he fails, then Europe risks becoming irrelevant or worse … In that event, Macron may have served, tragically and reluctantly, as the last president of Europe. (p. 213)

Germany: A Nation in Its Time: Before, During, and After Nationalism, 1500–2000
Helmut Walser Smith. London and New York: Liveright, 2020.
£30.00/$39.95. 608 pp.

This great work of historical analysis explores the emergence of a German nation and the evolution of the way in which its people thought about and related to it. Germany, according to Helmut Walser Smith, was not 'imagined' by nationalists; its inhabitants first related to places and spaces. The author shows that nations are real in different ways at different times – thus, there was, or is, 'a Germany before, during, and after nationalism' (p. xi). A second key argument of this book is that, historically speaking, Germany has not been particularly violent: during the eighteenth and nineteenth centuries, France and Britain were the principal martial powers.

So how did Germany succumb to the paroxysm of violence and industrialised murder perpetrated by the Nazi regime? Walser Smith traces this development through four parts. Part One, 'The Nation Before Nationalism', shows, mostly through the study of contemporaneous maps and the accounts of travellers, both German and foreign, how Germans came to think of themselves and their country as distinct. The 'Copernican Turn' (Part Two) towards nationalism as a particular – and potentially highly violent – ideology takes place in the eighteenth century. In sources from that time, the author finds the first references to what he calls 'sacrificial patriotism', a form of emotional attachment to one's country that includes a willingness to make sacrifices for it. At that time, however, Germany was many countries, not only Prussia and Austria, but also Bavaria, Württemberg and Sachsen, to name a few. Patriotism thus produced 'a nation deeply divided' (p. 87).

The shift towards *German* nationalism took place in the early nineteenth century – not, the author insists, during the Napoleonic Wars, as the conventional wisdom would have it, but in their aftermath. He writes that the age of nationalism, which Germany entered after the Congress of Vienna, was 'an era of relative peace' for the country: Britain, France and Russia were at war about three times as much during the period as was Germany or Austria (p. 196). During the second half of the century, Germany became a modern, industrial and increasingly urban nation-state, formally united through the war with France in 1870–71. Yet, as Walser Smith points out, 'German unification was never a foregone conclusion' (p. 197). However strongly the second Wilhelmian empire tried to mould its peoples into Germans, strong regional attachments continued even as a sense of belonging to the German nation grew.

This nationalism became tinged with fanaticism starting in the early twentieth century, but it was only after the First World War that Germans entered what the author calls the 'Nationalist Age' (Part Four). Just as Germany had experienced a shift towards nationalism in the aftermath of the Napoleonic Wars, the fallout of the First World War was to make nationalism Germany's dominant ideology (p. 294). The author uses two key concepts to help explain Germany's descent into the hell of nationalistic extremism: 'sacrifice for' and 'sacrifice of'. 'Sacrifice for' refers to the act of giving one's life for the higher purpose of the nation in war. Walser Smith illustrates the emotional power and destructive force of this kind of sacrifice by telling the story of Käthe Kollwitz, the famous artist and sculptor who lost her son in the first weeks of the First World War in 1914 and spent much of her career wrestling with that loss through her sculpture.

A willingness to 'sacrifice for' would eventually be twisted through humiliation, despair and rage into the perilous notion of 'sacrifice of' as nationalism turned inward against the country's Jews and outward in a racist push to secure *Lebensraum*. Chapter 12 ('Death Spaces') unsparingly summarises the mass murder committed by Germany before and during the war, not just in the Holocaust but in other settings too, as in the killing of about two million Soviet prisoners of war during the second half of 1941. Part Five ('After Nationalism') explores how Germans eventually managed to settle into what Willy Brandt called a 'dignified national life' (p. 410) after the catastrophe of Nazi rule, collectively developing what Dolf Sternberger described as a 'living and not a deathly concept of fatherland' (p. 425). In the epilogue, which brings the story to the present, the author argues that this last shift now seems deeply entrenched, despite the signs that a new, populist, right-wing nationalism is emerging. Germany has become a nation capable of compassion, he concludes. This erudite, beautifully written study provides not only deep insights into the evolution of modern Germany, but also a fresh perspective on nationalism itself, still one of the world's most powerful ideologies.

Tipping Point: Britain, Brexit and Security in the 2020s
Michael Clarke and Helen Ramscar. London: I.B. Tauris, 2020.
£16.99. 318 pp.

After what Michael Clarke and Helen Ramscar call the United Kingdom's 'complete nervous breakdown' (p. 237) during the 2010s, it seems that the country's many problems are only to be compounded in the 2020s by a range of domestic and international threats. In ten dense chapters, the authors provide a comprehensive stocktaking of these threats, detailing what they define as Britain's 'long-term challenges' (Part One), 'immediate challenges' (Part Two) and the 'Brexit challenge' (Part Three). The picture that emerges is not pretty: the authors present a world characterised by the return of traditional power politics, global economic turmoil, pervasive social upheavals and a deep crisis of liberal democracy. As they see it, the 2020s will challenge the security of all European countries, but the UK's departure from the EU will complicate things further, both for itself and for its neighbours. Brexit, they argue, has thrown the country into a constitutional crisis that threatens the very future of the United Kingdom, while its foreign-policy apparatus, weakened by a decade of neglect, displays a 'structural mismatch between the official aspiration to keep Britain on the front line of world diplomacy … as against constrained resources – people, money, experience' (p. 241). Keep in mind that this assessment was written before the coronavirus pandemic.

What is the country to do? Part Four explores what the authors term the UK's governmental and societal 'security capabilities' – the power resources, both hard and soft, that the country could mobilise to meet the challenges of the 2020s. The balance sheet shows strengths – Britain's still impressive (if badly stretched) military forces, its diplomatic and intelligence assets, and its vibrant, open society and economy – but also significant weaknesses, such as the comparatively poor performance of the British economy in terms of productivity, trade, investment and wages. The authors are moderately confident that 'Britain will remain the most significant military power in Europe' (p. 205), but note three important caveats having to do with the scale of Russia's challenge to European security; problems of overstretch, sustainability and credibility in the deployment of military force; and the pace of innovation in military technology.

As the authors see it, the next few years will be decisive. They advise that a 'strategic surge' is needed for the UK to avoid further disarray and international irrelevance. Such a surge, which the concluding chapter sketches in some detail, would mobilise the country's significant strengths to counteract a declining European ability to adapt to an accelerating pace of strategic change. In addition, the surge would reorient the UK away from its present 'national unhappiness' (p. 248) by 'moving decisively towards a more federal' political structure (p. 251), rebalancing the economy, and healing painful and disruptive social divisions. Implementing this surge could, in the authors' view, make Britain 'a European game changer' (p. 253).

Europe's Crisis of Legitimacy: Governing by Rules and Ruling by Numbers in the Eurozone
Vivien A. Schmidt. Oxford and New York: Oxford University Press, 2020. £25.00/$35.00. 358 pp.

Surplus Citizens: Struggle and Nationalism in the Greek Crisis
Dimitra Kotouza. London: Pluto Press, 2019. £22.99/$29.95. 291 pp.

The "Greek Crisis" in Europe: Race, Class and Politics
Yiannis Mylonas. Leiden: Brill, 2019. £121.00/€140.00. 259 pp.

Europe's Crisis of Legitimacy is an important book. It offers an impressively detailed, thorough and perceptive analysis of what happened in the eurocrisis and why, taking the European governments and institutions involved to task for imposing bad solutions on crisis-hit countries and sticking to them rigidly, and then taking corrective action without admitting their previous mistakes. Europe's crisis managers, argues author Vivien Schmidt, based their policy prescriptions for the crisis on the largely erroneous assumption that the problem was excessive public (rather than private) debt. In fact, public-sector indebtedness in Greece was the exception, rather than the rule; in most countries affected by the crisis, the problems were caused by reckless lending in the banking sector. On the basis of their flawed analysis, the EU imposed one-size-fits-all solutions on the widely diverging socio-economic dynamics of Cyprus, Greece, Ireland, Portugal and Spain.

Schmidt's indictment of this approach draws on the concept of democratic legitimacy, which involves governing effectively in the public interest and in accordance with common values while taking into account the voices of those affected by the decisions taken. Ultimately, legitimacy lies in the eye of the beholder; to benefit from it, governments must consider the wishes and concerns of their constituencies ('input legitimacy') and effectively address any problems ('output legitimacy'). Legitimacy can also be built by adhering to the principles of good governance in arriving at decisions, such as accountability and transparency ('throughput legitimacy'). Given the EU's highly complicated system of governance – its 'split-level legitimacy' (p. 57) – the main focus of Schmidt's analysis is its throughput legitimacy. She takes a close and critical look at the crisis-management performance of the EU Council and finds that its behaviour was sometimes consistent with that of a 'deliberative body' dedicated to decision-making based on extensive argument and reasoning, and sometimes consistent with that of a 'dictatorship' (p. 117). She sees the European Central Bank (ECB) as both 'hero' and 'ogre' (p. 150) – hero, because of bank chairman Mario Draghi's famous pledge to do 'whatever it takes' to protect the euro, which indeed turned out to be 'enough', but also ogre, because the ECB insisted on coercing the crisis-afflicted countries into highly destructive austerity policies that did not work. Schmidt also draws ambivalent conclusions about the performance of the European Commission, which she faults as 'Ayatollahs of austerity' but also credits with efforts to soften the rigid austerity policies as 'ministers of moderation' (p. 176). The European Parliament, meanwhile, was largely sidelined in the management of the crisis, and therefore remained a mere 'talking shop' (p. 208). Overall, Schmidt finds that the eurocrisis has seriously damaged the legitimacy of the EU, driving wedges between European institutions and the European people, but also between member states. The old permissive European consensus – in Schmidt's words, 'policy without politics' (p. 13) – has been shattered, and in its place we now have 'policy with politics', 'national politics against policy' and even 'politics against polity', as in the case of Brexit (pp. 14, 259). In her conclusion, Schmidt offers a range of ambitious and detailed policy suggestions for how the pernicious politicisation of European governance could be overcome.

What this crisis meant for Greece is laid out in two recent books written from Marxist – and, in the case of Dimitra Kotouza's *Surplus Citizens*, also feminist – theoretical perspectives. Kotouza relentlessly focuses on the internal tensions in the Greek Left's response to the crisis. Her analysis uncovers the sometimes hidden, sometimes barely concealed contradictions between allegedly progressive discourses and actions, and their tendency to develop pseudo-inclusive categories such as 'the nation' that actually separated and excluded people through what the author calls 'rigid racialized and gendered identities' (p. 9): Greeks vs migrants; white, male 'patriarchs' vs women; the Greek nation vs international (German, EU) imperialism.

Kotouza opens her study with a survey of the history of modern Greece (particularly since 1973), with a focus on her central themes of ethnicity/race, class and gender (Part One). The core of the empirical work assesses the development of group identities in the social struggle against the eurocrisis (Part Two), and the debates and struggles about migration and border management (Part Three). Although large parts of the book are hard going for anyone not particularly well versed in the arcana of Marxist and feminist theories (there is also a certain amount of repetition), Kotouza nevertheless provides interesting and thoughtful analysis of the narratives and activities of left-wing contestation, often based on first-hand observation.

While *Surplus Citizens* can be said to contain rigorous, sophisticated and reflective analysis despite its flaws, the same cannot be said for *The "Greek Crisis" in Europe* by Yiannis Mylonas, which offers 'critical discourse analysis' of the reporting of Danish, German and Greek media on the eurocrisis in Greece. Although the analytical categories of 'race' and 'class' are used in the book, they are deployed very differently than in *Surplus Citizens*, and it seems revealing that the category of 'gender' is completely missing in Mylonas's study. In his analysis of reporting by a select group of mass media, notably the German populist tabloid *Bild* and the almost equally sensationalist weekly *Der Spiegel*, he identifies a number of political and cultural stereotypes which are then castigated in equally stereotypical Marxist terms. Thus, his unsurprising conclusion is that the media coverage – said to be representative of mainstream, neoliberal thinking – was 'dominated by the strategic interests of the political and economic establishment of the capitalist democracies' (p. 218). No serious efforts are made to substantiate this proposition, and the methodology applied in the content analysis is anything but transparent. There may be something to be gained from Marxist-inspired analyses of the eurocrisis, but this volume demonstrates the potential pitfalls and limitations of this analytical approach.

Counter-terrorism and Intelligence
Jonathan Stevenson

Skin (film)
Guy Nattiv, writer and director. Distributed by A24, 2018.

Joker (film)
Todd Phillips, co-writer and director. Distributed by Warner
Bros. Pictures, 2019.

You Were Never Really Here (film)
Lynne Ramsay, writer and director. Distributed by StudioCanal
in the United Kingdom and Amazon Studios in the United
States, 2018.

During the Trump administration, the balance of professional counter-terrorism concern about home-grown threats shifted from jihadist ones towards far-right, white-supremacist ones. Several movies have explored the latter phenomenon. Guy Nattiv's *Skin* is a largely true story about a nasty skinhead (a convincing Jamie Bell, portrayer of ballet dancer Billy Elliot as a teen) who decides to leave an American white-supremacist group and his path of agony, which includes facial-tattoo removals that do some heavy symbolic lifting. Bill Camp and an especially creepy Vera Farmiga are very good as the group's insidious husband-and-wife ringleaders.

Equally telling about the polarisation of American society are higher-profile movies that have cropped up about the rise of far-left domestic extremism, which, though the Trump administration has highlighted it as a grave danger, poses a much less organised, less active and less substantial threat than the far-right variety. *Joker*, an origin story of Batman's nemesis and a hit for which Joaquin Phoenix won the 2020 Oscar for best actor, is a self-conscious fusion of Martin Scorsese's *Taxi Driver* and *The King of Comedy*. Set in the 1980s, Gotham City is a clichéd sewer patrolled by wilding teenagers, several of whom beat clown-for-hire, aspiring stand-up comic and classical downtrodden misfit Arthur Fleck to a pulp. He conjures a gun and murders three drunkenly abusive, yuppie financial types on the subway, becoming an anonymous folk hero to the have-nots and a spur to their billionaire Trumpian employer Thomas Wayne – father of Bruce Wayne, aka Batman – to run for mayor and clean up the city. Negative reinforcement of various types turns Gotham into hell and Fleck into the Joker, its presumptive Lucifer. The film is cynically manipulative as well as tiresomely derivative. Particularly perverse is the way it implicitly demonises the anti-fascist – 'Antifa' – resistance. The masses don clown masks as tribute and wreak violent havoc throughout the city in solidarity with an evidently psychotic murderer. The message is apparently that the underclass will lay bloody siege to its oppressors as a matter of human nature. Bong Joon-ho's exquisitely black comedy *Parasite* – which won Oscars for best picture and best foreign film, as well as the Palme d'Or at Cannes – is a far more inventive, sophisticated and searching take on class antagonism and the violence it could provoke.

Phoenix himself offers a much more poignant maladjusted anti-hero in Lynne Ramsay's *You Were Never Really Here*, based on Jonathan Ames's crafty pulp-style novella, for which Phoenix won best actor and Ramsay best screenplay at Cannes in 2018. Fragmentary flashbacks provide a diaphanous backstory for Joe, the protagonist. He's a PTSD-stricken ex-marine who, like Fleck, lives with his declining mother. He was an FBI agent until he went AWOL over a sting operation in which the perpetrators intentionally asphyxiated 30 Chinese girls in a truck. Now he's a vigilante for hire, rescuing underage girls from sexually depraved politicians, doing what he can to punish the worst and save the weakest. However savagely, he acts only on particular facts, and not on the basis of prejudged hatred. Despite his will to action, he knows he's ultimately powerless against evil forces with superior resources and connections. He's not a terrorist, just a desperate soul in a fallen world trying awkwardly to hang on to his humanity.

Crossfire Hurricane: Inside Donald Trump's War on the FBI
Josh Campbell. Chapel Hill, NC: Algonquin Books, 2019.
£22.99/$28.95. 276 pp.

Bluster: Donald Trump's War on Terror
Peter R. Neumann. London: C. Hurst & Co., 2019. £15.99. 254 pp.

The mere juxtaposition of the subtitles of these two books reflects the incoherence of US President Donald Trump's national-security policy: it's difficult to wage an effective 'war on terror' while trying to undermine the nation's primary counter-terrorism agency. The impetus for the latter effort was the FBI's counter-intelligence investigation of Russia's interference with the 2016 US presidential election, which the bureau dubbed *Crossfire Hurricane*, improbably but not inappropriately borrowing a term from the opening line of the Rolling Stones song 'Jumpin' Jack Flash': 'I was born in a crossfire hurricane.' A fair number of FBI employees must have ended up feeling that way. The investigation proved so incendiary and disruptive as to turn Trump against the bureau, driving him to constrict its counter-terrorism function.

Josh Campbell, who as a special agent served as FBI director James Comey's special assistant, left the organisation after more than ten years of service in order to 'speak out' as a matter of patriotic duty and institutional loyalty that he wears on his sleeve, often self-consciously (p. 9). Providing colourful and informative background, he tells the story, by now familiar and recently dramatised in Showtime's *The Comey Rule*, of the FBI's Russia investigation, Trump's unsuccessful attempt to cajole Comey into pledging blind loyalty to him, and the president's drive to discredit special counsel Robert Mueller's investigation of Russian interference as a 'witch hunt' (see chapter ten) after firing Comey. While Campbell arrays facts well and perceives clearly the iniquities of the Trump administration, he is also prone to going off on tangents and to breathlessly glorifying the 'awesomeness' of the American system (p. 230). And his hardwired respect for law-enforcement luminaries leads him to equate Mueller's shilly-shallying with noble objectivity in the face of 'extraordinary external pressure' (p. 204). But the author's overarching point is surely correct: pure spite and political survival were the key motivations for Trump's marginalisation of the FBI.

There were also devious policy reasons. The main one, perhaps, was Trump's compulsion to concentrate federal law-enforcement efforts on immigration rather than standing transnational terrorist threats, which had been their primary focus since 9/11, or on burgeoning, domestic far-right terrorist impulses that the administration itself was fuelling. In *Bluster*, Peter Neumann's sharp chronicle of the administration's cynical and disorganised counter-terrorism programme, the author notes that in the wake of its largely frustrated Muslim bans, a former FBI official characterised Customs and Border Protection's (CBP) National Targeting Center, celebrated by Trump, as doing 'little more than to feed "the [administration's] false narrative that there was an influx of terrorists related to weak immigration controls"' (p. 74). More broadly, this programme has tried to replace the putatively elite FBI with Immigration and Customs Enforcement, the CBP and Border Patrol as the ranking institutional heroes of federal law enforcement in the public mind, and to an extent it has succeeded. Trump's calculated, populist preoccupation with immigrants, Neumann suggests, 'has allowed him to advance a radical ideological agenda that has challenged widely accepted definitions of America' as a multicultural nation and a liberal exemplar (p. 158). Due to this and Trump's personal political priorities, law enforcement itself has become acutely politicised, to the clear detriment of US national security.

Unwanted Spy: The Persecution of an American Whistleblower
Jeffrey Sterling. New York: Bold Type Books, 2019. $28.00. 262 pp.

In 2015, Jeffrey Sterling, a former CIA operations officer, was convicted of violating the US Espionage Act by allegedly disclosing details to a journalist about the agency's failed effort – called *Operation Merlin* – to undermine Iran's nuclear-weapons programme by supplying its scientists with fraudulent warhead blueprints. He was sentenced to 42 months in prison, but he contends, credibly, that he did no such thing. Furthermore, his candid, thoughtful and angry autobiography resonantly places his CIA experience in the context of epochal grievances concerning institutional racism. In Sterling's view, his real offence was that he was 'a black man who'd dared to try to build a career serving [his] country as an officer of the CIA' (p. 3).

Sterling grew up in Cape Girardeau, Missouri – a racially divided town about 160 kilometres south of St Louis on the Mississippi River, and the birthplace of ultra-conservative radio personality Rush Limbaugh. Sterling experienced overt and occasionally violent racism as a child, and integration struck him as the most sensible prescription for African-American progress. He attended a predominantly white college in Illinois and the prestigious Washington University School of Law. Ambivalent about the law, he answered a newspaper ad for CIA operations officers emphasising the agency's quest for diversity, and was accepted. At first, he was 'damn proud to be learning how to be part of such an exclusive club' (p. 64). He soon discovered that racial openness at the CIA was a charade. Assigned to the Iran desk and posted to a European station, he was saddled with unrealistic recruitment goals, given poor cover and reined in because his superiors said he would 'kinda stick out as a big black guy speaking Farsi' (p. 116).

Exasperated, he moved to counter-proliferation and was sent to the CIA's New York office. There he worked on *Operation Merlin*, handling a Russian agent who would pass the flawed warhead plans to the Iranians. When Sterling pointed out that the scheme could backfire if they detected the ruse and decided to send back bogus information through the agent or used the flaws as guides to a functional design, his superiors were dismissive and threatened to impede his career if his attitude didn't improve. After eight acrimonious months, he returned to Langley and filed an employment-discrimination claim with the Equal Employment Opportunity Commission. Ostracised and marginalised, he lost (as he later did in federal district court). The CIA terminated Sterling's employment in May 2001 after eight and a half frustrating years. Black friends had warned him about trying to join a white boys' club and spurned him when he did. 'Black America didn't want me', he reflects, 'and now white America had tossed me out' (p. 149).

Sterling described his discriminatory treatment by the CIA to *New York Times* reporter James Risen, who published a story about it. On his own initiative, Sterling also informed two staffers of the Senate Select Committee on Intelligence about the risks of *Operation Merlin*. Friendless, depressed, broke and unemployed – the CIA had blackballed him – he half-heartedly attempted suicide but then rebounded, marrying and finding a good job. In 2006, however, Risen's book *State of War: The Secret History of the CIA and the Bush Administration* came out. It mentioned *Operation Merlin* and its pitfalls. The CIA and FBI essentially inferred that Sterling was Risen's source, and in 2010 the Department of Justice brought a criminal case against him, seeking key testimony from Risen. He famously refused to testify about his sources on First Amendment grounds and ultimately was not required to do so. But the government arrayed exclusively white CIA witnesses plus former secretary of state and national security advisor Condoleezza Rice, herself an African American, against Sterling in a completely circumstantial case. 'The feeling grew in me', he writes, 'that, from the moment I'd first complained about being subject to racial discrimination, a machine had begun to be assembled with the singular purpose of destroying me' (p. 228). It's hard to blame him.

Deep State: Trump, the FBI, and the Rule of Law
James B. Stewart. New York: Penguin Books, 2019.
£25.00/$30.00. 372 pp.

In Deep: The FBI, the CIA, and the Truth About America's "Deep State"
David Rohde. New York: W. W. Norton, 2020. £22.99/$30.00.
345 pp.

These two books by Pulitzer Prize-winning journalists offer compatible perspectives on Trump's stated conviction that a 'deep state' composed of career government officials – in particular, the FBI – has sought to undermine him and his administration. James Stewart essentially fleshes out, clarifies and crystallises previously reported news into a sharper picture of the struggle between the White House and the FBI, focusing on the latter's investigations of Hillary Clinton stemming from her use of personal, unsecured email accounts while serving as secretary of state, and of Trump himself for possible collusion with Russia on election interference and obstruction of justice. Covering much of the same ground, David Rohde undertakes a somewhat more expansive examination of what these matters imply about the fragility of US democracy.

Stewart's forensically invaluable account lets the facts he arrays speak for themselves. He rarely frames his own opinion, so when it does surface – mainly in the concluding chapter – it is especially noteworthy. In endorsing Mueller's assessment that an improper motive can render otherwise lawful conduct criminal obstruction – an assessment that Attorney General William Barr has sought to obscure – Stewart (who is a lawyer) notes that 'subjects of investigations may have many motives to conceal behavior that, while it may not be criminal, is nonetheless embarrassing, dishonest, or greedy. Countless defendants have been prosecuted for and convicted of obstructing justice where there was no underlying criminal activity' (p. 314). Pointedly, he adds that 'Trump would seem to be a textbook case, because the ways his campaign benefited from Russian interference undermined the legitimacy of his election victory, giving him a motive to conceal it' (p. 314). Sceptical of Trump and his supporters' hypothesis of a vast deep-state conspiracy against him, Stewart also remains chillingly uncertain about the FBI and the Justice Department's willingness to resist satisfying 'Trump's seemingly insatiable thirst for vengeance' (p. 331).

Rohde interjects his normative views a bit more freely. Fortunately, they are considered and judicious. To take one example: 'Barr likes to describe Trump as the heir to Ronald Reagan. But in some ways his administration, with its fixation on enemies and its willingness to bend laws for political gain, is more reminiscent of Richard Nixon's' (p. 230). Clearly Rohde shares Stewart's fears that Trump could enlist government agencies for personal retaliation. More broadly, while conceding that long-serving officials inevitably have their political biases, Rohde firmly dismisses any notion of a systemic deep state. Yet, he writes, 'under the guise of stopping a "coup" that does not exist, Trump is upending the checks and balances that are the foundation of American democracy' and creating a '"deep state" of his own' (p. 274).

Tonight We Bombed the U.S. Capitol: The Explosive Story of M19, America's First Female Terrorist Group
William Rosenau. New York: Atria Books, 2019. $28.00. 318 pp.

Timothy McVeigh, a far-right militant, perpetrated the most lethal domestic terrorist attack in US history when he blew up the Alfred P. Murrah Federal Building in Oklahoma City in 1995, killing 168 people. American white-supremacist groups are now considered as dangerous to the US homeland as transnational jihadist ones. Terrorist threats from scattered left-wing groups – inappropriately lumped together as 'Antifa' – do not constitute a major national-security problem. This follows the historical pattern: notwithstanding a brief and poorly executed bombing campaign against public officials in 1919, and possibly the horrific Wall Street bombing in 1920, alarm about anarchists and Bolsheviks arising during the 'First Red Scare' was overblown. But left-wing threats have not always been minor. Having usurped the largely non-violent Students for a Democratic Society in 1969, the Weather Underground Organization surged its violent activity in the mid-1970s, drawing strength from and lending it to black and Puerto Rican nationalist groups. Although the Weathermen disbanded in 1976, holdouts from that group and the Black Liberation Army tried to fill the void, to some effect.

In the assiduously researched *Tonight We Bombed the U.S. Capitol*, veteran policy analyst and former US counter-terrorism official William Rosenau briskly and cogently tells the fascinating story of a heretofore obscure terrorist group of that vintage: the May 19th Communist Organization, or M19. This group planned and helped pull off the chaotic 1981 robbery of $1.8 million from a Brink's armoured car in Nyack, New York, in which a Brink's guard and two policemen were killed. Unlike its predecessors, M19 was established and led by women. 'They'd created a new sisterhood of the bomb and gun' (p. 8). Not content with 'lesbian separatism', they wanted to forge a new world purged of sexual oppression and the ideologies they believed supported it – including capitalism, racism and imperialism – through national liberation. Men were allowed to join the group as long as they subscribed to this world view. Having attended top colleges such as Barnard, Berkeley, the University of Chicago and the University of Wisconsin, the leaders inconspicuously coalesced and lived communally in New York near Columbia.

While Rosenau's anecdotal and breezy approach is reader-friendly, the author wants M19, small and short-lived though it was, to be taken seriously and understood in context. He notes that it arose as left-wing militants operating outside the US – such as Carlos the Jackal, the Red Brigades, the Baader-Meinhof Gang and the 17 November Organisation – were perpetrating lethal and sensational attacks against American interests. By the late 1970s, the domestication of the American Left may have yielded a flaccid counter-culture, but some leftist militants, partly inspired by an energised international Left, saw complacency as opportunity. Within the Reagan administration, 'specters of America's recent radical past … managed to reanimate themselves' (p. 145). And M19's robbery spree did, in fact, trigger a concerted FBI response that produced the Joint Terrorism Task Force – a mechanism for New York City Police Department (NYPD) and FBI collaboration that anchored the post-9/11 national law-enforcement mobilisation (pp. 146–7).

Determined not to go down as a mere relic of the 1960s, M19 honed its bomb-making skills and advanced from robberies to higher-value symbolic targets. No one was killed or wounded in the Capitol bombing on 7 November 1983 – M19 provided a tactically calibrated five-minute warning, short enough to imperil lives and long enough to plausibly deny responsibility for any carnage – but the blast left a 4.6-metre crater in the wall that reportedly cost $1m to repair and destroyed a portrait of South Carolina senator John C. Calhoun, the South's foremost defender of slavery. M19's last major bombing, in retaliation for police brutality, was of the NYPD Patrolmen's Benevolent Association's Manhattan headquarters in February 1985. By then, M19 was 'living in an ideological cul-de-sac' and considered 'a bunch of crazy dead-enders' by less extreme leftists (p. 214). But it still had big operations planned when the FBI rolled up the key players that May. Rosenau notes that M19 shared relevant traits – including utopian delusions – with both jihadist and far-right groups, but judges leftist terrorism unlikely to re-emerge in the West on a significant scale. Crucially, he also argues that M19's relatively swift demise vindicates the FBI's low-key approach to counter-terrorism and the rejection of any attempt to militarise law enforcement.

Letter to the Editor

Spheres of Instability

Sir,

In your April–May issue, Evan Sankey argued for the rather interesting concept of spheres of restraint. I applaud Sankey's ingenuity and pithy writing. A closer look at his argument, however, reveals its internal contradictions. In addition, a preponderance of historical and contemporary evidence points to the futility of any sphere-of-restraint arrangement, especially as it applies to Sankey's examples.

Sankey lays out five prerequisites for a successful sphere-of-restraint arrangement: clear boundaries, asymmetric military capabilities, acquiescence at the receiving end, an absence of overlapping interests and recognition by other powers. The logic of these criteria is somewhat dubious. In particular, the boundaries of spheres are always murky; otherwise, interests would not overlap in the first place. Furthermore, the balance of military capabilities among powers changes in reaction to the shifting circumstances on the ground. For instance, China's military budget was on par with Taiwan's in the late 1990s. Beijing ratcheted up its defence spending and upset the regional balance.

Sankey's spheres of restraint appear tantamount to a more familiar concept in geopolitics: buffer zones. These have never worked as neatly as Sankey suggests. In 1885, Tokyo and Beijing agreed to leave Korea as a buffer and respect their mutual interests there. Ten years later, however, war broke out when Japan abruptly sank a Chinese vessel off the coast of Korea. Throughout the second half of the nineteenth century, Britain and Russia struggled over Central Asia. It required the rise of Germany for the decades-long 'Great Game' to end with the establishment of a neutral zone in Persia in 1907. As Sankey himself suggests, Russia and Japan failed to delineate a buffer dividing their respective spheres in Korea and Manchuria, leading to the Russo-Japanese War. In 1938, Neville Chamberlain ceded the Sudetenland to Germany in the hope of forging 'peace for our time'. The following year, Adolf Hitler cut a secret deal with Joseph Stalin to carve up Eastern Europe. Hitler chose not to recognise the putative spheres, ultimately invading both Western Europe and the Soviet Union. At the end of the Second World War, US secretary of state James Byrnes sought to establish spheres in Europe and the Middle East, but was soon disillusioned by the Soviet excursion into the Turkish Straits. His successor Dean Acheson's exclusion of the Korean Peninsula from the United States' line of defence in 1950 emboldened Pyongyang and Moscow, leading to the Korean War.

This record shows that buffer systems made possible by one-sided concessions do not work. It takes two to tango, so there also needs to be some basic agreement on the international modus operandi among parties involved, as with the Congress of Vienna. No such mechanism exists today between the United States and China on a wide range of issues, from freedom of navigation on the high seas and intellectual-property rights to less immediate but still important matters such as democratic norms in Hong Kong and human rights in Xinjiang. A revisionist power that does not accept the basic international rule of equality among states is unlikely to exercise restraint and stop its depredations where Sankey would like it to when presented with opportunities for expansion.

Sankey's fundamental argument – that extended deterrence is becoming burdensome for the United States – has some validity, and Washington may have to swallow bitter pills in certain areas. But the United States should first try to renegotiate the share of this burden with its allies and partners, which indeed it has been doing. It would be rash simply to ditch an 'unsinkable aircraft carrier' in the Pacific and drop a 'dagger' poised in the Far East, especially in an era of strategic competition in which revisionist powers are meddling in the western hemisphere.

Jaehan Park
Austin, TX

In Reply

My thanks to Mr Park for taking the time to read my article and pen a response. A few points are in order. Regarding my proposed five determinants of a stable sphere of influence, Mr Park oversteps in claiming that sphere boundaries are 'always murky'. No territory can be perfectly delineated but, excepting Berlin, the Cold War European spheres were fairly clear. Winston Churchill's description of the Iron Curtain – 'From Stettin in the Baltic to Trieste in the Adriatic' – remained a close approximation of reality until 1989. The 1907 Anglo-Russian agreement on Persia cited by Mr Park had even clearer boundaries: a Russian zone in the north, a British zone in the south and a neutral zone in the middle, all confined to certain geographic limits.

Militarily, it is of course true that the balance of national capabilities changes over time. Every approach to statecraft is doomed to face this problem. But where US liberal hegemony simply prescribes ever more deterrence, spheres at least offer the possibility of giving political expression or ratification to shifts in the underlying military balance. That makes them a key tool of statecraft, especially when the shifts in question are effectively permanent. Modern US foreign policy does itself a disservice by not leveraging that tool.

On buffer zones, I agree that there are many examples of unworkable sphere arrangements, but I claim that at least one of my five determinants of a stable sphere was absent or lacking in each case. Mr Park's aversion to 'one-sided concessions' should make it easy for him to see the merit in a sphere-of-restraint settlement. My article is clear that such arrangements have mutual recognition – and therefore reciprocity – at their core. The Cold War-era dispositions of Finland and Austria were based on reciprocal superpower restraint. Similarly, substantial US–China restraint underpins the current disposition of Taiwan. Any successful initiative to stabilise the broader US–China relationship will necessarily involve reciprocal restraint. Sphere arrangements will therefore be an attractive option, even if trans-Pacific diplomats never actually utter the word 'sphere'.

I do not claim that spheres are a recipe for international peace, only that they are not inherently unstable and that historically they have been useful tools of statecraft. The nuclear revolution and developments in conventional-weapons technology offer powerful reasons to expect that modern sphere arrangements will be more stable than those of the past. The emerging multipolar order could be a golden age of great-power diplomacy. The US should not tie its hands by refusing to avail itself of a potentially effective diplomatic tool.

Evan R. Sankey

Donald Trump's Legacy

Dana H. Allin

I

By June 2020, James Mattis had had enough. Until that month, the retired Marine Corps general – US President Donald Trump's first secretary of defense – had been a study in discretion. To be sure, his 20 December 2018 letter of resignation was clear enough for any reader with sufficient knowledge to squint between the lines. Mattis had resigned when President Trump abruptly pulled US special-operations forces from northeastern Syria, abandoning Kurdish partners to the wrath of invading Turkish troops. This followed years during which Trump – the flamboyant New York businessman, reality-television star, presidential candidate and then president – had voiced disdain for American overseas commitments and treaty allies. Mattis wrote in his resignation letter: 'One core belief I have always held is that our strength as a nation is inextricably linked to the strength of our unique and comprehensive system of alliances and partnerships.'[1] He was leaving the Pentagon, Mattis said to President Trump, because the president had 'the right to have a Secretary of Defense whose views are better aligned with yours on these and other subjects'. For the next 17 months, however, Mattis kept mainly quiet, citing the normative tradition of 'what the French call a devoir de reserve, "a duty of quiet"'.[2] He did stipulate, however, that this duty did not last forever.

Dana H. Allin is Editor of *Survival* and IISS Senior Fellow for US Foreign Policy and Transatlantic Affairs. A portion of this essay appeared on Politics and Strategy: The Survival Editors' Blog (under the title 'Trump, Biden and the Crisis of Transition') on 13 November 2020.

Survival | vol. 62 no. 6 | December 2020–January 2021 | pp. 259–270   https://doi.org/10.1080/00396338.2020.1851108

Mattis's reckoning came about 17 months later. A Minneapolis police officer had killed George Floyd, an African-American man arrested for allegedly passing a counterfeit $20 bill, by planting a knee bearing much of his body weight on Floyd's neck for over eight minutes, suffocating the prisoner as he pleaded for his life. Over the days that followed, impassioned demonstrations mixed with violent outbursts engulfed the United States on a scale unseen since the aftermath of Martin Luther King Jr's assassination in 1968. The 2020 demonstrations were multiracial and driven by a conviction that 'black lives matter' against overwhelming evidence that the disproportionate killings of African Americans by police was a consequence of systemic racism. A week after Floyd's murder, Trump acknowledged in a Rose Garden statement that 'Americans were rightly sickened and revolted by the brutal death of George Floyd', but then described the demonstrations in terms reminiscent of the 'American carnage' that his January 2017 inauguration speech had invoked and promised to end. Claiming that 'our nation has been gripped by professional anarchists, violent mobs, arsonists, looters, criminals, rioters, Antifa, and others', Trump warned that if mayors and governors failed to restore order he would send in US military troops to do so.[4] As Trump spoke, federal police deployed chemical tearing agents to drive peaceful demonstrators away from the northern edge of Lafayette Square in front of the White House. Astonished reporters then watched as the president left the White House on foot to stride across the square, flanked by an entourage that included his attorney general, his current defense secretary and the chairman of the Joint Chiefs of Staff in combat fatigues, to stand awkwardly in front of St. John's Episcopal Church, holding up a Bible that the president's daughter Ivanka pulled from a Max Mara bag.

It was this photo op that moved Mattis to break his silence. Calling himself 'angry and appalled', lauding the protests as 'defined by tens of thousands of people of conscience who are insisting that we live up to our values', and warning that a militarised response 'sets up a conflict … between the military and civilian society', Mattis castigated Trump as the 'first president in my lifetime who does not try to unite the American people – does not even pretend to try'.[5] A plethora of retired high-ranking military officers also condemned Trump's conduct. Secretary of defense Mark Esper and General Mark Milley, chairman of the Joint Chiefs, who had been part of the Lafayette Square entourage, made a point of distancing themselves from it and disavowing the deployment of active-duty US troops for domestic political purposes.[6] In the midst of overlapping crises caused by a global pandemic; consequent economic collapse; racial wounds emerging from four centuries of slavery, civil war and injustice; and bitter political divisions animated by deeply contested visions of American identity, the president had fomented a full-blown crisis of civil–military relations.

II

The US Constitution is a spare document, and whether its eighteenth-century assumptions are fully adequate for a twenty-first-century superpower is subject to debate. The Framers fretted over the design of the office of the presidency, anxious about monarchical aggrandisement, on the one hand, and factional weakness, on the other. Over the ensuing centuries, the power of the presidency has waxed and waned, with critics warning that it was becoming either imperial or dysfunctional – or, not implausibly, both at once.

One fairly constant assumption is that the influence of the office derives in part from moral symbolism. Even in a fiercely contested American polity, the president is supposed to convey gravitas and a unifying dignity, especially in times of crisis or great national tragedy. After the 9/11 attacks, George W. Bush was able to stand on the rubble in Manhattan with a megaphone and reach most Americans. Whatever his faults, Bush was fluent in the language and rituals of an American civil religion: vaguely, but not exclusively, Christian, embedded more broadly in foundational American texts and history, and an ecumenical deism within which the president's respectful visit to a Washington mosque in that week of genuine carnage made sense. Eight years later, Bush vacated the White House for Barack Obama, America's first black president – an apparent affirmation that the United States was becoming, in Obama's frequent use of the language of the Constitution, 'a more perfect union' that would overcome the legacy of slavery.

Trump, it is safe to say, did not fulfil this role. Many presidents have dissembled some of the time, often compelled in their own minds, no doubt, by *raison d'état*, and occasionally by sexual indiscretion (Bill Clinton) or criminal conspiracy (Richard Nixon). But Donald Trump is the first president to engage in a daily assault on the very notion of objective truth, elevating falsehood to a governing principle – from his campaign claim that Obama was not a native-born American to daily fabrications such as the assertion that thousands of New Jersey Muslims cheered with joy on 9/11. On the very day of his inauguration, Trump instructed his press spokesman, Sean Spicer, to insist with a straight face that the crowd assembled on the Washington Mall to celebrate his swearing-in was the largest such crowd in American history.

Historian Anne Applebaum was not the first to observe a familiar authoritarian trick here: the effect, arguably the purpose, was not to persuade but to corrupt, making subordinate officials, starting with Spicer and increasing in number, complicit in the subversion of reality.[7] Since many of Trump's lies were conveyed via Twitter, Republican members of Congress blithely waved them off as harmless. Abundant falsehoods, however, have strategic significance. The alternative reality propagated on social media and, most prominently, by the right-wing Fox News network hardened the epistemic bubbles dividing Americans into hostile political and cultural camps.

In 2016, Moscow targeted this febrile and vulnerable America to damage the candidacy of Hillary Clinton and to help Trump win the presidency. Clinton won the popular vote by a margin of three million, but the Electoral College went to Trump because of 70,000 votes across three key states. Whether or not the Russian intelligence operations through social media and the hacking and release of Democratic emails affected the election result, they certainly loosened the glue of America's unifying civil religion. So too did the Trump campaign's unconcealed interest in the success of the Russian influence operation. While Special Counsel Robert Mueller's investigation did not establish a criminal conspiracy between Russian operatives and Trump or his campaign, it did say that the campaign knew about and welcomed Moscow's work on its behalf.[8]

Worse still, Trump as president endorsed Russian President Vladimir Putin's protestations of innocence in the affair, in contradiction to unambiguous findings of the entire US intelligence community.[9] Before Trump ceases to occupy so much of our headspace, we should reflect on what an extraordinary moment this was in American history. No president or major presidential candidate in living memory had ever publicly expressed indifference to a foreign power subverting the American political process.

In the weeks between Trump's election and inauguration, Michael Flynn, his designated national security advisor, met with the Russian ambassador to urge Moscow not to retaliate against sanctions that Obama, still the president, had imposed to punish Moscow's election interference. Flynn was indicating that the new president, who had benefited from that interference, would return the favour by lifting the sanctions. The Mueller investigation resulted in Flynn's conviction on perjury charges based on that conversation, the conviction of four other members of Trump's campaign team, guilty pleas from incidental associates and the indictments of 12 Russian intelligence operatives. Mueller's report also laid out evidence that Trump obstructed the investigation, but due primarily to long-standing Justice Department guidance that a sitting president cannot be indicted, the investigators refrained from stating that he had committed a crime. Still, the report was damning enough: 'if we had confidence after a thorough investigation of the facts that the President clearly did not commit obstruction of justice, we would so state … We are unable to reach that judgment … While this report does not conclude that the President committed a crime, it also does not exonerate him.'[10]

Mueller testified before Congress about his investigation on 24 July 2019. The very next day, Trump called his Ukrainian counterpart, Volodymyr Zelensky, to condition the release of some $400 million in military aid, authorised by Congress, on Zelensky's public announcement of a spurious investigation into former vice president Joe Biden and his son, Hunter, who during the Obama administration had joined the board of a Ukrainian energy company. For the same coercive purpose, Trump was delaying the scheduling of a White House visit by Zelensky, who wanted a visible signal of US support against Russia. Trump also regurgitated to a presumably mystified Zelensky a bizarre conspiracy theory, promoted by Russian intelligence, that Ukraine and not Russia had intervened in the 2016 US election.[11]

The Democratic Party controlled the House of Representatives by virtue of the 2018 mid-term elections, but had viewed impeachment proceedings as a political dead end due to Trump's assured acquittal by a Republican-controlled Senate. Upon learning of the phone call from an anonymous CIA analyst using a protected 'whistle-blower' channel, however, the Democrats felt they had to rein in a president who was out of control, utterly unable to distinguish between the American national interest and his own narrow political interests in conducting foreign policy. This harsh judgement was confirmed beyond reasonable doubt by a series of government witnesses, some of whose careers in public service Trump subsequently endeavoured to ruin. Even so, the Senate acquitted Trump on a party-line vote, save for Mitt Romney, the Republican Party's previous presidential nominee, who stated: 'The president delayed funds for an American ally at war with Russian invaders. The president's purpose was personal and political. Accordingly, the president is guilty of an appalling abuse of the public trust.'[12] Ukraine is not a formal American ally, of course, but the basic point stands.

Trump's personal interests and proclivities caused broader damage to transatlantic relations. He clearly preferred Putin's company to German Chancellor Angela Merkel's. Trump's abrupt announcement in June 2020 that a third of the 35,000 US troops stationed in Germany would be withdrawn was apparently prompted by Merkel's decision, due to the COVID-19 emergency, not to attend the scheduled late-summer G7 meeting in the United States, forcing its cancellation. Beyond that, he has abundantly demonstrated he considers allies burdensome and redeemable only in transactional terms that they have not satisfied. It has been credibly reported that on several occasions the president told aides he wanted to withdraw the US from NATO.[13] Such a move would be at odds with one of the few points of bipartisan agreement among American elites, and of course radically overturn a bedrock of post-war foreign policy.

Yet it was the Trump administration's summer 2018 withdrawal from the Joint Comprehensive Plan of Action (JCPOA) – the Iran nuclear deal – that made allies see Trump's America as a real and not just rhetorical wrecking ball against international order. This abrogation, coupled with aggressive secondary sanctions against European companies that declined to end business with Iran, threatened European governments' profound attachment to multilateralism and their expectation that the transatlantic alliance would be stabilising rather than destabilising, empowering rather than subjugating. Biden should be able to return stability and amicability to transatlantic relations. But he probably cannot completely restore European allies' confidence in the United States given the severe damage Trump has caused, the manifest divisions in American politics and the real possibility that another Trumpian figure – perhaps even Trump himself – will be elected president in the not-too-distant future.[14]

III

It is also uncertain that the Trump administration's corrosive effect on democratic norms can be easily repaired. While this problem was manifestly exacerbated by the president's unusual personality and character, it also reflected structural flaws that appeared increasingly to threaten the legitimacy of the American political system. These include the Electoral College, whereby the loser of the national popular vote can be elected president. This happened only three times in the nineteenth century, and not at all in the twentieth. Yet, in the first 16 years of the twenty-first century, encompassing five presidential elections, it happened twice more.

The democratic unfairness of the Electoral College is especially toxic because it intimately involves race. In recent elections, Republicans have benefited from the Electoral College because many Democratic voters have been 'wasted' as a result of being packed into urban areas in big states such as California and New York. These voters are also disproportionately from African-American, Hispanic and other minority communities. Furthermore, as ethnic minorities grow and whites shrink as relative shares of the US population, the overwhelmingly white Republican Party has an objective interest in seeing fewer minority voters come out to the polls. This interest has fuelled false accusations of 'voter fraud' (most loudly from Trump himself), the enactment by Republican-controlled state legislatures of laws making it more difficult to vote, and a maldistribution of voting infrastructure between white and minority neighbourhoods. The COVID-19 crisis added another point of contention, as many states sought to protect voters from infection by affording them the option of voting by mail, which the president insisted was a Democratic plot to commit voter fraud.

That baseless claim was the source of Trump's surreal refusal, ongoing at press time, to concede that he had lost the 2020 election, violating the venerable American tradition of the peaceful and orderly transfer of presidential power. To publicly acknowledge defeat is a necessary confirmation of the legitimacy of the process. When Jimmy Carter lost his re-election bid in 1980, he spoke ruefully but graciously: 'I promised you four years ago that I would never lie to you. So, I can't stand here tonight and say it doesn't hurt.' He continued: 'About an hour ago I called Governor Reagan in California, and I told him that I congratulated him for a fine victory.'[15] Twelve years later, President George H.W. Bush spoke in the same spirit. 'Well, here's the way I see it. Here's the way we see it and the country should see it – that the people have spoken, and we respect the majesty of the democratic system. I just called Governor Clinton over in Little Rock and offered my congratulations.'[16] The best example is among the most recent. The late senator John McCain's concession speech on the night of his defeat by Barack Obama in 2008 stands as a masterpiece of personal class and political grace: 'My friends, we have come to the end of a long journey. The American people have spoken, and they have spoken clearly. A little while ago, I had the honor of calling Sen. Barack Obama – to congratulate him on being elected the next president of the country that we both love.'[17] McCain continued eloquently about the historical significance of America electing its first African-American president, then added something very personal: 'Sen. Obama has achieved a great thing for himself and for his country. I applaud him for it, and offer my sincere sympathy that his beloved grandmother did not live to see this day – though our faith assures us she is at rest in the presence of her Creator and so very proud of the good man she helped raise.'

Here is what Trump said at 03:30 on the morning after Election Day 2020:

> This is a fraud on the American public. This is an embarrassment to our
> country. We were getting ready to win this election. Frankly, we did
> win this election. We did win this election. So our goal now is to ensure
> the integrity for the good of this nation. This is a very big moment. This
> is a major fraud in our nation. We want the law to be used in a proper
> manner. So we'll be going to the US Supreme Court. We want all voting
> to stop. We don't want them to find any ballots at four o'clock in the
> morning and add them to the list. Okay? It's a very sad moment. To
> me this is a very sad moment and we will win this. And as far as I'm
> concerned, we already have won it.[18]

In September 2016, the conservative writer Salena Zito wrote of then-
candidate Trump that 'the press takes him literally, but not seriously; his
supporters take him seriously, but not literally.'[19] This was a clever line
that got a lot of attention. Like much cleverness, however, it obscured
more than it illuminated. That Trump has been a serious force in American
history can no longer be doubted, and in 2020, as in 2016, he has claimed
the serious loyalty of almost half the US electorate.

It is less obvious that we can safely discount the literal meaning of his
words. During his first campaign, Trump vowed to ban Muslims from
entering the United States; upon his inauguration his administration enacted
bans on travel from as many Muslim countries as it could get past federal
courts. He promised to build a border wall, and though he obviously could
not coerce Mexico or even the US Congress to pay for it, he financed some
construction by diverting money from the Pentagon's budget. After Trump
called immigrants 'animals', his administration seized immigrant children
from their desperate parents and put them into caged enclosures; some of
these families have not been, and may never be, reunited.[20] He demonised
sitting members of Congress in racist terms. And he tore up international
agreements, from the Paris climate agreement to the JCPOA.

For much of the year before this election, Trump insisted that only
fraud could prevent him from winning, but also that fraud was self-

evident in the use of mail-in ballots to protect a vulnerable electorate from a deadly pandemic. After Biden won the election by comfortable margins in states giving him precisely the same 'landslide' of 306 electoral votes that Trump claimed four years ago, the current president fulminated about fraud foretold. Most Republican leaders at least tacitly supported Trump's war against reality.

The rejection, 160 years ago, by 11 slave states of Abraham Lincoln's election culminated in secession and civil war. This comparison might seem exaggerated, although it is fair to observe that the regional fault lines, and some of the disagreements, are similar. A less dire comparison is the difficult transition between presidents Herbert Hoover and Franklin Roosevelt. In those days, a president's lame-duck purgatory lasted four months, until March, and a bitter Hoover spent much of that time trying to bend Roosevelt to the austere economic policies that had deepened the Great Depression following the 1929 stock-market crash. Hoover did not, however, deny the legitimacy of the election itself, and Roosevelt, upon taking office, was able to rally much of the country behind his crisis government and his New Deal policies.

The current transition crisis could be graver than that of the early 1930s. Trump's indifference to governing as he fought the phantom of a stolen election appeared to be an increasing problem as COVID-19 ravaged the United States. When Biden does take office, it is likely that Senate Republicans will rediscover their Hooverite adherence to balanced budgets – precisely what the US does not need in a demand-starved economy. And, since Trump's denial extended, as of mid-November, to refusing to accord the incoming administration the courtesies, resources and access to classified intelligence that are customary during a normal transition, America just has to depend on luck in avoiding a national-security crisis like the one that struck seven months into the George W. Bush administration.

These are relatively short-term problems, albeit grave ones. Longer-term, Trump and his allies are attacking the very idea of electoral democracy. Some non-trivial share of Trump voters believes his preposterous claims that the election was stolen. The city of Philadelphia (this author's birthplace, so I take it somewhat personally) has been put forward as a racialised totem of election fraud. There was a time in American history when elections in big cities could be rigged, but now watchful independent media, dedicated poll workers and judicial oversight preclude it. The idea of a conspiracy to fake hundreds of thousands of votes under such intense scrutiny is simply absurd.

Trump's are the tropes of illiberal autocrats. The rituals enacted by Carter, Bush, McCain and many others may seem sanctimonious and sentimental, like gauzy scenes from *The West Wing*. But the consequences of abandoning them are not trivial.

Notes

1   'James Mattis' Resignation Letter', CNN, 21 December 2018, https://edition.cnn.com/2018/12/20/politics/james-mattis-resignation-letter-doc/index.html.

2   W.J. Hennigan, 'James Mattis on Why *Call Sign Chaos* Isn't a Political Book About the Trump Administration', *Time*, 14 September 2019, https://time.com/5677440/james-mattis-call-sign-chaos/.

3   Conor Friedersdorf, 'James Mattis and the Duty of Reserve', *Atlantic*, 26 September 2019, https://www.theatlantic.com/ideas/archive/2019/09/mattis-duty-reserve/598894/.

4   Donald Trump, 'Statement by the President', White House, 1 June 2020, https://www.whitehouse.gov/briefings-statements/statement-by-the-president-39/.

5   Jeffrey Goldberg, 'James Mattis Denounces President Trump, Describes Him as a Threat to the Constitution', *Atlantic*, 3 June 2020, https://www.theatlantic.com/politics/archive/2020/06/james-mattis-denounces-trump-protests-militarization/612640/.

6   Helene Cooper, 'Milley Apologizes for Role in Trump Photo Op: "I Should Not Have Been There"', *New York Times*, 28 July 2020, https://www.nytimes.com/2020/06/11/us/politics/trump-milley-military-protests-lafayette-square.html.

7   Anne Applebaum, 'History Will Judge the Complicit', *Atlantic*, July/August 2020, https://www.theatlantic.com/magazine/archive/2020/07/trumps-collaborators/612250/.

8   Special Counsel Robert S. Mueller, III, 'Report on the Investigation into Russian Interference in the 2016 Presidential Election', Volume I of II, US Department of Justice, March 2019, p. 13, https://www.justice.gov/storage/report.pdf.

9   See, for instance, Jeremy Diamond, 'Trump Sides with Putin over US Intelligence', CNN, 16 July 2018, https://edition.cnn.com/2018/07/16/politics/donald-trump-putin-helsinki-summit/index.html.

10 Mueller, 'Report on the Investigation into Russian Interference in the 2016

Presidential Election', p. 220.

11 'Transcript of First Conversation Between Trump and Zelensky in April', Lawfare, 15 November 2019, https://www.lawfareblog.com/transcript-first-conversation-between-trump-and-zelensky-april.

12 Madeleine Carlisle, '"An Appalling Abuse of the Public Trust." Read Mitt Romney's Speech on Voting to Convict Donald Trump', Time, 5 February 2020, https://time.com/5778603/mitt-romney-speech-donald-trump/.

13 Julian E. Barnes and Helene Cooper, 'Trump Discussed Pulling U.S. from NATO, Aides Say Amid New Concerns over Russia', New York Times, 14 January 2019, https://www.nytimes.com/2019/01/14/us/politics/nato-president-trump.html.

14 See Fabrice Pothier, 'Joe Biden's Post-transatlantic Moment', Survival, vol. 62, no. 6, December 2020–January 2021, pp. 97–104.

15 Jimmy Carter, 'Remarks on the Outcome of the 1980 Presidential Election', 4 November 1980, The American Presidency Project, University of California at Santa Barbara, https://www.presidency.ucsb.edu/documents/remarks-the-outcome-the-1980-presidential-election.

16 George H.W. Bush, 'Transcript of the President's Speech, Conceding His Defeat by Clinton', New York Times, 4 November 1992, https://www.nytimes.com/1992/11/04/us/1992-elections-disappointment-transcript-president-s-speech-conceding-his-defeat.html.

17 'Transcript of John McCain's Concession Speech', NPR, 5 November 2008, https://www.npr.org/templates/story/story.php?storyId=96631784&t=1605555021209.

18 'Donald Trump 2020 Election Night Speech Transcript', Rev, 4 November 2020, https://www.rev.com/blog/transcripts/donald-trump-2020-election-night-speech-transcript.

19 Salena Zito, 'Taking Trump Seriously, Not Literally', Atlantic, 23 September 2016, https://www.theatlantic.com/politics/archive/2016/09/trump-makes-his-case-in-pittsburgh/501335/.

20 Julie Hirschfeld Davis, 'Trump Calls Some Unauthorized Immigrants "Animals" in Rant', New York Times, 16 May 2018, https://www.nytimes.com/2018/05/16/us/politics/trump-undocumented-immigrants-animals.html.

Correction

Article title: The Strategic Implications of China's Weak
Cyber Defences
Authors: Greg Austin
Journal: *Survival*
Bibliometrics: Volume 62, Number 5, pages 119–138
DOI: http://dx.doi.org/10.1080/00396338.2020.1819648

When this article was first published online, the fourth sentence on page 129 read as follows:

It is also unlikely that China is in a position to devolve decision-making on wartime cyber options to every level of command, as the US did in 2015.

This has now been corrected to read:

It is unlikely that China is in a position to set itself an aim for wartime, as the United States did in 2015, to devolve cyber operations to every level of command.

Also, when first published online, the first sentence of endnote 1 on page 132 read as follows:

One of the latest quantum-communication achievements from China (working with Australian physicists) was the teleportation of multidimensional states of photons.

This has now been corrected to read:

One of the latest quantum-communication achievements from China (working with Austrian physicists) was the teleportation of multidimensional states of photons.

These corrections have been made to the online article.